D1094071

Books by Francis Steegmuller

SAINT-BEUVE, SELECTED ESSAYS
(translator and editor, with Norbert Guterman)
LE HIBOU ET LA POUSSIQUETTE
BLUE HARPSICHORD
THE CHRISTENING PARTY
THE GRAND MADEMOISELLE
THE TWO LIVES OF JAMES JACKSON JARVES
MAUPASSANT, A LION IN THE PATH
FLAUBERT AND MADAME BOVARY: A DOUBLE PORTRAIT
STATES OF GRACE
FRENCH FOLLIES AND OTHER FOLLIES
THE MUSICALE
THE SELECTED LETTERS OF GUSTAVE FLAUBERT
(translator and editor)
MADAME BOVARY *(translator)*

(Under the name Byron Steel)

O RARE BEN JONSON
JAVA-JAVA
SIR FRANCIS BACON

(Under the name David Keith)

A MATTER OF IODINE
A MATTER OF ACCENT

Poet among the Painters BY

APOLLINAIRE

Francis Steegmuller

Farrar, Straus and Company NEW YORK

"Moonlight," "Song of the Poorly Loved," "The Emigrant of Landor Road,"
"Mirabeau Bridge," "Singer," from Apollinaire's Alcools,
edited by Francis Steegmuller, translated by William Meredith.
Published by Doubleday & Company, Inc. and reprinted with their permission.

Published simultaneously in Canada by
Ambassador Books, Ltd., Toronto.
Manufactured in the United States of America.

This book is dedicated to

MARCEL ADÉMA

LEROY C. BREUNIG

MICHEL DÉCAUDIN

Apollinaire scholars to whose work and generosity
it owes so much.

Preface

The name Guillaume Apollinaire has reached the ears even of those who do not read French poetry: Apollinaire has become part of our picture of the Paris of the brilliant days before the first world war. The name itself has an attractive quality that somehow engraves it on the memory; and although as a poet Apollinaire is perhaps more Dionysian than Apollonian, still the inevitable association with one of the gods of poetry lends an almost magical appeal both to the name and to the man. The name is furthermore associated with another name that has a magical appeal—Mona Lisa of the unfathomable smile. Newspapers in 1911 carried headlines announcing that the famous picture had been stolen from the Louvre and that a certain Guillaume Apollinaire—described in *The New York Times* as "a well known Russian literary man living in Paris"—had been arrested and held for questioning on suspicion of complicity. The story made quite a splash in those calm days. Apollinaire was soon released, but in that brief time he had achieved a notoriety which, as he himself said, he could well have done without.

Before that deplorable episode, what fame he had enjoyed was more restricted—yet more satisfying, one suspects, than most of today's much publicized reputations. It was no small thing to be part of a group of artists and writers in the Paris of the early twentieth century who felt

vii

themselves engaged in a great adventure, in the discovery of new worlds in art, revolutionizing poetry and painting. It was in just such a group of innovators that Apollinaire was known: he was friend, comrade, and equal of Derain, Vlaminck, Picasso, Braque, Marie Laurencin, Max Jacob. He shared in their audacity, their fervor, and their fun. To ward off the occasional wolf at the door he engaged in literary journalism and wrote and edited works of erotica.

Shortly after the episode of the Mona Lisa, Apollinaire, in his early thirties, did what he had been planning to do for some time: he put together some of his poems that had been appearing in magazines, wrote a few new ones, and published the collection in a volume which he called *Alcools*. The book was reviewed and talked about among a wider public, for by now there was an interest in Apollinaire as a personality. It was known, for instance, that he had an eccentric mother, of vaguely Slavic origin, who lived on the outskirts of Paris with her lover, an Alsatian gambler. His only brother was a quiet, respectable bank clerk. His father was a question mark. When asked about his past, he took pleasure in giving misleading answers. There was talk about his unhappy love affair with Marie Laurencin. The poems in *Alcools* were recognized as striking a new note, but such was Apollinaire's reputation as a prankster and mystifier that critics tended to hedge. This bafflement caused by his verse both reflected and enhanced that provoked by his person. There was an aura of mystery about him.

With the outbreak of the war in 1914 cultural activity in France was largely interrupted; then, in the midst of the life and death struggle, in 1916, Apollinaire re-emerged in Paris, a figure more legendary than ever. Now he was a war hero, wounded in the head, trepanned, awarded the Croix de Guerre: although of foreign nationality, he had enlisted and fought near Verdun. Young writers visited him in his hospital, looking up to him as the originator of an entirely new current in French poetry; a book of new poems, *Calligrammes,* some of them written in the trenches, appeared in 1918. A few months later he was dead, at thirty-eight, carried off by influenza. He was buried on November 13, two days after the Armistice; his funeral services were attended by all the *avant-garde* writers and artists not absent on military duty.

Following his death his reputation grew quickly, both among critics and the general public. Monographs about his work and life began to appear, but it was not until after the second world war that painstaking biographical research was undertaken. Among other things, these studies revealed that Apollinaire's own remark about the poems in *Alcools*—"Every one of them commemorates an event in my life"—was nothing but the truth. At last his personality began to emerge from the fog.

Much about him still remains unclear, but the facts unearthed are perhaps more fascinating than the legend they displace; and even the light they cast has not dispelled the aura of myth and unreality always associated with his name.

It is the facts of Apollinaire's life that are the subject of this book.

F.S.   ix

En chaque artiste est un homme, un être qu'il faut veiller aussi et cultiver. L'homme est peut-être le simple procédé pour l'œuvre de l'artiste.

ODILON REDON, *A Soi-Même*

CONTE DE FAIT

Il était une fois un homme qui s'appela lui-même Guillaume Apollinaire

et il eut beaucoup d'enfants.

GEORGES VERGNES

Illustrations

Illustrations

*Picasso drawings of Apollinaire preceding the title page and the first page of text are from
Picasso, CARNET CATALAN, courtesy Berggruen & Cie, Paris; for the photographs on the
title page, see page 279.*

xiii

Illustrations

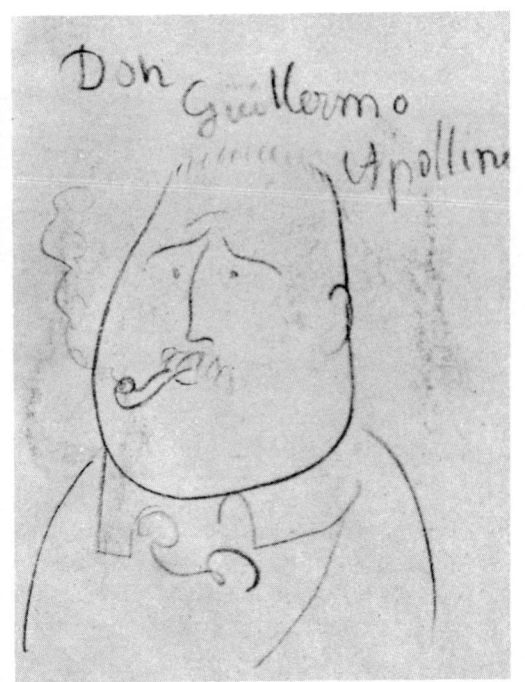

One

No one knows to this day, for a certainty, who the father of Guglielmo de Kostrowitzky was, and some people think that even when Kostrowitzky grew to manhood and was known as Guillaume Apollinaire he himself may never have been sure. At various times he hinted at being the son of an eminent personage—a noble, a prince of the blood, a heretic, a prelate, or even a pope. Perhaps it is in celebration of one of those references that Picasso made his drawing of Apollinaire on the throne of St. Peter, wearing the tiara— and a wrist watch.

At one-fifteen on the afternoon of August 31, 1880, a woman presented herself at the Municipal Records Office in Rome, declaring that she had come to report a birth. As the official in charge took down her testimony she identified herself as "Molinari Luisa in Boldi,"[1] a midwife, aged fifty-three, and stated that on August 26, at 5 A.M., a male child had been born in Trastevere (that part of Rome which lies "across the Tiber," as Parisians speak, with characteristically greater precision, of the "Left Bank" of the Seine) to a woman who "refused to be named." The midwife did not have the child with her, the official dutifully recorded, but "she gave it the name Guglielmo-Alberto and the family name Dulcigni."

[1] Italian legalese: Molinari was her maiden, and Boldi her married name.

3

Guillaume Apollinaire

The "family name Dulcigni" does not mean that the name of the child's father was Dulcigni, or even that the midwife said it was. In Italy, as elsewhere, the child of a known mother by a father who is unknown or unmarried to the mother is given the mother's family name, but the child of two unknown parents is presented with a surname by the municipal authorities. The "family name Dulcigni" was supplied, not by the midwife, but by the clerk.

Why "Dulcigni" rather than some other name? The clerk on duty when I visited the Anagrafe—the Rome Records Office—some seventy-five years later, replied to that question: "It must have been one of the days when they were giving out names beginning with 'D'." It was only recently that changes in Italian custom had made it the practice to assign inconspicuous surnames to children of unknown parents. Foundlings had formerly been branded "Esposito" ("Exposed") or "Diotiallevi" ("May God rear you"), or given ironic labels like "De Angelis" or "De Sanctis," indicating that they had come into this world as gifts of the angels or the saints. Only on October 31, 1955, was a law passed in Italy to omit from then on any mention of the name of the parents in all official records such as passports, driving licenses, and marriage certificates. Formerly, in the case of illegitimate children, the name of the father or mother or both was given as "N.N." (*Non noto,* "Not known.")

The clerk appended:

The deponent having requested that I leave said infant with her, promising in the presence of the undersigned witnesses to be responsible for its feeding and care, and to answer any inquiry

Apollinaire: One

about it by the authorities, I, finding no objection, have agreed and have consigned said infant to the deponent, who has affirmed that she will entrust it to a woman living in this city, Piazza Mastai, Vicolo Cieco No. 8. This document has been read to the interested parties and executed by the undersigned.

The two witnesses signed as "Cesare Giuli" and "Carole Guidi." Each identified himself as "clerk": perhaps they were clerks in the Records Office or some other office nearby, pressed into service for the occasion. The Piazza Mastai is in Trastevere, but it was not stated, at least in writing, whether the woman living there, to whom the baby was to be entrusted, was the mother who had refused to be named.

The mother was not long in coming forward, however. In the Archivi del Vicariato in Vatican City—that is, the library housing the old records of the various parish churches of Rome—the baptismal register of the church of Santa Maria Maggiore contains an entry for "Die 29 Septembris 1880" under the heading "De Kostrovvitzki Guillelmus (Via Milano No. 19)":

Guillelmum, Apollinarem, Albertum natum die 25 [sic] Augusti huj. anni hora 5 e Angelica de Kostrov-vitzki, f. Apollinaris, e "Pietroburgo" baptizavit R. D. Themistocles Auda Vice-Par. P.P. fuer. Laurentius Ciccolini, f.g. Benedicti, Rom; et Maria Gribaudi, F.G. Josephi, Taurinensis. Obstx Molinacci Aloissa.

Such, in the transparent Latin of the baptismal entry, is the first mention by name of the child's mother, Angelica de Kostrowitzky, "daughter of Apollinaris, of St. Petersburg." In the original document there is no mention of a father. A father's existence is acknowledged only in certain

5

subsequent versions, furnished by the parish as baptismal certificates, and in these he is accorded merely the two-letter abbreviation, "N.N."

A month and a few days later there was another development. On November 3 there appeared in the Municipal Records Office the same Signora De Kostrowitzky Angelica, "daughter of Apollinaris, born in Sweaborgin, Finland (Russian Sweden), and living in Rome, Via del Boschetto No. 40," to present a "true copy" of an act of acknowledgment "drawn up on November 2nd instant by the notary Signor Vincenzo Castrucci in his office on Piazza Aracoeli No. 34 and recorded in Rome the same day in Register 58, No. 5687 Public Acts," by which she stated her intention to recognize as her own lawful son the child born to her on August 26 of the same year and registered under the name of Dulcigni, Guglielmo-Alberto. By the same act she gave him her own family name, Kostrowitzky, and the names Guglielmo, Alberto, Wladimiro, Alessandro, Apollinare.

A new birth entry was accordingly prepared for the newly recognized child, and in this it is stated, as in the certificates of baptism, that he was the son "of father unknown and of De Kostrowitzky Angelina."[2]

[2] It is this new birth-entry, this single document only, that is shown to the seeker who merely asks at the Rome Records Office to see the entry of Guglielmo de Kostrowitzky for August 26, 1880 and presents the required acceptable reason for his request. Should the seeker ask permission to copy the document himself, or to make notes, permission is refused; and should he ask for an official copy, he is likely to be handed or mailed one that is incomplete: the copy is apt to omit the words "father unknown" and to replace them with a mere blank: "*di* ———— e di de Kostrowitzky Angelina." Who can deny the *gentilezza* of an officialdom so persistent in concealing or blurring or understating irregular circumstances of birth? Furthermore, the

6

In and among those various documents there is a certain confusion of names, dates, and places, quite apart from the change of name from Dulcigni to De Kostrowitzky. Although the Latin midwife Molinacci Aloissa of the baptism is doubtless the Italian midwife Molinari Luisa of the birth registry, neither of the witnesses at the baptism— neither the godfather Lorenzo Ciccolini, of Rome, nor the godmother Maria Gribaudi, from Turin—was one of the witnesses at the registry. The child's birth date is changed by a day. The mother's name is both Angelina and, correctly, Angelica. The child has more given names in the act of acknowledgment than in the baptismal entry. And if the latter is to be read as meaning that Angelica de Kostrowitzky herself, and not her father "Apollinaris," was a native of St. Petersburg, then there is more confusion, for in the act of acknowledgment she states that she was born in Sveaborg, Finland (then Russian territory), on April 29, 1858, and furthermore that she lives not in the via Milano but in the via Boschetto, which is nearby and parallel. (Portions of both streets are in the parish of Santa Maria Maggiore.)

Certainly, the birth of that baby in Trastevere was the occasion for much hocus-pocus.

official copy is likely also to be stamped: "No record of marriage"—meaning, "No record of this baby's ever having been married." And if you inform the official that this baby, i.e. Guglielmo de Kostrowitzky, was indeed married, in Paris, on May 2, 1918 to a pretty red-haired French girl named Jacqueline Kolb, he is apt to shake his head. "Very negligent of him not to inform us," I was told. "Everyone of Italian birth who marries outside the commune where his birth was registered should send news of his marriage to that commune. How else can we keep track of our babies and send them our congratulatory thoughts?"

Guillaume Apollinaire

On one occasion, Guillaume Apollinaire pointed to a photograph of an Italian army officer in his mother's house and said to a friend: "That is my father." And because his mother once told one of her few women friends that her elder son's father was named "Aspermont," a good deal that is persuasive has been written about a certain Francesco Flugi d'Aspermont, an Italian army officer, as Apollinaire's father.

It is a Parisian business man of literary tastes and with a flair for literary research, M. Marcel Adéma, who has followed the clues concerning this likely candidate for Apollinaire's paternity. M. Adéma's interest in Apollinaire was aroused by the fact that Mme de Kostrowitzky's confidante was one of his aunts; and in the course of his investigations he has accumulated a rich collection of documents concerning his hero and had written a biography of him to which later biographers will always be indebted.

Adéma found that the Flugi d'Aspermonts were an ancient Swiss clan, originating in St. Moritz and ennobled in the seventeenth century. Some of the Flugis remained at home, becoming Swiss ecclesiastics, warriors, or local poets; others made their careers abroad. Francesco, the man of the photograph, born in 1835 (and thus more than twenty years older than Angelica de Kostrowitzky), was a young officer on the staffs of Ferdinand II and Francis I, the last kings of the Two Sicilies. He was still in his twenties when the Neapolitan Bourbons fell to Garibaldi and Victor Emmanuel, and he resigned from the army, apparently too Bourbon himself to be willing to serve lesser masters.[3]

[3] Readers of the Prince of Lampedusa's novel The Leopard, (Il Gatto-

He did not marry, and for years wandered over Europe, doing no one knows what. During the 1870's and early '80's he spent some time in Rome, the home of several of his relations. His oldest brother, the head of the family, was a prelate, the Very Reverend Romarino-Maria Flugi d'Aspermont. Don Romarino was Abbot Primate—abbot-in-chief—of the order of the Black Benedictines, after having reigned from 1868 to 1871 over the diocese of Monaco with the title of Abbot Nullius—abbot without an abbey—appointed to that post by Pius IX in the days before the principality had been awarded a titular bishop. When Francesco became *persona non grata* to his brothers because of gambling debts and a series of entanglements—one of them, supposedly, with "a Russian woman" of whose child or children he was the father—they provided him with capital and persuaded him to emigrate to America, whether North or South is not specified. That was in 1884, and his family claims never to have heard from him or, except vaguely, even of him, again.

Perhaps Francesco Flugi d'Aspermont really was one of those ultimate eccentrics, one of the small, select company of mortals who succeed in dropping out of sight while still in this world. Such, at least, is the picture of him given to M. Marcel Adéma by the Flugi d'Aspermonts who spoke with M. Adéma in Rome, apparently frankly, in the late 1940's. At first, they said, the family was not too sorry that Francesco should have vanished, but later they tried to find him in connection with an inheritance, and

pardo), will be familiar with this moment in history and the class of officer to which Francesco must have belonged.

9

Guillaume Apollinaire

could learn only that at some time or other he had been "seen in St. Petersburg." There was also the rumor that he had never gone to America at all, but had left his ship at Messina and for a time rejoined his "Russian woman." But in *her* life—if she is really to be identified with Angelica de Kostrowitzky—his only recorded presence is in his photograph.

When M. Marcel Adéma presented his revelations concerning Francesco Flugi d'Aspermont as Apollinaire's probable father in the *Figaro Littéraire* in 1949 and 1950, he did so modestly and tentatively, always ready, he declared, to withdraw him should a more compelling candidate be advanced. Adéma never provided, nor claimed to provide, any indications of the time or place or circumstances of even a single meeting between Francesco and Angelica. In fact there is no record of their ever having met at all; none of their having been together at any time. Francesco is little more than a photograph—truly a thing of shadows. The case for his paternity rests on several exhibits: Apollinaire's pointing to a photograph and his mother's mention of a name; and the name "Baron d'Ormespant" (an anagram of Aspermont) given by Apollinaire to a character in the first draft of one of his stories; Marcel Adéma's knowledge that Don Romarino, Francesco's prelate brother, considered it his Christian duty to contribute for a time to the support of the Kostrowitzky children in Monaco; and, finally, another photograph, one of Don Romarino himself, given to Adéma by the Flugi d'Aspermont family.[4] In this photo-

[4] The largeness of view—one should perhaps call it gallantry—on the part of the Flugi d'Aspermonts in agreeing with Marcel Adéma that their

graph the then head of the Benedictine Order does indeed bear a startling resemblance to his supposed nephew, the poet Guillaume Apollinaire.

M. Marcel Adéma's persuasive nomination of Francesco Flugi d'Aspermont as the father of Guillaume Apollinaire was immediately and generally accepted as probable by those familiar with Apollinaire's life and work. No other candidate had ever been put forward at all persuasively. Recently, however, another possibility has been suggested, one that might be called the dubious fruit of a surrealist poet's intuition, as contrasted with the deductions and photographic confrontations of a literature-loving businessman.

In 1959 a Polish surrealist poet, Anatol Stern, was told by Kostrowitzkys still living in Poland that a male descendant of a branch of the Kostrowitzky family other than that represented by "Angelica, daughter of Apollinaris, of St.

erring Francesco was probably the natural father of Apollinaire is rather remarkable in a Roman family of the "black" or papal aristocracy, which might be expected to show reserve in a matter of this kind, especially one linking them to the world of the Cubists, Dadaists, and Surrealists. While following the trail so clearly blazed by Marcel Adéma in Rome, I received a most courteous letter from the present head of the family, Monsignore Mariano Flugi d'Aspermont, nephew of Francesco, in which he speaks of his uncle's "probable, very probable adventure with Mad. de K," and says further that the Italian poet, Ungaretti, a friend of Apollinaire's, had recently found in him, the Monsignore, "an unmistakable family resemblance" to his probable cousin. Perhaps it is purely coincidence that Monsignore Mariano Flugi d'Aspermont was until recently "Sacrestano" of the basilica of Santa Maria Maggiore, in whose baptistry the baby was christened. The Monsignore is a man of literary tastes, and for the catalogue of an Apollinaire exhibition held in Rome late in 1960 it was he who translated into Italian M. Marcel Adéma's biographical sketch of the poet who was probably his cousin.

11

Petersburg" was resident in Rome in 1880, year of the birth of the baby in Trastevere. Certain Kostrowitzkys had moved from Poland to Vienna very early in the nineteenth century, among them a certain Melanie. Melanie Kostrowitzky was known, by the family, to have frequented the Austrian imperial court at Schoenbrunn, and was further known, also by the family, to have conceived and borne in 1831, at the age of eighteen, a child fathered by a very exalted member of that court. "A very highly placed personage," ran the Kostrowitzky family tradition, "very close to the throne of France."

Now in 1831 at the court of Schoenbrunn there was no one "very close to the throne of France" except the twenty-year-old François-Charles-Joseph Bonaparte himself, Napoleon's son by his second empress, Marie-Louise, daughter of the Emperor Francis I of Austria. At birth he had been given the glorious title of King of Rome. When his father abdicated in his favor in 1814 he became, for a brief time at the age of three, Napoleon II. In exile with his mother, however, when the great Napoleon—"*l'Aigle*" (the Eagle)—was banished to St. Helena, the boy was re-titled the Duke of Reichstadt. He is often known as "l'Aiglon" (the Eaglet).

For the advent of her son Melanie was spirited to Rome, the Kostrowitzkys told Anatol Stern. He was raised not by his mother, but "in the care of the Vatican"; he was called Kostrowitzky; and for his support the Kostrowitzkys in Poland were proud to sell certain estates of which they would never have stripped themselves but for extraordinary reasons. The young Duke of Reichstadt died a year after the boy's birth, in 1832: gossip has credited him with fathering more than one child in his brief life, including Maximilian, Emperor of Mexico; but no one had previously heard of a son named Kostrowitzky who was raised in the Vatican.

Leaving her son in Rome, Melanie returned to Vienna, where she spent the rest of her life. She never married. In her later years she was known as "the old countess": her right to the title was guaranteed by eighteenth-century patents of nobility given to the Kostrowitzkys by Catherine the Great.[5] The old lady lived in a palace and dressed like a nun, "all in black, with a large cross on a heavy chain around her neck," but on her grey hair "a red skull-cap." She frequently visited her son in Rome, the family said, and when she died in 1888, the Vatican inherited her property. Shortly before, however, she had given her relatives in Poland, saying that she wished to dispose of "all her ties with the world—everything that reminded her of past joys and sorrows," some portraits and

a number of trunks, strangely shaped and very old, covered with leather and finely reinforced with iron and copper. The trunks contained a quantity of letters, documents, a few boxes containing engravings, drawings, watercolors and a number of unframed oil paintings rolled around wooden cylinders: on the back of several of these could be read the words "King of Rome"

[5] It has been estimated that in the eighteenth century about one and a half million Poles (a tenth of the population) were "noble," i.e. gentry of varying degrees of prosperity. To indicate their distinction Poles of this class living abroad frequently made use of the French particle "de"—in their estimation the equivalent of the Polish suffix "ski," often used in family names to show derivation from a place or an estate. In using the title "countess" Melanie may have taken certain liberties.

13

Guillaume Apollinaire

or "Duke of Reichstadt."

There were also copies of pictures in the Sistine Chapel. Somewhat anticlimactically, Anatol Stern had to report that his Kostrowitzky informants told him that all those boxes had disappeared from one of the Kostrowitzky houses in Poland during one of the world wars.

That is all that is known about Melanie's son: nothing about his life in Rome; not the date of his death; not even his first name. Why should the Vatican, traditionally hostile to the Bonapartes, have been charged with the rearing of a Bonaparte? Was he its prisoner? Officially this X—— de Kostrowitzky does not exist. The shadowy ne'er-do-well Francesco Flugi d'Aspermont is flesh and blood compared with him. His unsubstantiality forces one to remember that "descendants of Napoleon" are perhaps more numerous in mental hospitals than in history.

And yet the poet Anatol Stern believes that Francesco Flugi d'Aspermont was merely one of the numerous lovers of Angelica de Kostrowitzky, Apollinaire's mother; that the poet's father was indeed her distant cousin, X—— de Kostrowitzky, raised in the Vatican; and thus that Guillaume Apollinaire was the great-grandson of Napoleon. The Emperor and his poet great-grandson were alike born obscurely, outside France; both met their destinies as French geniuses.

It is true that if Melanie's son was living in Rome, with some Vatican connection and at the same time as Angelica, the two could scarcely have helped meeting; for as we shall see Angelica's father held a Vatican office. And it may also be true, as Anatol Stern says, that X—— de

Kostrowitzky's age of fifty, in 1880, as compared with Angelica's twenty-two, was no bar to a romance, especially if, as Stern puts it, "in Poland and not only in Poland fifty is considered the age of mature masculinity."

Stern's chief exhibit in support of his Napoleonic thesis—an exhibit as striking in its way as the photographic resemblance between Guillaume Apollinaire and Don Romarino-Maria Flugi d'Aspermont—is a story of Apollinaire's called "La Chasse à l'Aigle" ("The Hunting of the Eagle,") written when he was in his twenties and short enough to be printed here in full.

The Hunting of the Eagle

I had been in Vienna a week. It never stopped raining, but the weather was mild, midwinter though it was.

I made a special point of visiting Schoenbrunn, and felt full of emotion as I walked in the dripping, melancholy park, once the haunt of the tragic King of Rome, fallen in rank to be mere Duke of Reichstadt.

From the "Glorietta"—the name struck me as an ironic diminutive, one that must have made him dream of the glory of his father and of France—I stared a long time out over the capital of the Hapsburgs, and when night fell and all the lights came on I started to walk back toward my hotel in the center of the city.

I lost my way in the outskirts, and after many false turnings I found myself in a deserted street that was wide and dimly lit. I caught sight of a shop, and dark though it was and seemingly abandoned, I was about to go in to ask my way, when my attention was attracted by another pedestrian, who brushed lightly against me as he passed. He was short, and a capelet of the kind worn by army officers floated from his shoulders. I quickened my steps and caught up with him. His profile was turned to me, and as soon as I glimpsed his features I gave a start. Instead of a human

15

Guillaume Apollinaire

face the creature beside me had the beak of an eagle, curved, powerful, fierce, and infinitely majestic.

Concealing my agitation, I continued to walk ahead, staring attentively at this strange personage with the body of a human and the head of a bird of prey. He turned toward me, and as his eyes stared into mine a trembling, old-man's voice said in German:

"Have no fear. I am not a bad man. I am an unfortunate."

Alas! I could make no answer, no sound came from my throat, it was so parched with anguish. The voice resumed, now imperious and with a hint of scorn:

"My mask frightens you. My real face would frighten you more. No Austrian could look at it without terror, because I know I look exactly like my grandfather...."

At that moment a crowd rushed into the street, pressing and shouting; other people came out of shops, and heads peered from windows. I stopped and looked behind me. I saw that those who were coming were soldiers, officers dressed in white, lackeys in livery and a gigantic beadle who was brandishing a long staff with a silver knob. Some stable boys were running among them, bearing flaming torches. I was curious to know the object of their chase, and I looked in the direction they were headed. But all I could see before me was the fantastic silhouette of the man in the eagle mask, fleeing, his arms outstretched and his head turned as though to see what this danger was that was threatening him.

And at that instant I had a vision that was very precise and immensely moving.

The fugitive, seen thus from behind, his short cape spread wide over his arms, and his beak in profile above his right shoulder, was exactly the heraldic eagle in the armorial bearings of the French empire. That marvelous effect lasted barely a second, but I knew that I had not been alone or mistaken in what I had seen. The crowd pursuing the Eagle stopped, amazed by the sight, but their hesitation lasted no longer than the vision.

Then the poor human bird turned his beak away, and all we had ahead of us was a poor unfortunate, making a desperate effort to escape from implacable foes. They soon caught up with

16

him. In the gleam of the torches I saw their sacrilegious hands catch hold of the cornered Eagle. He screamed some words that so filled me with panic and so paralyzed me that I was incapable of even thinking of going to his help.

His last desperate cry was: "Help! I am the heir of the Bonapartes...."

But fists rained blows on his beak and on his head, and cut short his plea. He fell lifeless, and those who had just murdered him promptly raised him up and hurriedly bore him off. The entire crowd disappeared around a bend. I tried to catch up with them, but in vain; and for a long time, at the corner of the street they had taken, I stood motionless, watching their flickering torches fade away in the distance....

A short time after that extraordinary encounter I attended an evening gathering at the home of a great Austrian nobleman whom I had known in Paris. There were marvelously beautiful women, many diplomats and officers. For a brief moment I found myself alone with my host, and he said:

"Everywhere you go in Vienna just now you hear the same strange story. The newspapers don't speak of it, because it is too obviously absurd to be believed by anyone with common sense. Still, it is something that can't help interest a Frenchman, and that is why I want to tell you about it. People are saying that in a secret ceremony the Duke of Reichstadt married a daughter of one of our great families, and that son born of this marriage was brought up unknown even to those in attendance at court. The rumor is that this very important person, the true heir of Napoleon Bonaparte, lived in concealment until an advanced age, and that he died barely two or three days ago in particularly tragic circumstances, though precisely how is not known."

I stood there silent, not knowing what to answer. And in the midst of the brilliant party I had a vision of the old Eagle who had spoken to me. Condemned to be masked for reasons of state, wearing the superb sign of an august race. . . . Perhaps I had seen the son of l'Aiglon.

17

Guillaume Apollinaire

Anatol Stern calls attention to the "extremely personal" tone of that little story, and to the presence of another eagle-mask in Apollinaire's work—a mere mention, in a tale called "Cas du brigadier masqué" ("Case of the Masked Corporal,") of a Polish Count Polaski, with a castle near Cracow, who is seen in Vienna "bargaining with a junk dealer for a strange mask in the form of an eagle's beak." In fact Napoleon is mentioned fairly often in Apollinaire's work. On one occasion Apollinaire said that he thought of his own face as being "the mask of Napoleon," and on another that he had "Cæsar's profile," a belief that Napoleon entertained concerning himself.

And then, after the publication of *his* "discovery," Anatol Stern had the excitement of learning that Melanie, the old countess in Vienna, of whose existence he had no reason to suppose that anyone now living in France had ever heard, had indeed been known to both Apollinaire and his mother—in life to the latter, and in death, at least, to the poet. For on November 9, 1959—the forty-first anniversary of Apollinaire's death—Anatol Stern called on his widow, Jacqueline Apollinaire, and found that she knew Melanie's name quite well. She showed him a brooch that her husband had given her shortly before his death: it had been a present to his mother, he had told her, from Melanie. And Apollinaire had told her that he had visited Melanie's burial vault in Vienna when he had been there in 1902.

So Apollinaire, who thought his own face "the mask of Napoleon," knew the story of Melanie and the "heir of the Bonapartes" all along? What more had he known? Or had he intuited, supposed, believed, invented?

18

Apollinaire: One

For the present, it is in those vaguer realms that the "Napoleonic thesis" must be left, for alas! in a new pair of anticlimaxes—like the Polish Kostrowitzky's lame avowal that all of Melanie's treasures had "disappeared"—there has recently come word from the municipality of Vienna that there is no record of anyone named Melanie Kostrowitzky being interred in any Viennese cemetery in 1888 or in any other year; and the Vatican archives report that there are no documents or traditions concerning any Kostrowitzky except Michal Apollinaris, Angelica's father.

So, Apollinaire's paternity remains a mystery, and there remains the further mystery: why should it have been kept a mystery?

One thing is sure, however. The poet may not have been the offspring of either of those dim, silent figures, the brother of the Abbot-Primate of the Benedictines or the supposed son of the King of Rome, but he was certainly the son of Angelica de Kostrowitzky. And she was not dim, precisely. She was more like a poster by Toulouse-Lautrec.

Her father, Michal Apollinaris Kostrowicki (Polish spelling), had apparently been a Polish officer in the Russian army and had seen the family property in Poland confiscated by the Russian government following the participation of his two co-owners, his brothers Joseph and Adam, in the anti-Russian revolution of 1863. His brothers were sent to Siberia, and he, with his Italian wife, Julia Floriani, and their daughter Angelica Alexandrina, moved to Rome, presumably to be near his wife's relations.

19

Guillaume Apollinaire

Olga de Kostrowitzky

Perhaps the Florianis supported the Kostrowitzkys: nothing is known about either family, or about Michal Apollinaris Kostrowitzky's possible profession or employment or income in Rome beyond one fact: that he presumably drew the food allowance of thirty-six scudi a year (roughly the equivalent of 90,000 Italian lire today, or about $150), vulgarly known as *"la zuppa,"* to which he was entitled by his otherwise unsalaried position as papal chamberlain, *"cameriere d'onore di capa e spada."*

20

Apollinaire: One

Olga de Kostrowitzky   21

Guillaume Apollinaire

In the "Pontifical Family"—"family" being used in the Italian sense to embrace all members of a household, including paid servitors—the papal chamberlains are recruited from *"signori rispettabili e cavalieri laici"* (respectable gentlemen and secular knights), Romans, Italians, or foreigners, who have given proof of religious attachment to the Apostolic Seat. Their numbers vary with the various popes, their hours of duty are short, and they are seldom if ever all on duty at the same time; but some of them are always present at important papal events like canonizations, and some of them always preside over the pope's antechamber during audiences. Anyone who has been received by His Holiness has seen them, with their black capes and their swords, and their triple silver-gilt chains and sky-blue medallions. The office is by its very title an honorary one, and apart from *la zuppa* it is not known to bring any perquisites beyond a built-in certificate of respectability.

Such a man, a *chevalier* certified to be *sans reproche,* was Guillaume Apollinaire's one known grandfather. Perhaps some Polish prelate was influential in getting him his post; the papal nomination, dated 1868, refers to him as a "retired Russian captain." His noble lineage must have helped him: in 1851, before the revolution that scattered them, he and his brothers had proven their nobility for at least four generations in order to qualify for listing in a Polish almanac of heraldry.

The date of his death is not known. If he continued to live into the 1870's and '80's, one winces at the thought of the outrages perpetrated on his paternal feelings by his daughter Angelica. In 1866 she was admitted into the

Istituto di Educazione delle Dame del Sacro Cuore, the convent-academy maintained in Rome for children of noble families by the French nuns of the Society of the Religious of the Sacred Heart of Jesus. "Her father paid for only one trimester, fifty francs," says the entry in the Admissions Register of the school, and—most unusually—her parents' address is omitted. Dated September 26, 1874, when she was sixteen, is the record of Angelica's dismissal: "Extremely difficult child. We had to ask her father to remove her." It was six years later that she gave birth, supposedly in a room "across the Tiber," to "Guglielmo-Alberto Dulcigni," of father "N.N."

Two years later, in 1882, Angelica de Kostrowitzky bore another son, also in Rome and also of father "N.N." This younger boy, whom we shall encounter from time to time in the following pages, was endowed by the municipal authorities with the name Zevini—the Z's apparently having by that time been reached in the name file of the Roman Anagrafe. His first name was given to the clerk as Alberto, and Alberto Zevini he continued to be for the first six years of his existence. Only in 1888 did Angelica do for him what she had done earlier for his elder brother Guglielmo-Alberto —she "recognized" him, and his name was changed in the records to Alberto de Kostrowitzky. So he remained for the rest of his life, only dropping the *o* when living in France. There seems to be no indication one way or another as to whether the two boys had the same father. Alberto's paternity is even more of a mystery than Guglielmo Alberto's, and the arrival of a second illegitimate son to Angelica has never cast any light on the paternity of her

23

elder son.

Yes: if the respectable *cameriere d'onore di capa e spada* Michal Apollinaris de Kostrowitzky lived to know of his rather special grandfatherhood, one is almost glad that history is mute concerning his feelings. He was almost certainly gone by 1887, the year of an event that would probably have given him some relief were he alive: his daughter left Rome and went abroad to live.

On March 4 of that year "Olga de Kostrowitzky" rented a furnished apartment in the Principality of Monaco. She was accompanied, says her *fiche* (the normal police form for foreign visitors), by "her two children." Unlike the international "Angelica," "Olga" is a specifically Russian name: perhaps she took it to comfort the Russian princes, dukes, and other grandees who in those days thronged the Monte Carlo Casino, or perhaps "Angelica" had merely begun to have too ironic a sound. On April 2 she moved to a different furnished apartment and filled out a new *fiche*. By now she was accompanied by "three persons." She soon attracted the attention of the authorities. On April 6 the weekly report submitted by M. de Farincourt, Governor General of the Principality, to his sovereign, Prince Albert I, included the following item:

Mme Olga de Kostrowitzky complains that she is being refused a residence permit. She claims that her situation is absolutely regular and that she is the recipient of a pension from the Czar as the daughter of a colonel in the Russian army.

M. de Farincourt will inquire into details before taking definite steps regarding this lady. Her attitude suggests that in addition to her pension she derives an income from sources of

24

Albert and Wilhelm de Kostrowitzky

25

Guillaume Apollinaire

questionable morality, notwithstanding the fact that she has two small boys, one at the Collège Saint-Charles and the other, aged four, with her.

On May 12 the Governor General's report to the prince contained the following:

M. Jolivot, presently Deputy Government Commissioner, has just obtained the expulsion of several *femmes galantes,* whose names will figure in his next weekly report. The Casino, considering its recent losses, has agreed to this drastic measure, despite the protests of a number of persons, including several of high social standing, who vouch for the ladies in question.

And, a few days later:

M. Jolivot confirms the news that he has already given concerning the *femmes galantes* recently ordered expelled. They are: C. d'A.; J.B.; Olga de Kostrowiska; L.L.; and the one who goes by the name of "A."[6]

[6] Those three documents, previously unpublished, were kindly communicated to me by Monsieur A. Lisimachio, Conservateur des Archives et de la Bibliothèque du Palais de Monaco, following the gracious intervention of their Serene Highnesses Prince Rainier and Princess Grace of Monaco. M. Lisimachio exercised the greatest discretion in communicating the documents, which came to me in the form of typewritten copies. He explained that it was not possible to send photocopies of the reports, as I had requested, because one of them names not only Olga de Kostrowitzky but also five other persons described as *"femmes galantes."* Because this document is so "recent," and touches on the private lives of several persons, he felt it necessary to replace the other names by initials, and to send copies in that form. M. Lisimachio further urged me not to divulge these details concerning Mme de Kostrowitzky "in a brutal way," but rather to "use them to show the influence of Guillaume Apollinaire's childhood surroundings on his work." This is of course my only purpose in using the documents, and I hope that my remarks on pp. 55–57 may reassure M. Lisimachio in this regard, and justify his generosity in releasing the seventy-year-old information.

Apollinaire: One

A historically minded Monegasque has written more explicitly about the presence of *"femmes galantes"* in the Principality at that time:

The gossip sheets of those days had much to say not only about the crowned heads . . . but also about "the fine flower of cosmopolitan *galanterie*" and certain pretty *soupeuses* who were often seen with the most exalted personalities. Among those mentioned are: Liane de Pougy, Valtesse de la Bigne, Adèle Richer, Albertine Wolff, Nini Biadler, de Lagny, Petit Pois, Morainville, Suzanne d'Almont, Yvonne de Ricy, and still others. All this set crowded to applaud La Belle Otero in her Spanish dances, or Mlle Katinka conducting her gypsy orchestra. Another Polish lady, Mme de Kostvowicka [*sic*], said to have been financed by the Société des Bains de Mer as *"entraîneuse"* certainly figured in these raucous gatherings.

"Entraîneuse" (literally a woman who "leads men on" —to spend money at gambling tables or in night clubs), *"soupeuse," "femme galante"*—Olga de Kostrowitzky, ex-Angelica, daughter of the impoverished Polish papal chamberlain, was all those and mother besides. Her prelate brother-in-law outside the bonds of matrimony, that head of the Black Benedictines who apparently met the expenses of her sons' education in Monaco, never prevented her from making her own living in the way that "came most naturally." The men in her life seem to have been comparatively few—few, that is, for a courtesan—and little is known about them. During her years in Monaco she made several trips outside the Principality with admirers whom she presented to her sons as their "uncles"; at least one of them, a rich silk manufacturer with bookish tastes, allowed her to bring the boys to his home in Lyons, where Apol-

27

Guillaume Apollinaire

linaire later recalled reveling in a fine private library. Along with these adventures of her Monaco days she entered into a steady liaison with an Alsatian gambler named Jules Weil, eleven years her junior, who was also, at first, presented to the boys as their "uncle." It was a liaison that was to last until death, long outdating the sojourn in the Principality. Angelica was an original. Handsome, strident, living outside society in a strange kind of isolation, she constantly reminded her sons of their descent from northern nobles of the dim past, and scolded them if they kept what she considered unworthy company. Despite her troubles with the police she was something of a prude, let alone a snob. Apollinaire's friends record that when she was hospitably inclined she could spread a welcoming feast like any generous bourgeoise, but that in general she looked down on them as Bohemian, harum-scarum, loose-living. She despised her elder son's choice of profession. Perhaps the best description of her, especially as regards Guillaume Apollinaire, is found in the Journal of Paul Léautaud, the French man of letters, under the date of Monday, January 20, 1919, a little more than two months after Apollinaire's death at the age of thirty-eight. Léautaud was then employed by the *Mercure de France*.

It was ten minutes to six, and I was about to leave for the day, when a message came from the salesroom that a lady was there, claiming to be Apollinaire's mother and asking to be given copies of his books. Should she be given them? I asked that she be sent up to me.

The lady who came into my office was quite tall, elegant, rather unusual looking. She greatly resembled Apollinaire, or rather he greatly resembled her—the nose, something about the eyes, and especially the mouth, the expression of her mouth when she laughed and smiled. She struck me as being a very original character. Exuberant. Nothing run of the mill about her. In half an hour she told me her life story: Russian, never married, a great traveler—all over Europe, or almost. (I had the sudden thought that the mobility of Apollinaire's *imagination* came from her foot-looseness.) Apollinaire was born in Rome. She said nothing about his father.

She spoke about the man she has lived with for twenty-five years, her "friend," an Alsatian, great gambler, one moment rolling in money, the next penniless. She has everything she wants. Dinners at Paillard's, Prunier's, the Café de la Paix, etc.

She tells me that she "set up" Apollinaire several times—financially, that is—showered money on him. In speaking of him she always referred to him as "Wilhelm." She had nasty things to say about his wife. Mme Cayssac was in my office during the conversation and thinks that Mme de Kostrowitzky's furs were worth four thousand francs at least. Also silk stockings of expensive quality. She described Apollinaire as a not very affectionate son, interested in what he could get out of her, often vile-tempered, always asking for money, and very loath to give her any when he had some. She didn't hide her age: fifty-two. Very well preserved for that age, remarkably slender, graceful in her movements. Apollinaire seems not to have sent her his books. She knew nothing of *Alcools*. In the salesroom she had just bought *Calligrammes*. *Les Mamelles de Tirésias* had been staged without her knowing anything about it.

She talked about all the money that "women are earning" at this moment in Paris, what with all the Americans and English here. She uttered the word "earning" in a very special tone, with a very special emphasis.

Apollinaire died at thirty-eight. If she is really fifty-two, he was born when she was fourteen. Mme Cayssac thinks that she took off a few years in calling herself fifty-two.[7]

She told me: "I have another son, my son Albert. He works

[7] In 1919 Olga de Kostrowitzky was probably sixty. 29

Guillaume Apollinaire

in a bank in Mexico. He is a hard worker, a good son. He writes well, too. He writes articles for a Mexican financial journal." Obviously, to her that kind of writing is far more important than anything Apollinaire ever did. "Madame," I told her, "you certainly seem to have no idea of the great reputation Apollinaire had made for himself by the time he died."

Apollinaire: One

Two

...the *femmes galantes* recently ordered expelled.... C. d'A.; J.B.; Olga de Kostrowiska; L.L.; and the one who goes by the name of "A."....

Ordered expelled: but in the case of Olga de Kostrowitzky, at least, the order given by the Governor General or a Commissioner must have been rescinded, or simply not executed, following word from "higher up." For she continued to live in Monaco for the next twelve years, apparently unmolested, pursuing her career as *entraîneuse* at the Monte Carlo Casino that we still know today, that "splendid construction in the style of the Renaissance," as Baedeker calls it, "built chiefly in 1878, from plans by Charles Garnier, architect of the Paris opera house."

Those twelve years, from 1887 to 1899, were the seventh through the eighteenth of her elder son, originally registered as Guglielmo Dulcigni, baptized Guglielmo de Kostrowitzky, and for some reason henceforth called by his mother and nearly always officially known as Wilhelm de Kostrowitzky. They were the years that turned him into a French poet. Had he remained in Rome he might or might not have become a poet anyway, but it was the twelve years in Monaco that made his language French.

Olga de Kostrowitzky had probably set the stage for her son's Frenchification by her own eight-year attendance, during her Roman girlhood, at the Convent-Academy of

31

Guillaume Apollinaire

the Sacred Heart on the Pincian Hill, familiarly known, from the name of its church, as Trinità dei Monti. Both buildings, standing side by side at the top of the Spanish Steps, were built in the fifteenth century by order of King Charles VIII of France as a monastery and church for the Order of Minims, the Hermits of St. Francis of Paola, and ever since the property has been French, considered French soil, enjoying rights of extra-territoriality. In 1828, by French royal letters of patent and by papal brief, the monastery was made over to the Dames Françaises du Sacré Cœur as a convent and academy, "as our great desire is"— so run the papal words—"that children of our noble families should be educated in a manner suited to their position." The superior of the convent has always been, and still is, a Frenchwoman; a certain number of the nuns are French; the French language and French history and literature are required subjects of study. Though she was expelled from Trinità dei Monti at sixteen, Olga de Kostrowitzky had nonetheless been thoroughly Gallicized: all her life she spoke French without accent and wrote it perfectly.[1]

[1] A friend who attended Trinità dei Monti considerably later than Angelica de Kostrowitzky has been good enough to write me of its Gallicizing influence:

The pupils are on the whole Italian and the language spoken is Italian, but in my day in half an hour, for instance, of an hour's recreation, we were obliged to speak French, and we had a French class every morning plus our Italian, and it was not only French language but French history and French literature. The education of Trinità dei Monti in pre-Mussolini times would have certainly left any impressionable girl with a predisposition to things French, as it did me. I love France, the country, the language, the culture, the people, even my prayers are sometimes French from *force d'habitude*. . . . The old pupils have got, even now, a very strong French mark. I am sure that it was through the nostalgia of some of the French nuns for their towns and villages that when I was young I got to visit so much of France and to know so much of the real countryside.

Apollinaire: Two

In 1881, the year after the birth of Olga's elder son, a French school, the first in the Principality, was founded in Monaco, created as though expressly for the benefit of French poetry, in plenty of time for it to function smoothly by the time the Kostrowitzky boy arrived. Hitherto the culture of Monaco had been Italianate. The local language, Monegasque, is closely related to the Ligurian dialect of Italian, and the only secondary school had been the Jesuit Collegio della Visitazione, where instruction was in Italian. But since 1860, when the important city of Nice, only twelve miles away, had come under French rule, a process of Frenchification had been creeping eastward along the Riviera. When the Principality was finally awarded a true bishop, in 1886, some years after the departure of Abbot Romarino-Maria Flugi d'Aspermont, the first Bishop of Monaco was a Frenchman, Charles François Bonaventure Theuret, from Vars in the Haute-Saône. It was he who founded the French school, the Collège Saint-Charles, in an eighteenth century building known as the Maison de Millo, the present City Hall of Monaco. The nuns and the priests (at first "free priests," that is, secular priests not as-signed to parishes, and later Marianist fathers) who taught there were of varied nationalities, but instruction was in French and the program of study was that of French second-ary schools: modern languages and literatures, mathematics, and the various subjects suggested by the names of the last two years—"rhétorique" and "philosophie."

The Collège Saint-Charles is perhaps the only reli-giously directed school in history to have owed its creation in part to the glamor of the gaming table. The Monte Carlo

33

Casino had opened in the 1860's after gambling had been prohibited in Germany and such prosperous casinos as those of Baden, Wiesbaden, and Hamburg had had to shut their doors. It quickly became the gaming center of Europe. Every winter it attracted gamblers from every country in the world," as Baedeker puts it, to play roulette and *trente-et-quarante*. *"Faites vos jeux!," "Rien ne va plus!,"* and the other famous formulas were shouted from 10 A.M. until two in the morning; and since French was the international language of the gamblers even when they were outside the Casino, it was inevitable that the citizens of the Principality, who were excluded by law from the gaming tables that were so enriching their little country that they were, until recently, exempt of all taxes, should want to Frenchify themselves and their children, at least linguistically, the better to profit from the winter visitors.

The Collège Saint-Charles must have been an unusual school, with its international faculty and its mixed enrollment of native sons and the children of cosmopolitan gamblers, *entraîneuses,* and other officials, servants, and hangers-on of the Casino. The pupils included French boys, Italians, English, Germans, Belgians, Russians, and, as one chronicler puts it, "even a few Americans."

It was a shifting student body. "I was a half-boarder at this charming school," writes the son of a gambling mother, who knew Apollinaire there.

On Thursdays and Sundays Guillaume Apollinaire would be leading the line of regular boarders as they took their customary walk through Monte Carlo, and I would leave the table at the Café de Paris where I was sitting with my parents and exchange a

Apollinaire: Two

few words with him. He was an inspired talker if ever there was one, I would come away dazzled by the strange, carefully-turned sentences that took wing from his lips with the grace of a lyre-bird. I knew that he wrote "strange" poetry. Alas! At that time I had not gone beyond François Coppée: my mother used to recite his verses to me. Eventually we had to return to Paris: my mother had no luck with roulette.

Kostrowitzky was an oblong-faced adolescent, whose most prominent physical feature was a heavy jaw, rather like the jaw of the young Mussolini; his body was heavy and chunky—the "grace of a lyre-bird" was always to be a lyrical grace only. Besides being an excellent pupil and taking many prizes, he was encouraged by his mother the *entraîneuse* in the ways of piety, and he made his First Communion and became secretary of the Congregation of the Immaculate Conception. He quickly had difficulty with the first name she insisted he use. "Wilhelm," pronounced in France with the *W* as a *V*, the *h* silent and the second *l* slurred, sounds like "*vilain*," meaning "nasty". At the Collège Saint-Charles, that school of shifting students where he found himself after all his shifts of name, the boys chanted "Wilhelm vilain! Vilain Wilhelm!"

As to the "strange" poetry he was writing—it could only seem strange, indeed obscure and mysterious, to his friend Frick and others of his contemporaries who were then unfamiliar with French verse more recent than the clear, correct, "square" stanzas of Coppée and other so-called Parnassians, poems that read today like fluent journalistic prose with incidental rhymes. The very titles of some of the verses by the young Kostrowitzky—"Lilith," "The Death of Pan," "Winter Dawn," "Triptych on Man"—   35 announce their writer's adherence to the "new" school of the Symbolists, the so-called "School of 1885," the school of Verlaine, Rimbaud, and Mallarmé. Mallarmé had written a famous statement about the new poetry and the old a few years before:

> The contemplation of objects, the image that rises out of the reverie the objects provoke—those are the song. But the Parnassians take the thing in its entirety and point at it: thereby they lack mystery. They deprive the reader of the delightful illusion that he is a creator. To name an object is to destroy three-quarters of our pleasure in a poem—the joy of guessing, step by step. The ideal is to suggest the object. We derive the most from the mystery that constitutes the symbol when we evoke the object step by step in order to portray a state of mind. Or, the other way round, when we choose an object and derive a state of mind from it by a sequence of decipherings.

Into his notebooks young Kostrowitzky copied verses by the Symbolists and their followers: Stuart Merrill, Moréas, Maeterlinck, Francis Jammes, Fernand Gregh, and others. Many schoolboys have written verse that has been Parnassian, Symbolist, Futurist, Dadaist, or Surrealist, and have gone on to practical careers in politics or medicine or business; but there are signs that at the age of sixteen, in Monaco, Kostrowitzky was beginning not merely to write verse, but to inhabit almost exclusively a strongly personal world, a world of poetry and a rather special kind of erudition. He quickly became the very prototype of vastly read youth, particularly in the fields of history, mythology, linguistics, and literature. Nothing was systematic; his erudition was immense, but spotty and *"amusante,"* as a friend was later to call it. He never stopped reading, and his library, still in existence, is a strikingly heterogeneous collection. From these earliest days his writings were apt to be full of recondite references. "He already knew all the *bons mots,* all the little episodes that are outside the main current of history but that give history its flavor," a school-mate remembers. "He could tell us whether such and such a wizard wore blue brocade and a pointed hat; he could describe the period costume worn by such and such a good fairy. He knew all about the worries of the incubi and the succubi. He lived among legends and all the anecdotes of history. He was fascinating to us, teaching us everything we didn't know: he knew everything already." (Including, the same writer tells us, all about the great courtesans of the day—that "Liane de Pougy, who had the most beautiful blue eyes in the world, had tried to commit suicide because Jean Lorrain had left her; that La Belle Otero had, in such and such circumstances, worn the most beautiful jewels, and that she came from a very modest background," etc.) None of his verses did he sign "Wilhelm." Under some he wrote the signature "Guillaume Macabre"; under others, as early as this, "Guillaume Apollinaire."

"He came very early into possession of his poetic universe," Michel Décaudin has said, "and in a career whose aspects were many and seemingly contradictory, he was often only continuing along the path of his adolescent dreams and discoveries." His earliest memories were of Rome: the Carnival there, the celebrations of Epiphany, "those feasts of the Magi, when I ate so many dragées stuffed with orange peel, so many anis drops with their

37

delicious after-taste"; "I remember very well a certain brotherhood that one saw at Roman funerals, whose members wore hoods." There was the beautiful corner of the physical universe in which he was living, the dramatic stretch of the Mediterranean coast where the Maritime Alps, crowned by fortresses and the old Roman triumphal monument at La Turbie, plunge abruptly into a sea as iridescent as the scales of its angel-fish. Palm trees lining blue bays, terraces of oranges and lemons, more terraces of carnations, roses, and violets for the perfume factories at Grasse, the contrast of snow-capped Alp and tropical sun, the latter so broiling at one banana-growing corner of Beaulieu, between Monaco and Nice, that the spot is called "Petite Afrique." His work is dotted with descriptions of the region:

> Directly across was the expanse of the sea, calm and blue in spots as though enormous sapphires showed through the water. The rocky promontory of Monaco jutted out into it, massive and lofty, with its marvelous hanging gardens, and the still unfinished cathedral whose door faces the sea. Clinging to its perpendicular sides were flowering cactus, some of it already in fruit, wild pomegranates, heavy-leaved fig trees, clumps of red geraniums, and a pink-flowered vine. . . . To the east it was as though a royal fleet were ablaze offshore from a city of white houses, Bordighera, which supplies the palms for ceremonies in the Vatican.

Not everything was rural: old Nice was redolent of the "perfume of fruits and herbs, mixed with the odors of raw meat, sharp pasta, codfish and latrines"; in the noisy streets the Niçois played the Italian finger-game of *morra;* the carnival was a true festival in those days; in Monte

Apollinaire: Two

Carlo there was an annual season of music and theatre (Apollinaire saw Sarah Bernhardt act while he was still a boy), and, all along the coast, a winter-long parade of dukes and princes.

That parade, during the heyday of the French Riviera as a winter resort, had three main centers—Monte Carlo, Nice, and Cannes—and young Kostrowitzky knew them all, for in 1895 his "charming school" in Monaco closed its doors, and for two years (his last years of schooling; he had none after the age of seventeen) he became a commuting pupil, taking the train every morning, in 1896 to the Collège Stanislas in Cannes, run, like the Collège Saint-Charles, by the Marianist Fathers, and in 1897 to Nice, where he attended the French secular Lycée—that final year of his education corresponding roughly to the second year in an American or British college. Every night he returned to Monaco.

The transfer of a young student from one school to another, simple and banal as the change often seems from the outside, always has its particular reasons and circumstances. Those surrounding Apollinaire's becoming a commuter along the Côte d'Azur are peculiarly Apollinairian in their combination of intimacy, scandal, and comedy.

Today, if one asks the appropriate Monegasque official why the Collège Saint-Charles ceased to exist in 1895, the answer given is that "it was closed on orders from the Prince." Persistence brings further cloudy information: "At the request of the founder [Bishop Theuret], the Marianists had accepted the direction of the college on a trial basis. But in 1895, when the bishop asked them to pay

39

rent for the college building, they abandoned the enterprise, having at the time between seventy and eighty pupils. Since the bishop himself was unable to assume the financial burden, he found himself obliged to close the establishment." Only further inquiry, at less official sources, brings a reasonably clear story. It is true that the Marianists couldn't pay the rent—because their Bursar had "misused" the college funds. (In Monaco of all places it is easy to "misuse" funds: one suspects one knows where the Bursar laid out the money.) And following the scandal the Prince ordered the place closed.

But there was another element. The Jesuits, the original secondary schoolmasters of the Principality, had apparently been jolted by the establishment of the Marianist, French-speaking Collège Saint-Charles into recognizing the trend of the times, and belatedly set about "modernizing" their old Collegio della Visitazione, with its traditionally Italian instruction. They at first "added a French section"—that is, they imported, probably, a few French-speaking members of their order, or merely had some of the multilingual present incumbents change tongues—and they gradually transformed the entire college into a French-speaking school. The change-over was apparently timed with finesse: by the time the Bursar of the Collège Saint-Charles made his fatal misstep of misusing the Marianists' funds, the Jesuit director of the old Collegio della Visitazione, now renamed the Collège de la Visitation, may not have done anything so crude as to urge the Prince to close the scandal-ridden Marianist school, but he was able to announce that *should* it close its doors its pupils would be put to no inconvenience, accommodation for all of them being now available in the streamlined, French-speaking, Jesuit Collège de la Visitation.

Still, there remains the question: why was at least one of them, young Wilhelm de Kostrowitzky, not accommodated in the new school? Why should he have taken a train every morning for two years to Nice and Cannes, when his French education could have been pursued in Monaco? The answer—like so many answers to Apollinairian questions—may lie in the question mark of his paternity.

Governor General de Farincourt's report to Prince Albert I in 1887, that the *femmes galantes* ordered expelled from the Principality had been vouched for by "a number of persons, including several of high social standing," probably referred in part to two prominent personages who were doubtless responsible for Olga de Kostrowitzky's *not* being expelled. The money sent her by her Benedictine brother-in-law for the support or partial support of her sons was delivered to her, M. Marcel Adéma has found reason to think, neither directly nor in bulk, but in small amounts sent at intervals to two different residents of Monaco from whom she in turn collected them. These were Mme François Blanc, wife of the manager of the Casino, and, it would seem, Bishop Theuret himself. (The Bishop was a worldly prelate, and the regular visits paid him by the beautiful *entraîneuse* to pick up her funds were misinterpreted by some: this may well be the source of later rumors that Apollinaire was the son of a prelate— rumors that he took pleasure in encouraging.) One suspects that Don Romarino in Rome thus divided his remittances

Guillaume Apollinaire

for reasons of caution and control. Mme Blanc, the wife of Olga's employer, may have been directed to remit at her or her husband's discretion. And as for the Bishop, what was more natural than his insistence, if insistence was needed, that the funds passing through his hands be used to pay tuition at the Collège Saint-Charles, founded by himself? So it seems likely that when the Collège Saint-Charles closed its doors, and the Bishop's Marianists left Monaco discomfited, it may have been the Bishop himself who decreed that Wilhelm should continue his studies with them, even if it meant commuting to Cannes, rather than transferring to the victorious Jesuits in their Collège de la Visitation. Or perhaps it was Don Romarino, Abbot-General of the Benedictines, who decreed that his nephew should study even in the godless national lycée in Nice rather than with the priests of the rival order: better that he should commute and come home every night to the "Russian woman" than live with Jesuits.

Vague and trivial though such details may seem, they underline two aspects of Apollinaire: the role his illegitimacy played in determining events in his life, and the current of mystery and mishap that constantly swirled around him. He was always one to whom extraordinary things happened, a mortal whom the gods kept taunting: the boy who had to commute to Cannes when his school closed, rather than merely transfer to another school a few hundred yards away, grew into the man who was—to use his own words—"the only person arrested in France for the theft of the Mona Lisa," when that picture was stolen from the Louvre.

42

A curious gap of two years follows the termination of Apollinaire's schooling in 1897, two years during which almost nothing is known of the Kostrowitzky trio (or quartet, since Jules Weil had now joined it), except that they left Monaco. Don Romarino, although he lived until 1904, seems now to have disappeared from the Kostrowitzkys' lives: one can only surmise that he cut off funds—there must have been some drastic reason for removing as bookish and brilliant a seventeen-year-old as Wilhelm not merely from classes in Nice but from all classes. Perhaps, though the Monaco records make no mention of it, Olga finally achieved expulsion from the Principality. In any case, she and Weil became itinerant, one might say picaresque.

In 1899, when the curtain goes up again, the scene has shifted northward, to Stavelot, a small town nestled in the Ardennes in eastern Belgium, ten miles from Spa, that spa whose renowned waters have caused its name to be used as a general name for spas the world over.

From the newspaper L'Annonce [*Stavelot*], *October 8, 1899:*

Sensational Getaway

Here in our corner of the world, usually so tranquil, nothing is being talked about except the sudden departure in the dark of night of two young Russians, whose charming manners and honeyed words had won them the boundless confidence of Monsieur X, proprietor of a hotel in Stavelot. Imagine! Their names were William [in English in the original] and Albert de Kostrowitski; they claimed to be of the high nobility, Russian barons, sons of a Russian general. Aged respectively eighteen and fifteen,

43

they spoke several languages, including perfect French, having studied in some of the best French lycées. The elder of the two devoted himself to literature in his leisure moments; he wrote graceful verse, and in fact addressed a number of pretty madrigals to one of our local young ladies. The younger boy's tastes were more simple and rustic: he was constantly picking mushrooms—perhaps he intended to pay his share of the hotel bill with them. Both boys were quite handsome: the elder had chestnut hair and wore a broad-brimmed hat à la Rubens; the younger was distinctly brunette, and invariably wore a French sailor suit.

Alas, our two de Kostrowitzkis were nothing but a pair of common swindlers, who in connivance with their alleged uncle on their mother's side, a certain Jules W—— did Monsieur and Madame X—— out of a considerable sum.

Here are the details.

Last June there arrived in Stavelot a gentleman calling himself Jules W——. He was of French birth, and had lived at various periods in Paris, London, and other capitals. Our little town took his fancy, and he rented a room in the X——'s hotel in the Rue Neuve. The price of room and board was agreed on at three francs a day, plus extras.

W——'s face was not particularly prepossessing. He read numerous French newspapers and claimed to be a former army officer. After a two or three weeks' stay he asked whether the hotel would be willing to accommodate his nephews: they were in need of fresh air, he said. The price of room and board agreed on with the hotelkeeper was three francs per Kostro, or six francs a day for the two nephews, plus extras.

By mid-July the family, or rather the trio, was ensconced in the hotel. One fine day the uncle announced that he was obliged to absent himself for a brief time, and left without paying. That should have aroused the hotelkeeper's suspicions. W—— wrote from Namur and from Ostend that he was detained by business, but that he would soon return to rejoin his two nephews (left as security) and would settle all bills. He was never seen again.

The two de Kostrowitzkis had more than one trick in their

44

bag. They frequently stated that their mother lived in watering places, that she moved about from Monaco to Ostend to Spa, etc. After a certain time they announced that in reply to a letter they had sent their mother (?) she had written asking that the itemized bill for the boys and their uncle be mailed to her in Paris, whence she would send a remittance covering the total. A week went by and nothing happened. About September 22 Madame X——, pretending certain urgent expenses, asked for 200 francs. The mother, written to again, replied that she would soon be in Spa and would come to Stavelot and pay the bill in person. That second maternal letter was never shown to the X——s, but according to the boys their mother would arrive in Stavelot on October 5 to redeem her two long-absent darlings.

As we see it, the "mother" was none other than our friend W——, who had probably concocted a plan of escape for his two nephews.

The latter quite simply decamped, sneaking out of the Hotel X secretly during the night of Wednesday—Thursday, October 4–5, carrying with them a little wicker trunk and two suitcases. In their bedroom they left behind one old suitcase, containing worn-out shoes.

What was the amazement of Monsieur and Madame X—— the next morning to find the cage empty and the two birds flown! *"C'est un z'oiseau qui vient de France,"* says the song; in the present case, it was two migrants returning south at the approach of cold weather.

Monsieur and Madame X—— immediately filed a complaint with the police, putting the amount of the swindle, uncle and nephews together, at more than 600 francs.

Telegrams have been sent in various directions. We will keep our readers informed, but we greatly fear that Monsieur and Madame X—— will never recover a single penny.

From the same newspaper, the following Sunday:
Sensational Getaway
Sequel to the Flight of the Two de Kostrowitzkis

45

Guillaume Apollinaire

Nothing has so far been heard from the two young Russian barons, William and Albert de Kostrowitzki, who absconded during the night of October 4–5, forgetting to settle a bill of 600 to 700 francs at the local Hotel C.

Investigation by the captain of the local police has brought to light the fact that the two young confidence men took the earliest morning train, about 5.50 A.M., at the station of Roanne-Coo. They first asked for two tickets to Jeumont, the French frontier station. But the agent could provide tickets only as far as Namur, whence they continued their flight to France.

The investigation also revealed that the two young Russians had planned their flight in advance. Two days before their departure for *la belle France,* the older, probably William, checked a parcel at the Roanne-Coo station, and the following day the younger, Albert, did likewise.

The night of their escape, our two smuggler barons took along two empty suitcases and a small wicker trunk ditto. The rest of the story is known....

The author of those articles in the Stavelot newspaper would not have written "As we see it, the 'mother' was none other than our friend W——," had he seen the police report from Spa:

...having sought in this city for the persons named Wel [*sic*], de Kostrowisky Albert and William, we have been able to obtain no information concerning these three individuals. They are included in no list of foreigners nor are they known at the Cercle des Jeux.

The Cercle des Etrangers has no record of an Olga Kostrowisky, but a person who wishes to remain anonymous has declared to us that said Olga was in Spa, that she was refused admittance to the Cercle des Etrangers, that she had no permanent residence; this same person states that he had seen her in Monte Carlo and Nice, that she had no regular source of income, and that he had no knowledge of her two sons or of the above-

Apollinaire: Two

mentioned Wel. Most likely, he says, she lives in Paris and her two sons have joined her there.

Said Olga was living in great opulence.

P.S. We have just learned that Olga Kostrowisky lived for three or four weeks in July at the Hotel de la Clef d'Or, Rue de l'Hotel de Ville. She lived alone. The above-mentioned Weil and her two sons, living in Stavelot, often came to see her. The proprietors of the Clef d'Or do not know their present address nor where they stayed when in Spa and Stavelot.

Following a report by the stationmaster at Namur that two second-class tickets to Paris had been sold on the morning of October 5 to two young men answering the descriptions given out by the police, the Belgian police asked their Paris counterparts to check hotels and rooming houses, and the two boys were quickly discovered in the heart of the city, in a furnished room at 9, Rue de Constantinople, near the Gare Saint-Lazare. They had arrived on October 6, and their room had been taken for them by their "aunt," a "Madame Olga Karpoff," who had been living at the same address since early September. On her arrival she had declared herself to be "twenty-six years old, born in Russia, coming from Ostend."

In November the trio was summoned before an investigating magistrate in Paris for questioning, a charge of fraud having been brought against the boys by the Belgian court of Verviers, near Stavelot. "William," speaking for himself and his brother, declared that he was amazed at the charge. "I fail to understand," he said, "why we should be accused of fraud. It is true that we had to leave Stavelot without paying our bill. But we always supposed our mother would take care of it. We live with her. She sup-

47

Guillaume Apollinaire

ports us. We have no private resources."

And "Olga Karpoff," who had by now admitted her true name and identity, found her sons' conduct quite justifiable. "It cannot be denied that they left without saying anything," she admitted, "but I suppose it was too embarrassing for them to say that I couldn't send the money. They're nothing but children, after all, and like children they must have wanted to avoid harsh treatment." She explained that gambling losses had made it impossible for her to pay the Hotel-Pension Constant in Stavelot. Her sons had left some of their possessions behind, she said, including a box of books that would cover part of the bill, and she protested that certain items on the bill were far too high anyway.

Olga must have been superb that day, a slender, handsome, "twenty-six-year-old" mother fiercely protective of her nineteen-year-old elder son and his fifteen-year-old brother. The magistrate—his name was Lascoux—readily agreed with her that certain items on the bill seemed suspiciously high, and took it upon himself to reduce the total. Olga promised to pay as soon as she could, if the charges of fraud were dropped. Judge Lascoux chivalrously approved that bargain. On January 18, 1900, the Belgian court dismissed the charge.

"The elder of the two devoted himself to literature in his leisure moments . . . ."

What did "William" de Kostrowitzky and his brother have except "leisure moments" those three months they passed in penniless suspension in Stavelot?

Apollinaire: Two

Guillaume Apollinaire, about 1899, on his return from Stavelot

49

Guillaume Apollinaire

"In their bedroom they left behind one old suitcase, containing worn-out shoes": one of the items on the disputed hotel bill was "Numerous repairs to shoes"—the boys hadn't even the wherewithal to pay cash for cobbling. Inhabitants of Stavelot who remembered the Kostrowitzkys were repeatedly interviewed about them in later years, when Apollinaire's youth became a subject of interest; they all remembered the boys' disintegrating shoes and clothes—Wilhelm's solitary blue jacket and trousers, and Albert's inevitable sailor suit: they seem to have had no change of clothing in three months. "There was," the Stavelotains remember, "an almost painful contrast between the cultivation and charming manners of those boys and the condition of their clothes." Ragged and ill shod, they spent their days roaming the moors and peat bogs of the old Wallonian province. "Sandwiches" is another item on the hotel bill—they had to charge their noonday picnics; and one suspects it was not merely an interest in mycology that caused Albert to be "constantly picking mushrooms" while William "devoted himself to literature."

Still in existence are William's so-called "Stavelot notebooks," the earliest samples of his writing extant except for the few schoolboy verses preserved by friends. Their contents have been partially published, and it is clear that many lines and phrases found in Apollinaire's later poems were originally written, either as parts of complete poems or as fragments, during his "leisure moments" that summer of 1899 in the Ardennes. The early efforts served as material out of which the poet built other poems when his years and skill increased.

50

One poem, never published by Apollinaire during his life and printed for the first time only in a collection of his works issued in 1952, has survived intact and unchanged from the Stavelot summer during which the nineteen-year-old poet wrote it:

Vae Soli[2]

Hélas s'en sont venus à la male heure
Diogène le chien avec Onan
Le grimoire est femme lascive et pleure
De chaud désir avec toi maintenant

Or la bouche
Que voudrait ta caresse est lointaine
Des Reines
Désirent entrer dans ta couche
Car delà le réel ton désir les brula

Hélas tes mains tes mains sont tout cela
Et l'estampe est chair douce

Woe To The Lonely

Alas there have come at the evil hour
Diogenes the dog with Onan
The spell is a lewd woman and now
Like you she weeps with hot desire

The mouth
That you would caress is far away
Queens
Long to enter your bed
For beyond the real your desire scorched them

Alas your hands your hands are all that
And the engraving is tender flesh

(Except where noted, all translations in the present volume are by the author.)

[2] Cf. the French text of Diogenes Laertius's life of Diogenes the Cynic [Gr. κύων = "dog"]:
    Un jour où il se masturbait sur la place publique, il s'écria: "Plût au ciel qu'il suffit aussi de se frotter le ventre pour ne plus avoir faim!" . . . Pendant un repas, on lui jeta des os comme à un chien, alors s'approchant des convives, il leur pissa dessus comme un chien.

51

Guillaume Apollinaire

It would be difficult to find a poem that fits more exactly than "Vae Soli" the requirements of Symbolism as stated by Mallarmé: "To name an object is to destroy three-quarters of our pleasure in a poem—the joy of guessing, step by step. The ideal is to suggest the object. We derive the most from the mystery that constitutes the symbol when we evoke the object step by step in order to portray a state of mind." The "object" of "Vae Soli" is certainly never named, and just as certainly it is evoked step by step to portray a "state of mind," until we learn that the lonely poet is staring at an engraving in a book as he satisfies his desires. "Vae Soli" is orthodox—one might almost say primary—symbolism.

Apollinaire also used the Ardennes background more than once in his prose writings, which often rival his verse in beauty and fantasy. His prose extravaganza *Le Poète assassiné,* which he began in Stavelot or shortly thereafter and kept reworking for years until it was finally published in 1916, opens with a rather remarkable description of the procreation of a poet:

Two leagues from Spa, on the road bordered by gnarled trees and bushes, Vierselin Tigoboth, an ambulant musician who was coming on foot from Liège, struck his flint to light his pipe. A woman's voice cried: "Ho! Monsieur!"
He lifted his head, and a wild laugh burst out:
"Hahaha! Hohoho! Hihihi! Your eyelids are the color of Egyptian lentils! My name is Macarée. I want a tom-cat."
Vierselin Tigoboth perceived by the roadside a young woman, brunette and formed of nice spheres. How charming she was in her short bicyclist's skirt! And holding her bicycle with one hand, while gathering wild plums with the other, she

52

ardently fixed her great golden eyes on the Wallonian musician.

"*Vs'estez one belle bacelle,*" said Vierselin Tigoboth, smacking his tongue. "But, my God, if you eat all those plums, you will have the colic tonight, I'm sure."

"I want a tom-cat," repeated Macarée and unclasping her bodice she showed Vierselin Tigoboth her breasts, sweet as angels' buttocks, whose aureola had the tender hue of pink sunset clouds.

"Oh! oh!" cried Vierselin Tigoboth. "They're as pretty as the pearls of Amblevia. Give them to me. I shall gather a great bouquet of ferns for you, and of irises, color of the moon."

Vierselin Tigoboth approached to grasp this miraculous flesh which was being offered to him for nothing, like the holy bread at Mass; but then he restrained himself.

"You're a sweet lass, by God, you're nicer than the fair of Liège. You're a nicer little girl than Donnaye, than Tatenne, than Victoire, whose gallant I have been, and nicer than Rénier's daughters, whom old Rénier always has for sale. Mind you, if if you want to be my love, 'ware o' the crablouse, my God."

Macarée
They are the color of the moon
And round as the wheel of Fortune

Vierselin Tigoboth
If you fear not to catch the louse
Then I should love to be your spouse

And Vierselin Tigoboth approached, his lips full of kisses: "I love you! It is marvelous! O beloved!"

Soon there was nothing but sighs and birdsong, and little russet hares, horned like imps, fleet as seven-league boots, went by Vierselin Tigoboth and Macarée, overcome by love behind the plum trees.

Then Macarée was off on her bike.

Macarée soon became aware that she had conceived by Vierselin Tigoboth.

53

Guillaume Apollinaire

"Does not that story of a child to be born to an independent young woman, proud of her sensuality, make one think of Apollinaire's own destiny?" Michel Décaudin says of *Le Poète assassiné* in one of his excellent academic studies of the poet. It does, of course, in many a rococo detail, especially when one reads on in the extravagant book and finds that the pregnant Macarée wins money at baccarat, marries a baron named François, buys elegant clothes in Paris, visits Rome with her husband, and has an audience with the Pope. She dies during the birth of the son she had conceived by the "ambulant musician," the "tom-cat," the birth taking place on the French Riviera and being brought on by Macarée's laughter at the baron's loud farting. The baron, the infant's putative father, has him baptized "Gætan-Francis-Etienne-Jack-Amélie-Alonso" and takes him to Monaco. There the baron loses everything at the Casino and shoots himself.

More autobiographical, perhaps, than any of those explicitly written embroideries on actual Apollinairian vital statistics, fantastic in themselves, is the *core* of the story of *Le Poète assassiné.* What has happened in that high-flown opening passage is that a poet has received his begetting, or one of his begettings (for Apollinaire believed in superfetation), in the countryside of the Ardennes, a short distance from Spa; and that, of course, is no embroidery, but simply the not-so-sober truth of what happened in that place during Wilhelm de Kostrowitzky's "leisure moments."

In a lonely grove of firs between Stavelot and Spa, overlooking hills and heaths, there now stands a monument

Apollinaire: Two

to Apollinaire. In Stavelot itself the ex-Hotel-Pension Constant, from which the poet fled at night with his brother and his wicker trunk, leaving the long bill unpaid, is now known as the Hotel du Luxembourg, and bears a plaque stating proudly that "Apollinaire lived here."

Apollinaire's irregular childhood has always interested psychologists, and they have written with differences that are sometimes amusing about the nature and the effect of his early experiences.

Guy Dupré, for example, has emphasized the "freedom" of Apollinaire's early years. In his view Apollinaire escaped the fate of French poets in the rebel tradition, like Baudelaire and Rimbaud, who became bitter enemies of bourgeois society, because he was not subjected in his childhood to the constraints of family life. His being born out of wedlock, in conjunction with the fact that he was not of French nationality, accounts for his ability to see French society as an outsider, and to write lightly about it. It is significant, according to Dupré, that the hero of André Gide's novel *Les Caves du Vatican* is a bastard: "As if only a 'natural' child could be endowed with the complete irresponsibility, the *grace,* that seems to be embodied in Apollinaire—Apollinaire the man without nationality, Apollinaire the love child."

Bernard Guillemain, on the other hand, sees chiefly the "torments" arising from Apollinaire's abnormal situation: the poet's childhood, far from being sunny and unconstrained, must have been full of "horribly wounding" experiences. His life with his mother, who was footloose

55

in more ways than one, is reflected in bitter lines in his verse, such as

Ton père fut un sphinx et ta mère une nuit

—lines "dictated to the poet by his pitiless unconscious"; but because he was a foreigner he was able to surmount this trauma by his humor.

Certainly young Wilhelm de Kostrowitzky's declaration of "amazement" before the investigating magistrate in Paris and his impudent "I fail to understand why we should be accused of fraud" are too striking to pass unnoticed. They are not sober statements, there is no "sincerity" in them: they represent a deliberately assumed attitude. Perhaps his mother suggested it to him as suitable for the occasion—if indeed at this point in his life he still needed her guidance at such moments. For although this declaration before the judge is the first recorded instance of Apollinaire's attitudinizing, it must have been far from the first in fact. Life with Olga in Monaco, life at school as Olga's son, life in Stavelot while awaiting word from Olga—all of it cannot but have been rich in false situations, putting a constant demand on the boy for inventions, quick answers, and bold fronts; and since the extraordinary circumstances of his life were to him not extraordinary, but merely the daily facts of existence, the constant assuming of attitudes inevitably became his "second nature." As time went on and an increasing circle of friends and acquaintances accepted him at the picturesque face value he placarded on himself, and as he accepted their acceptance, Apollinaire grew to be rather like a Bohemian character out of an early novel by Aldous Huxley. However, his day-to-day life as a Bohemian poet often strikes one as being a façade fitted over something never seen, merely hinted at. "What he was really like" remains more of a riddle than in the case of most humans.

Guided by his statement that every one of the poems in his first collected volume, *Alcools,* commemorates an event in his life, sensing his implication that more than in the case of other poets (whose poems, too, after all, commemorate events in their lives) his verses contain autobiographical revelations, one records the events of his life as they are known, one savors the poems as *objets d'art* unquestionably "made by human hands": but the humanity that went into the making is often heavily veiled behind the deliberately assumed attitudes.

What an artist's biographer looks for are the cracks in the mask, the rents in the veil. A man, a biographer stubbornly feels, is always more precious than any art he may produce, even the greatest, and rightly or wrongly he believes that discovery of the man intensifies perception of the art. In Apollinaire's case there is a quantity of what is known as "biographical data," but despite it all—and there are many anti-biographers who will feel that this is a blessing—the man Kostrowitzky behind the posturing Apollinaire remains hard to unravel. But the biographer persists, happy to obtain as many clear strands as possible, leaving the inevitable knots and snarls to his successors. Fortunately, the "biographical data," the documents, continue to be picturesque in themselves.

Guillaume Apollinaire

Three

A grim time in Paris followed the flight from Stavelot in 1899. A letter dated "Villa Holterhoff, Honnef-on-Rhine, Germany, July, 1902," to an otherwise obscure schoolfriend named James Onimus tells us what it was like:

> In Paris, a hard winter. It looked as though we were going to have to eat bricks. I even wrote addresses in an office at four sous an hour, the lowest work imaginable, along with jailbirds, broken-down ex-lawyers, adventurers back from the gold mines. Plenty of them would have been glad to enlist for the Transvaal if they had been eligible; I was one of this starving rabble. At the end of the month I was left with the 23 francs 50 I had earned: it was handed to me by the *patronne* of the establishment . . . she paid the poor wretches herself, burning perfume-papers so as not to smell their odor. The lowest I ever sank.
>
> I hang around jobless. Meet up with old Esnard whom I knew in Monaco. He is a Bohemian lawyer who has a novel to write for *Le Matin* and is too busy to do it himself. He asks me to help him. He already has another assistant, Gaillet, a Bohemian newspaperman with a pretty daughter—now he is publisher of *Tabarin*. I write a few chapters and *Le Matin* publishes the novel serially under the title "Que Faire." Other serial-writers imitate my chapters. During this time I often go to the Mazarine Library. Meet Léon Cahun, the orientalist, uncle of Marcel Schwob. He introduces me to the latter, but it doesn't go any further. I'm often invited to the Cahuns, meet Albert Delacour of the *Mercure*, Maxime Fourmont *(Gil Blas)*, Ravaisson, Mollien the philosopher and his sons. At home I make a meal of a herring. Esnard forgets to pay me for the trash I wrote for him. I see a lot of him anyway, and make his mistress, twenty years old to his 53. Finally

a want ad gets me a job with a shady brokerage outfit called the Bourse Parisienne. No cash in the till—in two months I make 50 francs. But I meet the nephew of Lagoanère, manager of the Théatre Renaissance just before its bankruptcy. From then on I get free theatre tickets. I also get to know a little Jew who has since become my friend and is at present doing his military service at Blaye—his sister is a doll. I see a lot of the family. The father teaches dancing at St. Cyr. I leave the Bourse Parisienne and take up writing again. I learn stenography and Hebrew. Get to know St.-Georges Bouhélier, Maurice le Blond, and especially my dear Walkenaer at the Mazarine. Old Cahun dies. Before the end he tells his nephew and everybody else he sees that I'm going to be somebody. The dancing teacher gives me an order for a book, *La Grace et le Maintien français,* which he signs, naturally, and which you can buy for two francs. Meanwhile I begin a story, "L'Hérésiarque," which I take to the *Revue blanche,* where I meet with a chilly reception. I begin a novel, still unfinished, which is going to make a stir. Then I run into an old friend from Cannes who writes for magazines. He introduces me at *La Grande France* and I publish some poems over my real name because the directors A/M Leblond won't let me use my pseudonym.

It is in the September, 1901 issue of *La Grande France* that one can find Apollinaire's first three printed poems, over the name Kostrowitzky.

One of these, ten lines long, is called "Lunaire": its opening words, *"Lune mellifluente,"* are scribbled in one of the Stavelot notebooks. Youthful though it is, it has many of the qualities that give a poem life, and twelve years later, when Apollinaire chose the poems to be included in his first published volume of verse, *Alcools*—a choice which, as we shall see, was a work of art in itself—he not only retained "Lunaire" (the only poem written so early that he did retain), but altered it scarcely at all, omitting only one

59

line and changing the title first to "Nocturne" and finally to "Clair de lune."

Clair de lune

Lune mellifluente aux lèvres des déments
Les vergers et les bourgs cette nuit sont gourmands
Les astres assez bien figurent les abeilles
De ce miel lumineux qui dégoutte des treilles
Car voici que tout doux et leur tombant du ciel
Chaque rayon de lune est un rayon de miel
Or caché je conçois la très douce aventure
J'ai peur du dard de feu de cette abeille Arcture
Qui posa dans mes mains des rayons décevants
Et prit son miel lunaire à la rose des vents

Moonlight

The honeyflowing moon is on every madman's tongue
Tonight, and makes gluttons out of orchard and town.
The stars can stand for the bees who gather this
Luminous stuff that cloys the very trellises.
And look, all saccarine as they pour from the skies,
The rays of the moon are in fact honey-rays,
Hidden gold. I dream of some sugary happening,
But I fear the bee Arcturus and his fiery sting,
Who having put these slippery beams in my hands
Took his lunar honey from the rose of the winds.

Translated by William Meredith.

Now "Nocturne" and especially "Clair de lune" are even triter, more conventionally stock "Symbolist" titles than the original "Lunaire"—Symbolist poetry is famous for being moon-drenched—and the fact that Apollinaire should deliberately use so conformist a title in his first collected volume, which he clearly intended to strike a new

60

note in poetry, would tend to confirm certain suspicions that a reader might have had in reading "Lunaire" in *La Grande France* in 1901. For *La Grande France* was a resolutely anti-Symbolist little magazine, in the sense that it encouraged writers who were trying to break away from the school or give it a new direction. (Its directors, Marius and Ary Leblond, the "A/M Leblond" of Apollinaire's letter, were to be founding members of the anti-Symbolist *Nouvelle Revue Française* in 1908.) Why should it publish so seemingly orthodox a poem as "Lunaire"? One wonders how many readers recognized "Lunaire" for what it was— a gentle gibe at Symbolism. The madmen speaking of the moon as "dripping honey," the dry tone in which stars are allowed "to stand for the bees": naturally such conceits were welcomed by the editors of *La Grande France*.

One of them, Fernand Gregh (whose verses had been reverently copied into Monte Carlo notebooks), always remembered young Kostrowitzky:

One day a young man appeared at my house, bringing me some poems for the magazine. They were written on scraps of paper that were a little crumpled from being carried too long in a pocket along with books, a knife, keys, and change—not too much of the last-named, no doubt. The handwriting was extraordinarily variable; in two successive lines the same words seemed not to have been traced by the same person. The verses were still a little hesitant, but they breathed a dreamy and ardent poetry, which rose like a warm mist and reflected the author's mixed Italian and Polish ancestry. We were friends at once. He treated me as an elder—in the eyes of youth a difference of four or five years is considerable—and even as "master"! I laughed about it *in petto*, concealing my amusement so as not to lose face. Kostro-

61

Guillaume Apollinaire

witzky, who like all the young was eager for a fight, took up the cudgels in behalf of my nonconformism so enthusiastically that only a few days after we met he wrote and published, in a little weekly called *Tabarin,* if I am not mistaken, a ballad in praise of humanism and against the symbolists. What wouldn't I give to lay my hands on it! I repeat: against the symbolists—against the very ones who have since adopted Apollinaire as one of their most typical representatives up to the time he himself created surrealism. . . .

Ever since Fernand Gregh wrote that, the curious have worn thin the pages of *Tabarin* in a vain search for the "ballad in praise of humanism and against the symbolists": it would be interesting to see in just what terms young Kostrowitzky attacked the symbolists explicitly. And some of the curious have wondered about "Lunaire": was it a joke from the beginning? Or had the young poet of Stavelot —still, perhaps, a symbolist—begun it "straight" and turned it into a parody as he quickly acquired sophistication in Paris?

The letter to James Onimus [continued]:

Then thanks to Lagoanère I meet the Vicomtesse de Milhau, German widow of a Frenchman. I give French lessons to her daughter for 100 francs a month from 9 to 11 in the morning, and at the same time I find three other pupils at one franc an hour. Gaillet founds *Tabarin,* an amusing little financial and political weekly. I do my first publicity for an election campaign, using my new name, Guillaume Apollinaire; the candidate is Francisque Michaux, son of the inventor of the bicycle. The Vicomtesse decides to leave Paris for Germany. She buys an auto and plans to drive to Germany in it. She asks me if I'd like to accompany her at 200 francs a month. I accept and we leave August 22, 1901.

62

Apollinaire: Three

The Vicomtesse's family name was Hölterhoff; it was her mother's villa at Honnef-on-Rhine from which Apollinaire was writing those lines to Onimus, in 1902; the two ladies were the widow and the daughter of a Cologne businessman said to have grown rich in the slave trade with the United States. The Vicomte de Milhau had recently shot himself at his country house on the Normandy coast: there is no record of the circumstances. Indeed there is no other record of the Vicomte, except that his head was ornamented by a cyst so prominent that German villagers near his wife's estate called him "Count Unicorn." The automobile that his widow bought for the drive to Germany was a De Dion-Bouton. Those were the days when the sight of a car caused crowds to gather and horses to rear; many highways and all lesser roads were unpaved; the Vicomtesse herself drove the five hundred miles to Cologne, whither her mother, her daughter Gabrielle, and a governess had preceded them by train. It took her and the tutor a week to make it, and shortly thereafter the household of four established itself in the Vicomtesse's country house, "Neuglück," in the hamlet of Bennerscheid, near the village of Oberpleis, across the river from the university town of Bonn, in a picturesque, rolling portion of the Rhineland called the "Siebengebirge," the Seven Mountains.

The son of the Oberpleis pharmacist of those days has left memoirs in which he describes the Vicomtesse as a "nasty, eccentric, smallish woman with rusty red hair, piercing eyes and a hawk-like nose"; charm bracelets jangling with jewels and coins clattered on her wrists, and in summer she shocked the countryside by going bare-

63

Guillaume Apollinaire

armed and bare-legged, displaying to all the scurf-like eczema that covered her neck and hands and arms and caused her to be called, by the same rustics who had baptized her husband "Count Unicorn," "the countess with the fish skin." At the wheel of the De Dion-Bouton she wore a "bibi"—a stiff, round felt hat—with a dark veil; and as she dashed into the village or across the countryside, sounding the klaxon and leaving a trail of fumes behind her, the Rhenish peasantry (a lumpish lot even today) looked on her as a witch in her coach. At times the auto went more slowly, dragged home or to Bonn or Cologne by a nag pulling at chains and straps: these were occasions for the villagers' rejoicing—the witch-like chatelaine was not an amiable neighbor or shopper, and the pharmacist's memoirist son recalls a slap she gave him in return for his prying, little-boy investigation of her car.

The scaly witch-countess is gone—she died in 1928 after marrying a Greek second husband named Dr. Zervoulakos, brother of another Zervoulakos who is said to have been the husband of none other than her own daughter, thus making mother and daughter sisters-in-law—but something remains that is her monument: the "Historisches Waldschlösschen Haus Neuglück, Café-Restaurant," as it is now called, Apollinaire's home in Germany for the better part of a year.

It has to be seen to be believed, this half-timbered toy-village, gingerbread manor house in the taste of Arthur Rackham or Walt Disney, if one may thus mention together those two very different exponents of the Hansel-and-Gretel, gnomes-and-elves style. Built on the site of a

64

ruinous peasant's hut that had served as foreman's dwelling at old lead and zinc mines in the nearby woods, it extends its red-painted timbers and white plaster, its tile and slate roofs, its gables and spires and belfries and balconies around two sides of a courtyard—now a parking lot for the couples who come out from Bonn of a Sunday for beer in the witch's ex-dining-room or for a tea dance in the queer old airborne parlor, propped up from below on spindly white posts carved with gargoyles. Set close beside a fir wood, the weird little property bristles with what can only be called "features"—grotto, stream, bridge, pool, and shrill painted warnings: "Caution!" "Forbidden to enter— danger to life!" "Traps!" "Automatic shooting at trespassers!" The house has many rooms, but it gives an impression of littleness, so mean are the proportions, so cramped the rooms and passageways, so pitiful the carved frosting of masks and gargoyles. There is an alcove called a chapel, with modern French stained glass and statues of the apostles; coffered ceilings are amateurishly painted with the signs of the zodiac and the arms of the French provinces. All this is the work of a single remarkably under-endowed local jack-of-all-trades, employed by the Vicomtesse to the exclusion of all architects, carpenters, painters, and masons; each fall she left orders for the work he was to do the following spring, and each summer on arrival she quarreled with him and called for changes: one year she made the luckless masterbuilder crawl along the roof-ledge and saw off a turret he had just finished constructing with his own hands. It is easy to believe the Oberpleis pharmacist's son's description of the Vicomtesse de Milhau: Neuglück bears the 65

Guillaume Apollinaire

stamp of a personality not only eccentric, but childishly petty. A remark made by a recent visitor to the place probably contains the poetic truth: "The poor lady must have had her doll's house snatched away from her when she was a child."

The letter to James Onimus [continued]:

Since then I've seen all of Germany and sleep with the English governess, 21, what curves!

As to the governess. . . . In 1915 Apollinaire, writing to a friend about his poetry, spoke as follows about his long love poem, "La Chanson du Mal-Aimé:"

"Aubade," which is not a separate poem but an intermezzo inserted into the "Chanson du Mal-Aimé," which dates from 1903, commemorates my first love, when I was twenty. She was an English girl whom I met in Germany. It lasted a year; each of us had to return to his own country, and we stopped writing. Many of the expressions in the poem are too severe and abusive considering that the girl understood nothing about me, loved me, and then was dismayed to find herself loving a poet, a creature of whims. . . . She was keen and gay, however, and I missed her greatly when she was away. . . . I went to see her twice in London, but marriage was impossible, and the whole thing ended with her leaving for America. . . . "L'Emigrant de Landor Road" . . . commemorates the same love.

In 1946, thirty-one years after Apollinaire wrote those words, an English lady named Mrs. Annie Playden Postings, living in California, received several letters from a 66 gentleman in Belgium, unknown to her, named Robert

Annie Playden in 1901

67

Guillaume Apollinaire

Goffin.[1] He informed her, much to her surprise, that a young man named Kostrowitzky, with whom she had worked in a household in the Rhineland many years before, had become a famous poet under the name Guillaume Apollinaire. She learned that she herself was celebrated as "Annie" in several of his love poems, and was regarded by Apollinairians as a kind of modern-day Beatrice or Laura. In 1951 Mrs. Postings visited New York, where she consented to be interviewed by an American friend of Goffin's, LeRoy Breunig, and in an account of the interview, published in the *Mercure de France,* Breunig revealed to the world the story of Apollinaire and the English governess.

Breunig found Mrs. Postings still astonished by Goffin's revelations: she remembered the tutor "Kostro" well, but had not even known that he wrote verse. She had not heard from or of him in almost fifty years, and had not known whether he was alive or dead. She had never heard the name Apollinaire. Now in her seventies, she was "a very energetic lady," Breunig reported, "short and simply dressed," with refined, English features, a dimple in her chin, and blue eyes that were bright but cold. "Everything she told me about her faraway youth was uttered with enthusiasm but with noticeable detachment, as though the young girl of Neuglück and the lady from California were two very distinct people." Breunig's account continues:

[1] Goffin, a lawyer, poet, and admirer of Apollinaire, had learned the name of the viscountess's English governess from two Germans, Professor E. M. Wolf at the University of Bonn and Johannes Dahs, a Bennerscheid farmer. Then in the London directory he had found "Playden, Landor Road," and had secured Mrs. Postings' new name and address from her family by telephone.

Apollinaire: Three

Miss Annie Playden was born in 1880—thus she was the same age as Apollinaire—and spent her entire youth in Clapham, a small suburb ten miles southwest of London, where she was raised in the rigid atmosphere of a middle-class Victorian family. Her father was an architect who demanded from his family such strict observance of the rules of the Anglican church that on Landor Road he was known as "the Archbishop of Canterbury." Annie herself organized a small Sunday School for the German children of the neighborhood as soon as she reached Neuglück. At twenty she was a very pretty young woman with light brown hair, but ever since her childhood she had been made to believe that there was something shameful and scandalous in her beauty. Other girls told her that there was something "perverse in her eyes"; her two brothers kept telling her that she should cover her face whenever she went out; and first her mother, and later the Vicomtesse de Milhau, taught her to distrust all men because of her beauty.

In 1900 Annie Playden came to Paris directly from Clapham to live as governess in the home of the Vicomtesse, who was still in mourning following her husband's suicide. She remained there a year and learned a little French before the move to Germany. It was in the Vicomtesse's home that she met Guillaume Apollinaire, shortly before the departure in August, 1901. She has described the meeting in a letter to M. Goffin:

"I remember that the day he came to apply for the situation he kept smiling at me as he talked. Later I learned that the countess had engaged him and that he was to be with us during our travels in Germany. When he came to know me he told me that his friends had asked him whether the countess was charming, and he replied: 'No, but the governess is, and that's what made me decide to take the job.'"

Frau Hölterhoff, the mother of the Vicomtesse, was a Cologne bourgeoise who according to Miss Playden was very proud of her daughter's title, hence very snobbish, and "stingy and boring" besides. The Vicomtesse herself seems to have been scarcely more glamorous. When I asked Miss Playden whether Apollinaire had been the lady's private secretary her answer was:

Guillaume Apollinaire

"Certainly not; she never had anything to write." The only halfway attractive member of the family was Gabrielle.

At Neuglück Apollinaire had a tiny room, poorly lighted and poorly heated, at the end of a wing. The governess and the tutor were not allowed to forget that they were mere hired help; Miss Playden recalls that Frau Hölterhoff insisted that they take their meals separately while traveling, until she discovered that it cost more to have two tables. Life at Neuglück was not very social. The only visitors during the entire year, according to Miss Playden, were the young schoolmaster from Bennerscheid and his mother.

The family spent most of the winter in Frau Hölterhoff's villa at Honnef-on-Rhine, where the climate is milder and more cheerful than at Neuglück. In a letter written to his mother on October 19, 1901, Apollinaire announces: "This week we leave Neuglück for Honnef, but you can still write me here. We shall stay at Honnef long enough (a few weeks) to furnish the villa: the Queen of Sweden is to come." Miss Playden assured me that the Queen of Sweden never came to the Villa Hölterhoff—on the contrary, there were scarcely any guests, despite the livelier atmosphere of Honnef, "the Riviera of the Rhine," and that the vicountess and her mother led the same dreary and isolated existence as at Neuglück.

So it is scarcely surprising that Apollinaire, who had such need of friends, should have sought amusement elsewhere. And it was especially among the common people that he found his most congenial companions: at Honnef workmen, servants and gypsies, and at Neuglück the Bennerscheid peasants. Miss Playden well remembers the farmer Johannes Dahs. In the evening he and Apollinaire often went to the tavern in the next village; Johannes played the flute—"that's about all he did do"—and Apollinaire very quickly learned German and the lieder of the peasants. Sometimes he took his meals with the Dahs family rather than at Neuglück, and he was the life of the party at Bennerscheid when the rustic citizens chopped up new cabbage for sauerkraut, singing as they chopped.

70

Apparently Apollinaire's love for Annie Playden developed slowly during the months that followed the first August meeting in Paris. In our conversation Miss Playden emphasized the young man's exquisite courtesy, and his attentiveness to her from the very first day, as exemplified in the pretty compliment already quoted in the letter to M. Goffin. This attentiveness caused Miss Playden to believe until 1951 that Guillaume de Kostrowitzky belonged to the high nobility, that he expected to inherit a great fortune at any moment, and that he meanwhile wished his mother wouldn't spend quite so much time in the Monte Carlo casino.

But later, as his passion deepened, he began to display a more somber and fierce aspect of himself, and the English girl's cold resistance brought on accesses of jealousy, and acts of cruelty so excessive that she feared for her life. He was wildly jealous of her liking for the Bennerscheid schoolmaster, and forbade her to have anything to do with him, threatening her with dire punishment should she disobey. The most upsetting experience was his proposal of marriage. For this Apollinaire chose the most romantic spot in the Seven Mountains, the top of the Drachenfels, where Siegfried, the hero of the Nibelungen, is reputed to have slain a dragon. There he offered her his title of nobility and his huge fortune. The young miss from Clapham declined. At that point Apollinaire coldly pointed to the precipice yawning at their feet, and made her understand that he could easily explain the "accident" when her corpse was discovered. Terrified, she accepted him, but took back her promise when they reached the foot of the mountain. In Munich, which they visited with the family in April, Apollinaire displayed the same frenzied feelings, now shaking her brutally by the shoulders until she wept, now sending a huge bunch of flowers to her hotel room with a fervent message. When the moment came for him to leave Neuglück in August and he realized that he might never see her again he was again lovelorn. "His eyes were sombre and velvety," Miss Playden recalls. . . .

The letter to James Onimus [concluded]: 71

Guillaume Apollinaire

I see the Rhine, Bonn, Cologne, Hanover, Berlin, Dresden, Prague, Vienna, Munich. Stay in Munich three months. I get a copy of the *Revue blanche* containing my story ["L'Hérésiarque"]. It had been out two months without my knowing they'd printed it. It was lying in a drawer in the office and Mendès saw it and decided to use it. Meanwhile I had written a few articles on Germany for *La Grande France* under the name of Kostrowitzky. Now I'm taking the name of Guillaume Apollinaire for good. Wrote to the director of the *Revue blanche,* Natanson, and he wrote me, congratulating me and asking me for something else, as well as for my novel. I sent him an article on the Pergamon in Berlin. It has appeared, but I haven't seen it yet; also a fairly good story, "Le Passant de Prague," which appeared June 1. Also sent more poems to *La Grande France*. I leave Munich, visit Nuremberg, Stuttgart, Spires, Heidelberg, Darmstadt, Frankfurt, Wiesbaden, Mayence, Coblenz, Treves, Ems, and back to Honnef. I've been so lazy ever since that I haven't answered a letter from the director of the *Revue blanche,* who is pressing me. I'm afraid of being cuckolded and am miserable. Console me! My brother is well; he's had good jobs and is now with a bank. I'll be back in September. I'd like to see you again. Hope you will destroy this letter, and in any case don't write to me at home in Paris—my mail is opened. Answer immediately.

"I'm afraid of being cuckolded and am miserable. Console me!" A reference to young Kostrowitzky's jealousy of the village schoolmaster, probably, if it is a reference to anything real. But the word "cuckolded" is almost surely put there to mislead Onimus, and so, probably, was the earlier statement: "I sleep with the English governess." In writing about sleeping-with and being cuckolded, that year in Germany, Kostrowitzky seems to have been once again "continuing along the path of his adolescent dreams": so, at least, we shall be tempted to conclude when we read "La Chanson du Mal-Aimé." Apollinaire wrote many poems in the Rhineland, and those that are love poems are apparently inspired chiefly by frustration: not for nothing did Mrs. Postings refer to herself, in her conversation with LeRoy Breunig, as having been a "silly girl" with a puritan upbringing. But had things been otherwise the Rhineland love poems might not have been written at all, or at least not then and there. Later in his life, when Apollinaire had a different kind of a love affair, there were no love poems until it was over.

A witch-like Vicomtesse to pay one's wages, a blue-eyed English girl to live in the same house with and be frustrated by, the Rhine a few miles off, with the Drachenfels and the rest of the Seven-Mountains country with its legends and its peasants and artisans, so picturesque or so easy to make sound picturesque,[2] a tour of central Europe as far as Vienna and Prague:[3] those are rich ingredients for a poet's Wanderjahr that came at the right time.

And there was one more ingredient, less tangible, but of an importance not to be underestimated:

[2] "At Honnef, on the banks of the Rhine," Apollinaire wrote in the *Revue blanche* shortly after his return to Paris from Germany, "I saw . . . an old man, very strange, who lived like a hermit and had nothing to do with anyone except tourists who came to buy his so-called antiques. His specialty was the faking of Siegburg pottery. He took a liking to me, and I once saw him kneeling in his little garden dirtying new pieces with damp earth. He sold them a few months later to a Protestant minister, a collector of Rhenish antiques. Nothing made him so happy as to put the finishing touches on some fake. He would look at it admiringly, and smile, and say 'Look at the god I've made, the prettiest little false god I've ever seen.' Then he would take his guitar and twist his toothless mouth as he sang old German songs about Kaetchen von Heilbronn or Schinderhannes."

[3] Apollinaire later told André Billy that in Central Europe he had "traveled on foot, without money, and that for two days in Prague he ate nothing but a Camembert cheese." A perfect tale to tell a Frenchman.

Guillaume Apollinaire

"*Ma chère Maman, Mon cher Albert,*" young Kostro-witzky wrote on the 19th of October, 1901, when he had been in Germany less than two months, "I have been travel-ing for the past week. We spent a night in Rhöndorff be-cause of motor trouble, and then we traveled by train for seven days. I saw the Apollinaris spring near the Rhine. . . ."

And at nearby Remagen he saw the Apollinaris church, the Apollinariskirche, built by Zwirner, nineteenth century architect of the Cologne cathedral, on the site of an ancient chapel, goal of generations of ailing pilgrims, atop the vineyard-planted bluff called the Apollinarisberg, beside the Rhine. Here reposes the miracle-working head of none other than St. Apollinaris, first Christian bishop of Ravenna, patron saint of all subsequent Apollinari, Apolli-narises, and Apollinaires. Baedeker tells the local legend: "The Emperor Frederick Barbarossa having given to Rainald von Dassel, archbishop of Cologne, the head of St. Apollinaris, bishop of Ravenna, the prelate desired to have it brought to Cologne in 1164; but the ship that was carrying it stopped in mid-Rhine off Remagen, and was held there by a mysterious force until the head of the saint was placed in the chapel that had just been built." In 1852 a mineral spring was discovered at nearby Bad Neuenahr, beside one of the pilgrims' roads leading to the Apollinaris shrine. It was promptly given the name of the saint whose head worked miracles, and Apollinaris Water (now the property of the Dortmund Union Brewery) has been bottled and sold throughout the world ever since.

In 1907 a minor Paris newspaper called the *Censeur politique et littéraire* published an article in which Guillaume

Apollinaire was described as entering a café, a little drunk, and calling for Apollinaris water, crying *"C'est mon eau! C'est mon eau!"* Apollinaire promptly sent two of his friends to demand a "formal retraction" from the journalist, refusal of which, he ordered them to say, would constitute acceptance of a challenge to a duel. André Billy, another friend of Apollinaire's, was secretary at the *Censeur,* and handled the matter in his own way. "One morning the poet's two seconds, wearing very shiny top hats, rang at the office door," Billy has written. "I would have been happy to open it for them, but I wasn't there. They wrote, but I was rather careless about the mail, and the letter would still be lying on the mantelpiece at the *Censeur* if the building hadn't later been torn down."

Clearly, Apollinaire didn't insist on having the journalist's blood, but equally clearly the journalist had scored a hit: for Apollinaire, Apollinaris water *was "mon eau"*—anything Apollinairian was his and had importance. Born in a corner of Trastevere, assigned a name out of an alphabet by a clerk, reassigned the Slavic name of a more or less nobly born adventuress mother, his father a silence and an absence—this French poet needed a name of his own. All his life he was to speak mysteriously or grandiloquently of his ancestry, as with Annie Playden he laid claim to high nobility and fortune. "I am descended from Rurik, the chief of the Varangians, the first king and first law-giver of Russia," he announced to a friend in one of his last years. In his poem "Cortège" he wrote:

Guillaume Apollinaire

Un jour je m'attendais moi-même
Je me disais Guillaume il est temps que tu viennes
Pour que je sache enfin celui-là que je suis. . . .

It must indeed have been even harder for young Kostro-witzky than it is for most of us to know who he "really" was. *"Ton père fut un sphinx et ta mère une nuit"*: who and what could be the product of such a union as that?

The name Apollinaire was neither sphinx nor night. In one language or another it was the name of his grand-father, the papal chamberlain, and his own, as testified to in a baptismal certificate; in French it has a particularly at-tractive sound, and in French, through efforts entirely his own, he had made it peculiarly his. Germany saw the end of "Kostro," as Annie called him; while he was there his first poems were published in Paris, and: "Now I'm taking the name of Guillaume Apollinaire for good." The miracle-working head of Bishop Apollinaris was just up the Rhine, on the hill at Remagen; and if the Bishop could give his name to a nearby spring, why not to a nearby poet, a young man who by birth and education was not immune to the prestige of bishops? Especially since Bishop Apolli-naris, Christian though he was, had been born in the pagan world and bore a name derived from that of the god who was a patron of poets.

Small wonder then that Apollinaire's Rhine year was one of those heady, youthful, vocation-confirming experi-ences like Flaubert's voyage to the Near East, as well as an *annus mirabilis* in itself like those twelve months in 1882–83 when Maupassant wrote not only *Une Vie* but several dozen of his best tales. Either during the year in Germany or out

76

of that year Apollinaire wrote several dozen of his poems that have stayed the freshest. Short lyrics, most of them, full of word play, humorous and sentimental, usually with the Rhine flowing at the poet's feet or the firs of Neuglück close by, often with strange little Rhineland characters as protagonists or witnesses or chorus.

In the Rhine poems he has become expert at conveying, in a few words, a strong physical picture:

Les sept montagnes dormaient comme les bêtes

or launching a concentrated blast, like one at Rhenish crooners:

Des châtrés enrhumés en métal ces ténors

or evoking romance:

Ruines au bord du vieux Rhin
On s'embrasse bien dans votre ombre

Slightly later came "La Chanson du Mal-Aimé." But to reach that high point of power the poet had to return from isolation among Rhenish ruins to the world of living artists.

Guillaume Apollinaire

Four

Among the many cafés of Paris there is one in a location more striking than most, situated not far from the cathedral of Notre Dame, at the corner of the Place Saint-Michel and the Quai Saint-Michel, or, to put it differently, at the corner of the "Boul' Miche" (the main stem of the Latin Quarter) and the Seine itself. This café is called Le Départ: on the lower level of the *quai* at this point stands the Saint-Michel station of a railroad much used by commuters, and in the late afternoon many an office worker stops off at the café for a glass of wine or something stronger before making his *départ* for the suburbs. Le Départ is not a popular café with students of the University of Paris, who throng rival establishments only a block or two up the boulevard, nor is it attractive to Paris personalities or to tourists: despite its distinctive location there is an aggressive lack of character about the place, both within and without, which makes it the opposite of sympathetic. And yet it does a steady nondescript business. Somebody recently called it "the café where nobody ever goes but where the terrace is always full."

This was not always true of Le Départ.

If you enter the place and (avoiding the busy *garçons,* who are apt to return an indifferent answer) ask the gray-haired lady at the cashier's desk, or the stocky manager, whether this is the place with the famous cellar, you are

78

likely to receive a quick smile, a nod, and a invitation to inspect the *sous-sol*. Downstairs is anticlimax: a cellar like the working cellar of any other café, divided into bins for the storage of hundreds of bottles of wines and spirits. There are walled-up windows: before the *quai* was reconstructed to accommodate the railroad, the manager will tell you, the street level of the intersection with the Boulevard Saint-Michel was much lower than it is now, and this cellar was a ground floor, with windows overlooking the river. (Below it, he tells you, is another cellar, the "true" cellar.) As you remount the stairs, having found it quite impossible to imagine these cluttered wine bins as a rendezvous of painters, poets, and singers, the manager will tell you that "Only last week an old gentleman came and asked in a quavering voice if he could take one last look at the place where he sang and recited at the turn of the century." And later in the day when you ask an old friend, a Parisian painter in his eighties, who had told you that he frequented the *caveau* "in the old days," whether it was at that time a cellar or a ground-floor with a river view, he answers: "Oh, it was already a cellar. We always went downstairs to listen to Verlaine."

It was in the cellar of the Café du Départ[1] that Apollinaire made his public debut in Parisian poetic society, on April 25, 1903, at one of a series of Saturday evenings called Les Soirées de *La Plume—La Plume* being a magazine of poetry under whose auspices the affairs were held.

[1] "Le Départ" was a new name for the café at the time of Apollinaire's debut. It had long been known as "Le Soleil d'Or," and before that as "L'Avenir." Today there exists another "Soleil d'Or," located in full view of "Le Départ" across the Pont Saint-Michel on the Ile de la Cité.

79

Guillaume Apollinaire

On his return from Germany he had brought with him a testimonial:

I hereby certify that Monsieur Wilhelm de Kostrowitzky has been employed by me in my home as tutor from August 21, 1901, to August 21, 1902. I have nothing but praise for his ability and his character. He is leaving me at his own request.

Vicomtesse E. de Milhau.

Neuglück bei Oberpleis
Kreis Sieg
August 24, 1902

That quickly got him a job as a bank clerk, and for the next five or six years he was to be clerk by day in a series of small banks and at least one financial weekly, and poet by night. He lived in a flat in the Rue de Naples with his mother, his brother and probably his "uncle," Jules Weil. During that summer and winter he had a few poems, stories, and articles published in the *Revue blanche* and in *L'Européen,* a Parisian pacifist publication: at this moment and somewhat earlier Apollinaire expressed a few vaguely anarchistic and pacifist sentiments, the closest he ever came to political utterance.

La Plume was a magazine that had been founded early in 1889 and offered its pages to numerous *avant-garde* poets, artists, and critics of diverse tendencies, Symbolist and otherwise, whose work had previously appeared in various reviews that had been unable to survive. That was the summer of the Exposition Universelle and the Eiffel Tower, and amid the swarms of visitors to the fair the *avant-garde* artists were more than usually vehement in their denunciations of the vulgarity of the masses and of the so-called social elite. It was toward the end of the summer that *La*

Plume inaugurated its Saturday soirées, which were held almost from the beginning in the cellar of the often re-baptized café at the corner of the Place Saint-Michel. One of the organizers stated that the purpose of the soirées was to *"ajouter une note d'art vrai aux bruits cosmopolites de l'Exposition Universelle."*

"Shall we attend one of these gatherings?" an historian of the Soirées de *La Plume* invites us.[2]

It is nine P.M. Streams of students, poets, and artists, recognizable by their corduroy suits and broad-brimmed felt hats, keep coming from Montparnasse, Montmartre, and Batignolles and flowing into the café. The main room is quiet; it looks like a café in the provinces; many tables are empty; the cashier is drowsing at her desk; for the sake of economy only every other gas jet has been lit; people from the neighborhood are playing cards in a corner; the waiter is putting away the morning newspapers. But do not stop; cross the room, follow the group just coming in; go down the stairs leading to the basement; open the door in front of you. For a moment you stand motionless, suffocated by the noise, the heat, and the smoke. A strange sight is before you: a long narrow cellar is filled to overflowing with a wildly gesticulating crowd. Two rushing, harried waiters seem unable to cope with the avalanche of orders and complaints, and can scarcely make their way among the clutter of chairs and tables laden with beer glasses. In a space that could barely accommodate forty persons, a hundred and fifty or two hundred are packed. . . . At the

[2] Ernest Raynaud, "Les Samedis de *la Plume*," *La Plume*, April 15, 1903. Ernest Raynaud was an unusual figure in that he was not only a Symbolist and "Romanist" poet, but also a Commissaire de Police. He became an admirer of Apollinaire after the latter's debut at the Soirées de *La Plume*, and called on him at his mother's flat in the Rue de Naples—purely a visit of respect from one poet to another. Apollinaire was not at home, and although Raynaud was in civilian clothes and introduced himself as a poet, Mme de Kostrowitzky was too experienced to be fooled. "What have you done now?" she demanded of her son, when he returned. "The police have been looking for you" (André Salmon, *Souvenirs sans fin*, I, 51.)

Guillaume Apollinaire

far end, a tiny stage framed by "curtains" of painted wood; a few brushstrokes on the end wall suggest a seascape and a symbolic moon.

At the left, a ramshackle piano . . . near the stage, a podium for the chairman [Léon Deschamps, founder of *La Plume*] . . . and grouped all over the floor, following the law of sympathies, Parnassians, Brutalists, Instrumentists, Magi, Kabbalists, Humorists, Decadists, Symbolists, Romanists, and those who will be known tomorrow as Naturists. Forgive me if I don't name all the names. There are too many. . . .

The chronicler does cite a number of names, but even among those poets whom he mentions out of the "hundred and fifty or two hundred" packed in few are remembered today: the French Charles Le Goffic, Charles Maurras, Jules Renard, Paul Verlaine, Maurice Barres; the Greek Jean Moréas, the American Stuart Merrill, the Belgian Camille Lemonnier. One wonders about some of the lady habituées: who was "Princesse Nadedja, *fleur de la Russie*," or "Marie Krysinska, who claims to be the mother of Free Verse?"

There was apparently something sympathetic about the soirées:

How simple and cordial and good-natured these gatherings are, very different from those of the Chat Noir, for example, where art quickly turns into puffism and parody. People went to that cabaret of Salis' because it was the thing to do, as they might go to a zoo, with the hope of catching a glimpse of a strange beast or two; one felt that the real purpose of those displays of art was business, lucre. I know that the poets who read their verses there had to be pretty thick-skinned and bent on success at any cost to stand the insolent lorgnettes and hostile monocles of the audience. An audience made up of snobs, amateurs, and bored society women, creating a music-hall atmosphere in which any poet had soon to become a ham actor. At *La Plume,* on the contrary, everyone felt at home. Everywhere, in every corner, were the faces of people one knew, friends who had come with the sole intention of listening to poetry. No attitudinizing.

Now the evening begins:

Come sign the attendance sheet: this is a must. Scarcely are we seated when there are cries of "Silence!" The chairman tinkles his bell and introduces *"notre cher camarade"* whoever he is, usually a singer: the evening usually begins (and ends) with singing—it takes the crashing chords of the piano to drown out the conversation and the clinking of beer glasses. . . . Then, when the pianist is dripping with sweat from his exertions he is relieved, and the poets begin. . . . Yann Nabor, a monologue. . . . Dubus, anything from puns to sobs. . . . About ten o'clock thick, Vesuvius-like smoke begins to rise steadily from the tables, forming heavy clouds at the ceiling and seeping out through the vents with a slowness that makes you think of eternity. Action is called for, and a few good-natured members of the audience, sitting near the wall, pull the cords that regulate the transoms to let in some air, and everyone pretends to feel better.

But what is happening now? Why the commotion, the jostling? Why is everyone standing? A police raid? No! It is the great Verlaine who is coming in. "His felt hat is his halo," as Aimé Passereau put it, and among his retinue are the hollow-eyed Jules Tellier and Henri d'Argis, pale after his fatal trip. Verlaine walks with a limp, leaning on his cane, the more dignified for feeling the effects of the drinking he has been doing. All make way before him, and—lo, oh miracle of Genius!—how joyfully, how reverently a group of lovely women welcomes this "tramp who looks like a thief"!

Verlaine could be elegant. Even at the Soirées de *La Plume* I used to see him actually wearing a fashionable English collar and a high silk hat that had doubtless been retrieved one moving-day from behind a piece of furniture. He was very proud of this hat.

83

Guillaume Apollinaire

He had to give it up only because a certain strand of his hair was really too rebellious and spoiled the esthetic effect. . . . However, one forgot all such incongruous details once he began to speak—his deep, gentle eyes transfigured him.

As the evening progressed, our chronicler tells us, there were "thunderstorms of applause"; *"le lyrisme est déchainé";* and toward midnight came the most popular, the most beloved if not the most admired, phase of the evening, the café singers from Montmartre.

Finally:

Now it is over. Midnight is striking; it is time to go. Far from pocketing the receipts, like Salis, the chairman is obliged to pay the waiters out of his own pocket for some drinks left unpaid for by some of the less scrupulous members of the audience. He does it with a discreet spontaneity that enhances the graceful gesture. The crowd is slow to disperse: groups intently discussing some point of esthetics block the corridors and the doors; and strollers on the Boulevard Saint-Michel stare at this unusually large number of people coming out into the night.

Such were the Soirées de *La Plume,* held continuously for six years from the founding of the magazine in 1889, when Wilhelm de Kostrowitzky was a nine-year-old school-boy in Monaco. There were also certain Dîners de *La Plume,* at which "Emile Zola, François Coppée, and Jules Claretie did not disdain to preside." Verlaine, *"Prince des poètes,"* was the bright star of such affairs, but he was a lonely one, and those who frequented the soirées uneasily felt that this was "a period of transition," as one of them expressed it, "in which nothing definitive is being created." Verlaine died in 1896; during his last years he was increasingly sick and feeble; perhaps his more and more frequent

84

absences from the soirées had something to do with their discontinuance.

In 1900 died the founder of the magazine, Léon Deschamps, the chairman who had so often tinkled his bell and paid for drinks; and in 1903 the new editor, Karl Boès, reinstituted the soirées. Boès felt that Paris literary life had been the poorer and the more acrimonious for the absence of the fellowship of the soirées: "In Paris," he said, "where life is so busy, this is the only practical way of seeing each other and thus clearing up in a few moments misunderstandings which the absence of personal contact tends to worsen. It is because poets and artists don't see enough of each other that they increasingly lose the spiritual contact that all those who really love Beauty should maintain. Let us not waste our hatreds on each other: let us make better use of them, against bad artists and bad writers." It was in honor of the re-institution of the soirées by Boès that the chronicler we have been quoting, Ernest Raynaud, wrote his sketch of the earlier soirées and proclaimed the beginning of the new:

The café de l'Avenir, which became the café du Soleil d'Or, [he says] today is the café du Départ. The new name is a good augury for young poets and artists.[3] May they come in crowds! They will find welcoming, attentive ears and a stage still warm with past triumphs.

There was a more official announcement on the last page of the April 15 issue of *La Plume:*

At the request of a large number of our contributors, friends, and subscribers, we have decided to resume the Soirées de *La*

---

[3] Because in French *"départ"* means "start" as well as "departure."

Guillaume Apollinaire

Plume, interrupted for several years. They will take place every Saturday, at nine P.M., in the same place as before, the Caveau du Soleil d'Or, 1 Place Saint-Michel. They will be preceded by a dinner of friends at the Restaurant du Palais, 3 Place Saint-Michel. These evenings will be *strictly private.* Cards of invitation must be presented at the door. Men of letters and artists wishing to attend these soirées may register every day at the offices of *La Plume.* The first soirée will be held Saturday 18 April.

In his memoirs, André Salmon laughs at the stern insistence on "cards of invitation" for the soirées. "I was to find, when Saturday finally came," he writes, "—that Saturday of the Soirées de *La Plume,* so feverishly awaited— that there was no need for a card, and that anyone who wished to come in could do so freely: after all, it was a café. And not only did nobody ask to see your card, but if you had the naiveté to show it to the café proprietor or one of his waiters it was looked at with curiosity and suspicion. However, you did have to sign the attendance sheet."

Apollinaire's signature is among those on the attendance sheet for the second of the new series of the Soirées de *La Plume,* held on April 25, 1903. To modern eyes this list, like Ernest Raynaud's earlier list, contains few familiar names: the ever-faithful American, Stuart Merrill, Paul Fort who had been elected "Prince des poètes" following the death of Verlaine, Jules Romains, André Salmon. It is to Salmon that we owe our picture of Apollinaire in the cellar of Le Départ. Both young men were clerks by day; neither had seen or heard of the other; both made their debuts that night:

Henri Vernot, the chairman, announced Guillaume Apollinaire. I see it now.

86

Apollinaire stood up, heavily. . . . From his mouth he removed a little white clay pipe decorated in black, green, and red: a *Narcisse,* so called because of the head that formed the bowl, preferred by him above all other models. Looking sombre, almost angry, a bit of reddish moustache half-hiding an almost feminine pout, he walked straight to the piano, leaned firmly against it, and began to declaim vehemently, in an intense, low-pitched voice, the poem "Schinderhannes," from a series then called *Le Vent du Rhin.* . . .

He had brought back from Germany, or had composed while thinking of Annie . . . enough poems for a volume to be called *Le Vent du Rhin.* But he was uncertain as to whether to make these Rhine elegies merely a part of the collection he wanted to publish—a collection whose title he hadn't yet chosen. Should it be *Le Violon,* perhaps? Or *L'Olive?* Of course it was to be neither the one nor the other, since the poems were not to be published in a volume until 1913, ten years after that Soirée de *La Plume,* and then the book would be called *Alcools* and would include nine of the Rhine poems, pieces taken from the projected *Vent du Rhin.*

At any rate, that night Apollinaire read "Schinderhannes," and when he came to the lines:

> *On mange alors toute la bande*
> *Pète et rit pendant le dîner*
> *Et s'attendrit à l'allemande*
> *Avant d'aller assassiner*

he stressed a little too complacently, perhaps, the word "pète," he declaimed, chanted the rest in his deep voice, and at the end positively shouted:

> *Avant d'aller assassiner*

I was among those who applauded furiously. The person sitting beside me—I learned later that it was Maurice Magre, well known since 1898—leaned over to me (I was utterly unknown in that gathering) and remarked: "He does it up brown, doesn't he?"

Apollinaire then pulled a thin manuscript out of one of the pockets of his ragged trousers and read part of "L'Ermite," a

87

poem which, when it appeared in *Alcools,* was dedicated to Félix Fénéon in gratitude for having introduced him to the *Revue blanche.*

Vertuchou Riotant des vulves des papesses
De saintes sans tetons j'irai vers les cités. . . .

I have never cared for those lines—I disliked them the first day I heard them, or rather that first night I heard them. They are the kind of thing a young man composes not to impress other people, but to impress himself, even when he is the young Guillaume Apollinaire. Nevertheless, that evening I was ready to defend those lines against those in the audience whom I saw turning up their noses.

André Salmon goes on to tell how, after Apollinaire returned to his seat, he himself was asked to recite and how, when the verses he declaimed were well applauded, Karl Boès immediately declared that they were accepted for publication in *La Plume.* "That audience of the soirées," says Salmon, "composed of the well known and the unknown, were Boès's reading committee." The "reading committee" chose some verses by Apollinaire, too, and in an early issue the magazine printed a poem called "L'Avenir." Perhaps the title was a glancing tribute to one of the former names of the café where the poet had found his first live audience, although André Salmon tells us that almost alone among the habitués, whose practice it was to speak of the place as Le Soleil d'Or, Apollinaire always gave it its proper new name, Le Départ, as though it were "a symbol of a splendid start toward fame." For some time Apollinaire faithfully frequented the Soirées de *La Plume,* his first poetic forum: he enthusiastically agreed with Karl Boès that poets and artists should see each other. In its issue of August 1 the magazine printed "Le Larron," the poem that contains the line so frequently quoted in reference to Apollinaire himself: *"Ton père fut un sphinx et ta mère une nuit."*

"Le Larron" is a heavily Symbolist poem, probably written in large part several years earlier, before the limpid Rhine poems. It has always been celebrated for its obscurity and for its plethora of learned allusions: it is one of the highwater marks of Apollinaire's employment of his wide reading as a device for "suggesting the object." Although he constantly made fun of the Symbolists, Apollinaire was almost always to remain what might be called a recurrent Symbolist himself: his poetic roots were deep in Symbolism, and for one with so vast a stock of assorted information, Symbolism offered too many opportunities for display to be discarded easily. Even in his last years someone said of him: "When Apollinaire's muse goes to Montparnasse, she goes there from the Bibliothèque Nationale."

That November Apollinaire traveled to London.

Annie Playden, the English governess, had stayed on in Germany in the service of the Vicomtesse a few months longer than he, and had then resigned and returned to her family's house on Landor Road in Clapham. Now, after she had been in London about a year, he went to see her.

There are few details extant concerning the visit, and it is not clear whether or not he gave her notice of his coming. "When he arrived at Landor Road," says LeRoy Breunig, further reporting his conversation with Annie Playden Postings in 1951,

Annie was out and her younger sister opened the door. He introduced himself to her in English, "which he spoke," [Annie

89

reminisced, in the interview] "very carefully and correctly, and he gave my sister a little bracelet that he had bought especially for her." Despite all his efforts to make a good impression on the Playden family he was not well received. He stayed with an Albanian friend, Faïk beg Konitza, who lived all the way across London. Annie once went there for dinner, but since her mother insisted that she be home every night before 9 o'clock they usually went out together only in the afternoon. "One night he rang our bell late: I didn't want to open the door, but my mother said if we didn't he might break it down. We lived in constant dread of his fits of rage."

Fits of rage. . . . The result of a frustrated passion, commentators on Apollinaire have usually said—his passion for the blue-eyed little English governess who had inspired so many of the Rhine poems, whom he told his friends he had slept with and "missed greatly when she was away," and who now in London refused his offer of marriage as she had refused it earlier after climbing safely down from the Drachenfels. What kind of an object was she for a poet's passion? And what was this passion that had been biding its time in Paris for well over a year and now, after a trip across the Channel, began to inspire a long poem of insufficiently requited love? Such is a fairly accurate description of "La Chanson du Mal-Aimé," among the most splendid of Apollinaire's poems, which he was to begin to write on his return from this first visit to Annie in London. Was Apollinaire's love for Annie deeper than ever, after the fourteen months that had elapsed since their farewells in Neuglück? Did her new refusal in London cause him anguish? One may be permitted to doubt it. That Annie inspired Apollinaire with passion cannot be doubted, but one suspects that what had happened during the interval,

90

that period of his maturing as a poet and his beginning to find an audience, was a growing realization of the poetic possibilities inherent in the ambiguous relationship.

"Despite all his efforts to make a good impression on the Playden family he was not well received. . . ." He gave Annie's sister a little bracelet. What did his other efforts to make a good impression on the pietistic Playdens consist of? Ringing the doorbell late at night? Indulging in "fits of rage?" Staying with "an Albanian friend, Faïk bég Konitza," perhaps? We know a little about Konitza. Apollinaire himself conjures him up for us quite vividly:

Of all the men whom I have known and remember with the greatest pleasure, Faïk bég Konitza is one of the most singular. He was born in Albania, forty years ago or so, of a family that had remained faithful to the Catholic religion. This Chkipe[4] was brought up in France, and at about the age of twenty was so devout that he wanted to become a novice at the Grande-Chartreuse. He did nothing about it, however, and gradually his religion changed not to indifference, but to a kind of resolute anticlericalism rather like that of Merimée. He continued his studies, but since he was filled with a love for his native Albania he returned to Turkey, engaged in conspiracies, and, as he relates, was twice condemned to death *in absentia*. He returned to France, of whose language and literature he had an excellent knowledge, and came into close contact with everyone who had anything to do with Albania. However, he found the degree of liberty permitted the individual in France insufficient, and went to live in Brussels, Rue d'Albanie, where he founded a learned review, *Albania,* which dealt with political matters and even more with literature, history, and phil-

[4] Apollinaire probably meant to write the word which we would spell Shquiptar, meaning, in Albanian, simply "an Albanian." The word "Shquipte" also means "Albanian," but in the sense of "the Albanian language."

91

Guillaume Apollinaire

ology. Thus he greatly vitalized the pro-Albania movement. By purifying the Albanian language of corrupt or parasitical terms that had found their way into it, he succeeded within the space of a few years in changing a patois used only in low sailors' dives into a beautiful language, rich and flexible.

However, liberty as it was understood in Brussels pleased him no more than in Paris. One day he got into trouble when a policeman accosted him in the street. "Your nationality?" the policeman asked. "Albanian." "Your address?" "Albania Street." "Your profession?" "I am editor of *Albania*." "Do you know, I really don't think I believe you," said the policeman, and the Albanian patriot spent the night in a stationhouse.

Faïk bég Konitza took great pains with the publication of *Albania*. On the cover, as a kind of emblem, were the arms of the future kingdom of Albania, designed by a talented French sculptor whose name I forget and who died a few years ago in the outskirts of New York by a fall from a balloon. However, because of the meticulous care with which Faïk bég Konitza wrote his articles, and his slowness, his magazine always appeared considerably behind time. In 1904 only the issues for 1902 came out, and in 1907 the 1904 issues appeared quite regularly.

Fed up with Brussels, Faïk bég Konitza left for London. He abandoned his beautiful printing press, composed exclusively of Plantinian characters, on which he had himself composed and printed various small books, extremely rare today. That activity had been of short duration because his one and only employee somehow managed to ruin all his type.

It was in London that I knew Faïk bég Konitza, in 1903. He was living in Oakley Crescent, City Road, E.C. I had never seen him. He had invited me to spend a few days with him, and had promised to meet me at the station. Some sign was necessary by which I would recognize him. It was agreed that he would wear an orchid in his buttonhole. My train arrived very late, and on the platform of Victoria Station I saw that all the gentlemen there were wearing orchids in their buttonholes. How would I recognize my Albanian? I took a cab and arrived at his house just as he was setting out to buy his orchid.

My stay in London was charming. Faïk bég Konitza had a passion for the clarinet, the oboe, and the English horn. In his living room he had an old collection of these instruments. In the morning, as we waited for lunch, which was always late, my host would play me twangy old tunes, sitting at his desk with lowered eyes and a serious air.

Lunch was *à l'albanaise,* in other words interminable. Every other day dessert was custard, a dish I care for not at all. He loved it. The alternate days there was blanc-mange, which I love: he ate none of it.

The lunches lasted so long that I was unable to visit a single museum in London—we always arrived just as the doors were closing.

However, we took long walks and I came to know Faïk bég Konitza's refined and cultivated intellect.

Like almost all Albanians of good ancestry he had a tendency to morbid anxieties, and I was all the more touched by the friendship that he showed me—I could see that it was a commodity that he didn't squander.

His anxieties took the most bizarre forms. After buying something in a shop he was always terrified to leave lest the shopkeeper come running after him and accuse him of stealing it. "How in the world would it be possible for me to prove that I hadn't stolen it?" he always said.

When I saw him in London, Faïk bég Konitza had just improved his library. He had sold all his books and replaced them with those English editions in which the text is printed in such small characters that you need a magnifying glass to read them. In this way he had formed a considerable new library, all of it contained in one small cupboard.

Of his old books he had kept only two dictionaries, Bayle's —he considered Bayle his master—and Darmesteter's.

His greatest literary admiration was M. Remy de Gourmont, and later, when I sent him a portrait I had found of that writer, he was very grateful to me.

Faïk bég Konitza, like the other Beyle, has always had a passion for pseudonyms. He changes them very often. At the time

93

when I knew him, he called himself Thrank-Spirobeg, from the name of the hero of a historical novel by Léon Cahun, which is by way of being a masterpiece and is the best book inspired by Albanian history. But seeing that typesetters invariably spelled his pseudonym Thrank-Spiroberg, Faïk bég Konitza soon decided to use that version himself.

That lasted only two or three years. Then he took another pseudonym, which he used to sign a very solid, well written book entitled *A Treatise on Artificial Languages*. That new pseudonym was Pyrrhus Bardyli.

At least half invented, probably. But even so. . . . Not that Faïk bég Konitza seems to have been in any way disreputable. Still, his eccentricities underline Apollinaire's own. Including the eccentricity of taking all the way across London, to visit this revolutionary with whom he had chosen to stay, a girl who had to be home before nine and on whose family he was, supposedly, trying to make a good impression because he wanted, supposedly, to marry her! A serious suitor. . . .[5]

If a young writer is an artist of much originality, the ambiance of a magazine under whose auspices he makes any kind of a debut seldom seems interesting to him for very long unless it changes along with him, and rather soon Apollinaire and his friend André Salmon began to sabotage the rather orthodoxly, one might almost say primly, Bohemian soirées of the fifteen-year-old *Plume*. In a later article, on Alfred Jarry, Apollinaire spoke of the soirées as he had come to think of them:

[5] For an account of another visit with Mrs. Annie Playden Postings, eleven years after LeRoy Breunig's of 1951, see Appendix II of this volume.

Apollinaire: Four

The first time that I saw Alfred Jarry, it was at the Soirées de *La Plume,* the second series, said not to be up to the first. The café du Soleil d'Or had changed its name: it was called the café du Départ. This melancholy name probably hastened the end of the soirées, and probably the end of *La Plume* itself: the name was an invitation to travel, and it made us all take our leave quite quickly. Still, in the cellar in the Place Saint-Michel there were some delightful evenings, and a number of friendships had their beginnings there.

According to André Salmon, he and Apollinaire both began to find it rather ridiculous for poets to read their verses "more or less propped up against a music-hall piano," and they were soon behaving rebelliously. Apollinaire took to appearing in clothes so ragged as to constitute almost a burlesque of the other Bohemian costumes present—Salmon calls this Apollinaire's "torn-trousers snobbery." They insisted on declaiming mock elegies whenever the belated Symbolists present declaimed "sincere" elegies: in their opinion, Symbolism had been overdoing the elegy. One evening Apollinaire tried everyone's patience by bringing with him a guest who was, or whom he declared to be, the editor-in-chief of a newspaper in Salonika, and solemnly requesting that particular consideration be shown this personage because his newspaper was "read by the Sultan himself." In these buffooneries one can perhaps see the influence of the supreme buffoon Jarry. Apollinaire, a great admirer of *Ubu roi,* walked part way home with Jarry the night of their meeting at Le Départ, and claims to have seen him point his revolver at a man who presumed to ask him a street direction. In his article on him he shows great appreciation of Jarry as a man, as a "case," and as an artist, and

95

in it he included a celebrated description of a visit to his weird lodgings, which he called his "Grande Chamblerie," in the Rue Cassette:

"Monsieur Alfred Jarry?"
"Second floor and a half."
I was somewhat puzzled by that answer from the concierge. I climbed up to where Alfred Jarry lived—second and a half turned out to be correct. The stories of the house had seemed too high-ceilinged to the owner, so he had cut each of them in two. In this way the house, which still exists, has fifteen stories, but since it is actually no higher than the houses around it, it is but a reduction of a skyscraper.

For that matter, reductions abounded in Alfred Jarry's abode. His second and a half was but the reduction of a story: Jarry was quite comfortable standing up, but I was taller than he, and had to bend. The bed was but reduction of a bed—a pallet: low beds were the fashion, Jarry told me. The writing table was but the reduction of a table: Jarry wrote on the floor, stretched out on his stomach. The furnishing was but the reduction of furnishing, consisting solely of the bed. On the wall hung the reduction of a picture. It was a portrait of Jarry, most of which he had burned, leaving only the head, which made him look like a certain lithograph of Balzac that I know. The library was but the reduction of a library, to put it mildly. It consisted of a cheap edition of Rabelais and two or three volumes of the *Bibliothèque rose*. On the mantelpiece stood a large stone phallus, made in Japan, a gift to Jarry from Félicien Rops. This virile member, larger than life, Jarry had kept covered with a purple velvet sheath ever since the day when the exotic monolith had frightened a literary lady. She had arrived breathless from climbing up to this second floor and a half, and bewildered at finding herself in this furnitureless "Grande Chamblerie."

"Is it a cast?" she inquired.
"No," answered Jarry. "It's a reduction."

96

Before long, Apollinaire's rebellion against *La Plume* took a more concrete form.

As a result of "a number of friendships" made at the soirées, he was in the habit of eating frugal dinners, those nights when he was not obliged to dine *en famille* in the Rue de Naples, with a small select company in the more-than-modest Restaurant Odéon in the Rue de Seine. Here a full portion of meat cost twelve cents and a half portion eight, credit often being extended to the artists for those amounts by the kindly Auvergnat *patron,* Père Jean; and here Jarry one night entertained the company by taking a spoonful of Pernod after every spoonful of his soup, until he had to be removed. Apollinaire, after several times informing his dining companions at the Odéon that he was considering founding a magazine of his own, to be called *Le Festin d'Esope (Aesop's Feast),* took them one night, as though to mark a great occasion, to a different and even more modest establishment, a *"sinistre brasserie,"* André Salmon calls it, in the Rue Christine, and announced that the magazine henceforth existed. As they skeptically listened, Apollinaire informed them that he himself was editor-in-chief of this verbally existent review, that Salmon was secretary, and the poet Nicolas Deniker *gérant*—that is, the member of the staff responsible, under French law, in case of violations or lawsuits. Young Deniker was son of the librarian of the Museum of Natural History in the Jardin des Plantes, the Paris zoo, and was known within his own family as "the only poet born in the menagerie."

Apollinaire was so rapidly acquiring a reputation for jokes, mystifications, and various strange habits à la Jarry— 97

Guillaume Apollinaire

among others, Salmon tells us that he was an accomplished *pétomane,* never failing to *"péter sec"* on the cakes displayed on a stand outside a certain Left Bank pastry shop, and a *chieur* very discriminating in his choice of locale[6]—that *Le Festin d'Esope* must have seemed to his intimates, well acquainted with his lack of funds, just another, more refined, Apollinairian fantasy. The strange thing is that the magazine not only materialized, but lasted for nine brown-covered issues, from November 1903 to August 1904, the issue for May being skipped.

The title refers to a well known anecdote in the life of Aesop:

His master, Xantus, who was giving a banquet for friends, ordered him one day to compose a meal of the best ingredients he could buy. Aesop served a banquet in which every dish, from the soup to the dessert, was made of tongues prepared in various ways. When Xantus reproved him Aesop replied that he had followed his orders to the letter, since the tongue [French *langue*] being the organ of language, is also the vehicle of truth, reason, science, social life, and all things that make life precious. Next day Xantus ordered Aesop to prepare a meal consisting of all the worst ingredients. Aesop again served the same dishes, explaining that the tongue as the organ of language is also responsible for all the worst things in the world—quarrels, dissensions, lawsuits, civil strife, war, lies, slander, blasphemy, and so on.

The first issue contained a manifesto:

Le Festin d'Esope will publish works of all kinds, literary contributions with imagination and ideas. As it does not represent any particular school, its sole concern will be to deserve by the

[6] The *chieur* and the scholar are curiously combined in a formidably learned-sounding article about the Thaïs legend which he published at this time. ("L'Exil de la Volupté, Un Roman sur Thaïs en 1611," *Mercure de France,* July 1904.)

Apollinaire: Four

justice of its criticisms and the quality of the work it publishes, its subtitle of "A Review of Belles-Lettres."

There were no editorial offices, or rather the editorial address required by law was given in the first issue as 244 Rue Saint-Jacques (where Salmon occupied a furnished room) and later as 23 Rue de Naples, residence of the Kostrowitzkys. Expenses were probably slight, but the printer had to be paid, and Salmon declares that it was always a mystery to him where the funds came from. Certainly not from himself or from Apollinaire, nor from the magazine's "advertising": "I don't imagine that the Criterion Bar in the Gare Saint-Lazare paid more than a round of drinks," he says, "for the 'advertisement' which it inserted for its 'Burton Beer, invented by Lord Burton, sincere friend of His Majesty Edward II.'" Salmon hazards one guess as to a financial source:

Someone who must have helped out with money—he had plenty of it—was Jean Sève, who had become a friend of Guillaume's long before me. . . . Guillaume always showed great cordiality to this young fellow, who was very nice, idle, *sportif,* and not too bright. In him Guillaume found an attentive listener who never contradicted him. What makes me think that Jean Sève more or less helped out in the very hazardous enterprise of the *Festin d'Esope* is something I once heard him say to Guillaume in a bar that was stylish enough to make it suitable for Jean Sève to pay for the drinks. "I'm no writer, it's true," he said, "but don't you remember, Guillaume, that I told you I'd like to sign some little thing in your review? Really the least little thing; not an article, of course—I don't know what, exactly—a bit of gossip, maybe, or just a filler."

A little while later Apollinaire, who was to take such an emphatic position in favor of modern art, thought he saw a good

99

opportunity to attack the official art that was still respected by public institutions but which was already beginning to crumble before the rising tide of the Fauves, following fast on the rehabilitation of the Impressionists. Guillaume composed a tiny paragraph more derisive than critical, but splendidly calculated to annoy the illustrious Gérôme, member of the Institute and painter of various grandiose daubs with titles like "Socrates Seeking Alcibiades in the House of Aspasia." He showed it to me, I laughed as much as he did, and he asked me: "André, don't you think we might have Jean Sève sign this?" I saw no reason to disapprove.

After the issue had appeared, we ran into Jean Sève in another bar. Guillaume, beaming, asked: "Have you read it? Are you pleased with your bit about Gérôme?" More in sorrow than in anger, Jean Sève answered: "Yes, I've read it. Didn't you know that Gérôme is my uncle?"[7]

The post of *gérant* of *Le Festin d'Esope* soon passed to a young man named Jean Mollet, who had been captivated by Apollinaire and André Salmon when he heard them read their poems at one of the Soirées de *La Plume,* and who was their inseparable from then on. Because of the distinction of his dress and his love of special kinds of elegance, Apollinaire dubbed him "Baron," and in some

[7] Jean Sève was indeed the nephew of Gérôme, but the rest of the anecdote is dubious. If there exists a "tiny paragraph" in one of the issues of the *Festin* concerning Gérôme and signed "Jean Sève," the present writer has not found it. The issue of July, 1904 contains an article entitled "La Légende des Lérins," signed "Jean Sève." It is a not at all uninteresting discussion of the islands off Cannes, and is so precise and enthusiastic in its explanation of a number of Provençal terms that one could suspect, especially after reading Salmon's anecdote, that Apollinaire had written it. However, Marcel Adéma supplies the information that Jean Sève was considerably brighter than Salmon makes him out to be, that he possessed a *carte de journaliste,* and, having been a fellow-student of Apollinaire's on the Riviera, was quite capable of writing such an article. "Of course," M. Adéma adds, "Apollinaire may have rectified the text."

100

Apollinaire: Four

writings about the period he is referred to as "Baron Mollet, Apollinaire's secretary." But in a light-hearted interview that he gave a reporter from *L'Intransigeant* in 1936 Mollet said: "I am going to destroy your illusions and demolish a legend: I was no more Guillaume Apollinaire's secretary than I am a baron. It was he who dressed me up with those fantastic titles, and I am proud of them because of him." Mollet doubtless performed occasional services for Apollinaire, some of them quasi-secretarial and others of a nature that may be conjectured from a charming booklet, *J'avais un secrétaire,* written about him by a subsequent writer-employer, Francis Carco. In Carco's service Mollet provided lessons in the one-step and impersonated his employer's father in certain delicate situations. Known as "Baron Mollet" to this day, he is a delightfully lunar character, a kind of non-writing neo-Jarry.[8]

Also associated with the *Festin* was a Norwegian, Arne Hammer, an editor of the pacifist *L'Européen* and

[8] In that same interview in *L'Intransigeant,* Mollet paints an engaging picture of Apollinaire the poet and the man:

"What was Guillaume's method of working? A man like him could have no method. He lived his poems himself. He wrote when he felt the need to externalize himself. . . . Before writing anything, he made notes, then he wrote his poem and let it sleep for a while. Later he took it up again and rewrote it almost entirely. Sometimes it was only after ten or so rewritings of this kind that I had the honor of hearing him read it. He would ask me my opinion, and never believed a word of what I told him; he was never satisfied with what he did.

"He loved his friends terribly. He was delightful to be with, and had an extraordinary wealth of fantasy. He never seemed the same, and greatly enjoyed surprising people. Many who knew him slightly used to wonder, when they saw him a second time, whether he was the same man they had met before.

"He had fervent admirers. Among the writers older than he, Remy de Gourmont and Elémir Bourges especially admired him. He was particularly susceptible to the praise of his elders. . . ."

further identified by André Salmon as "godson of Bjoernstjerne Bjoernson, Ibsen's rival."

As for the magazine itself, it is chiefly Apollinaire's own contributions that "justify" the nine issues. Not too interesting is a tale from his Stavelot days, "Qu'vlo'v," so full of Flemish dialect that one of his friends protested: "When you have to know the patois of Eupen and Malmédy to understand French prose, count me out." But there are several of the Rhine poems, including "Schinderhannes," which Apollinaire had read with such effect at an early soirée, versions of "L'Adieu" and the poem now known as "La Dame," and, in five installments, "L'Enchanteur pourrissant," a kind of Arthurian prose and verse dreamlike vaudeville à la *Tentation de Saint-Antoine,* in which countless characters—animals, snakes, druids, sphinxes, an abbot, Vivian the Lady of the Lake, Behemoth, etc.—declaim around the tomb in which lies rotting the body of the enchanter Merlin. Apollinaire was always a lover of the legends surrounding Arthur, *"roi passé, roi futur"*; portions of "L'Enchanteur pourrissant" reproduce verbatim passages from the ancient *Lancelot du lac.*

Otherwise, there were contributions more or less serious or significant by André Salmon, Alfred Jarry, Jean de Gourmont, and Nicolas Deniker; but for the most part Apollinaire, apparently straining to avoid the mawkishness of the soirées, kept the contents light, almost to the point of farce. There is a translation by Henry Vernot of "Mandalay," by Rudyard Kipling, and there are two pieces by the Albanian "Thrank-Spirobeg," one entitled "Outline of a Method of How to Succeed in Winning Applause from the Bourgeois," and the other "The Most Colossal Mystification in the History of the Human Species." Apollinaire contributed a feature called "Notes du mois." Among these is a quotation from the *London Morning Advertiser,* which had asked Lady Tree for some autobiographical details and had received from her four brief lines of verse; after passing through the hands of the *Festin's* French printer these appeared as:

> This is the life
> Of little me:
> Jam the wife
> Of Berbohm Tree.

Le Festin d'Esope was that kind of a magazine—a few of the most delicate of Apollinaire's own traceries silhouetted against a background of rather crazy cobwebs.

And then, after its ninth issue, it ceased. Apparently that was about an average life span for a little magazine in those days. "When they had a good tail wind," André Salmon says, "the little magazines could make it to the tenth issue. Several put out their first number in December, in order to have the childish joy of printing the words 'Second Year' on the cover of the next. As for the little magazines that really lasted more than a year, they were no longer considered little magazines."

During the life of the *Festin,* Apollinaire went to London again in May, the month no issue appeared.

"He became still more insistent," Annie Playden Postings told LeRoy Breunig in their conversation of 1951. " 'Finally I told him that I had to leave for America, where

I had a fiancé waiting. It was the only way I could get rid of him.' Trapped by her own lie, Annie Playden felt obliged, the next day, to go to an employment office and ask whether there was a situation as governess abroad. A request had just been received from the United States, and ten days later, after saying her final farewell to Apollinaire at Waterloo Station, she was on her way to the new world. . . .

"Miss Playden continued to receive letters from him, forwarded by her parents from Landor Road. She has not forgotten a postcard on which he had written a single line, a quotation from Oscar Wilde: 'For each man kills the thing he loves.' Interpreting the phrase literally, and fearing lest he follow her to America, she sent her parents strict orders never to give her address, under any pretext, to Guillaume de Kostrowitzky. Until his death he heard nothing more from her."

On this second visit to London, Apollinaire stayed with his same Albanian friend.

On another occasion I once again spent some time in London with Faïk bég Konitza, who had married and was living at Chingford. It was spring, we took walks in the country and spent hours watching people play golf.

Shortly before my arrival, Faïk bég Konitza had bought some hens, in order to have fresh eggs; but when he had them he found it impossible to eat them. And in truth, how can you eat the eggs of hens whom you know personally and whom you feed yourself? The hens soon began to eat their own eggs, and this horrified Faïk bég Konitza to the point where he looked on the poor birds with revulsion; he no longer let them out of the little hen coop, where by now they were killing and eating each other,

104

Apollinaire: Four

except for one which survived and lived on, lonely and victorious. It was at that time that I saw her. She had become fierce and mad; and since she was black and had lost much weight, she soon came to look like a crow; by the time I left, she had lost her feathers and was metamorphosed into a kind of rat.

When the Turkish revolution came, Faïk bég Konitza planned to return to his country. But things did not turn out as he wished, and just when revolt was being fanned in Albania he left abruptly for America. . . .

Then, back in Paris, Apollinaire resumed publication of *Le Festin* and busied himself with the polishing and finishing of two very considerable poems, both of which owed their inspiration to the daughter of "the Archbishop of Canterbury"—"La Chanson du Mal-Aimé" and "L'Emigrant de Landor Road." Both poems are aesthetically and biographically fascinating. Except for Annie Playden's revelations to LeRoy Breunig, most of what we know about the relationship between Annie and Apollinaire is contained in them.

Guillaume Apollinaire

La Chanson du Mal-Aimé

À Paul Léautaud

Et je chantais cette romance
En 1903 sans savoir
Que mon amour à la semblance
Du beau Phénix s'il meurt un soir
Le matin voit sa renaissance

Un soir de demi-brume à Londres
Un voyou qui ressemblait à
Mon amour vint à ma rencontre
Et le regard qu'il me jeta
Me fit baisser les yeux de honte

Je suivis ce mauvais garçon
Qui sifflotait mains dans les poches
Nous semblions entre les maisons
Onde ouverte de la mer Rouge
Lui les Hébreux moi Pharaon

Que tombent ces vagues de briques
Si tu ne fus pas bien aimée
Je suis le souverain d'Égypte
Sa sœur-épouse son armée
Si tu n'es pas l'amour unique

Au tournant d'une rue brûlant
De tous les feux de ses façades
Plaies du brouillard sanguinolent
Où se lamentaient les façades
Une femme lui ressemblant

Song of the Poorly Loved

To Paul Léautaud

I made this song in nineteen-three
Before my love was clear to me:
He is a phoenix bird who dies
Tonight and will tomorrow rise

In London on a dismal night
I met a hoodlum in the street
Who might have been my love—
He looked so much like her his gaze
Made me blush and drop my eyes.

I trailed him as he slouched along,
Hands in pockets, whistling:
The street became a trough,
Two billows of the Red Sea rose
And I was Pharaoh, he the Jews.

Oh if I have not loved you well,
Let that brick ocean comb and fall.
I am the King of Egypt,
His chariots, his sister-wife,
If you are not my only love.

I turned then down a street that glowed
With fire along its whole façade,
So that the house-fronts wept.
Where sores of fog were bleeding flame
I met a woman who looked like him.

106

C'était son regard d'inhumaine	Nothing but that inhuman look
La cicatrice à son cou nu	And the long scar on her bare neck
Sortit saoule d'une taverne	As she lurched out of a bar—
Au moment où je reconnus	And I knew again what I'd known before
La fausseté de l'amour même	That love itself is false as air.
Lorsqu'il fut de retour enfin	It was the old dog at his feet
Dans sa patrie le sage Ulysse	Who recognized and knew to greet
Son vieux chien de lui se souvint	Ulysses home from war,
Près d'un tapis de haute lisse	While at her thick-piled tapestry
Sa femme attendait qu'il revînt	His wife kept watch for him by sea.
L'époux royal de Sacontale	And Sacontale, whose royal mate,
Las de vaincre se réjouit	Tired of conquest, found it sweet
Quand il la retrouva plus pâle	That she was pale with woe:
D'attente et d'amour yeux pâlis	Love and delay made those eyes pale
Caressant sa gazelle mâle	While she caressed a male gazelle.
J'ai pensé à ces rois heureux	How happy in those wives they were!
Lorsque le faux amour et celle	But false love and the love of her
Dont je suis encore amoureux	I have been faithful to,
Heurtant leurs ombres infidèles	Flailing their ghosts in faithless strife,
Me rendirent si malheureux	Have made a torment of my life.
Regrets sur quoi l'enfer se fonde	Regret, on which hell builds his house,
Qu'un ciel d'oubli s'ouvre à mes vœux	For which oblivion hears vows
Pour son baiser les rois du monde	As for a kind of heaven—
Seraient morts les pauvres fameux	Ah, kings would have perished for her kiss,
Pour elle eussent vendu leur ombre	Poor famous souls unshrived for less.
J'ai hiverné dans mon passé	I have stood frozen in my past
Revienne le soleil de Pâques	Like the forty martyrs of Sebaste
Pour chauffer un cœur plus glacé	On the pond where they were driven.
Que les quarante de Sébaste	Now may some Easter sun make hot
Moins que ma vie martyrisés	My chill heart and its chillier fate.

107

Guillaume Apollinaire

Mon beau navire ô ma mémoire	O pretty ship, my memory
Avons-nous assez navigué	Isn't this far enough to sea,
Dans une onde mauvaise à boire	And the sea not fit to drink?
Avons-nous assez divagué	Haven't we drifted far and lost
De la belle aube au triste soir	From fair dawn to dreary dusk?
Adieu faux amour confondu	Farewell false love, I took you for
Avec la femme qui s'éloigne	The woman that I lost last year
Avec celle que j'ai perdue	Forever as I think:
L'année dernière en Allemagne	I loved her but I will not see
Et que je ne reverrai plus	Her anymore in Germany.
Voie lactée ô sœur lumineuse	O Milky Way, sister in whiteness
Des blancs ruisseaux de Chanaan	To Canaan's rivers and the bright
Et des corps blancs des amoureuses	Bodies of lovers drowned,
Nageurs morts suivrons-nous d'ahan	Can we follow toilsomely
Ton cours vers d'autres nébuleuses	Your path to other nebulæ?
Je me souviens d'une autre année	For I remember another spring,
C'était l'aube d'un jour d'avril	An April dawn when all I sang
J'ai chanté ma joie bien-aimée	Was one long lover's round,
Chanté l'amour à voix virile	When the year was at its time of love
Au moment d'amour de l'année	And I sang with a voice I was master of.

AUBADE CHANTÉE A LÆTARE UN AN PASSÉ · AUBADE SUNG IN LÆTARE IN A PAST YEAR

C'est le printemps viens-t'en Pâquette	*It's spring again, Paquette, come walk*
Te promener au bois joli	*In the pretty woods. The chickens cluck,*
Les poules dans la cour caquètent	*The dawn is making a pink bed*
L'aube au ciel fait de roses plis	*For Love to try your maidenhood.*
L'amour chemine à ta conquête	
Mars et Vénus sont revenus	*Venus and Mars are back, they kiss*
Ils s'embrassent à bouches folles	*Immoderately in the woods*
Devant des sites ingénus	*And rosebushes share their excess*
Où sous les roses qui feuillolent	*And naked goddesses and gods.*
De beaux dieux roses dansent nus	

Apollinaire: Four

Viens ma tendresse est la régente
De la floraison qui paraît
La nature est belle et touchante
Pan sifflote dans la forêt
Les grenouilles humides chantent

Beaucoup de ces dieux ont péri
C'est sur eux que pleurent les saules
Le grand Pan l'amour Jésus-Christ
Sont bien morts et les chats miaulent
Dans la cour je pleure à Paris

Moi qui sais des lais pour les reines
Les complaintes de mes années
Des hymnes d'esclave aux murènes
La romance du mal-aimé
Et des chansons pour les sirènes

L'amour est mort j'en suis tremblant
J'adore de belles idoles
Les souvenirs lui ressemblant
Comme la femme de Mausole
Je reste fidèle et dolent

Je suis fidèle comme un dogue
Au maître le lierre au tronc
Et les Cosaques Zaporogues
Ivrognes pieux et larrons
Aux steppes et au décalogue

Portez comme un joug le Croissant
Qu'interrogent les astrologues
Je suis le Sultan tout-puissant
O mes Cosaques Zaporogues
Votre Seigneur éblouissant

Come, it is all my tenderness
That has brought on this blossoming;
Nature is shy, she counts on us.
Pan whistles and the wet frogs sing.

So many of these gods have died,
Christ Jesus and the great Love god,
That in my Paris courtyard I
With willow trees and tomcats cry.

I've made a song for the poorly-loved
And songs for everything I grieved—
For unaccompanied slave and shark,
For queens who've gone into the dark.

But at this death of love, I tremble;
I follow creatures who resemble
Him, and like some grieving widow
I wake and sleep for his dead shadow;

Like dog to master, vine to trunk,
And like those pious, bawdy drunk-
en cossacks in the painting who
To their steppes and decalogue held true.

"Zaporozhian Cossacks, take
And wear the Crescent like a yoke
As faithful servants to your Lord:
This is the fiery Sultan's word."

109

Guillaume Apollinaire

Devenez mes sujets fidèles
Leur avait écrit le Sultan
Ils rirent à cette nouvelle
Et répondirent à l'instant
A la lueur d'une chandelle

The cossacks laughed to read these rules
And scurrilously that very night
Declined to be his sacred mules.
They answered him, by candlelight:

REPONSE DES COSAQUES ZAPOROGUES
AU SULTAN DE CONSTANTINOPLE

REPLY OF THE ZAPOROZHIAN COSSACKS
TO THE SULTAN OF CONSTANTINOPLE

Plus criminel que Barrabas
Cornu comme les mauvais anges
Quel Belzébuth es-tu là-bas
Nourri d'immondice et de fange
Nous n'irons pas à tes sabbats

"*What dirty Barrabas are you,*
You horny, stinking Lord of Flies,
Fed on shit-and-garbage stew?
We won't attend your revelries.

Poisson pourri de Salonique
Long collier des sommeils affreux
D'yeux arrachés à coup de pique
Ta mère fit un pet foireux
Et tu naquis de sa colique

"*Does putrid Salonikan fish*
And festered eye compose your flesh
Or is it as your friends report,
Your mother let a liquid fart?

Bourreau de Podolie Amant
Des plaies des ulcères des croûtes
Groin de cochon cul de jument
Tes richesses garde-les toutes
Pour payer tes médicaments

"*King of ulcers and putrescence,*
Snout of pig and arse of mare,
Keep your diamond-studded crescents
To buy veterinary care."

Voie lactée ô sœur lumineuse
Des blancs ruisseaux de Chanaan
Et des corps blancs des amoureuses
Nageurs morts suivrons-nous d'ahan
Ton cours vers d'autres nébuleuses

O Milky Way, sister in white
To Canaan's river and the bright
Bodies of lovers drowned,
Can we track laboriously
Your steps to other nebulæ?

Regret des yeux de la putain
Et belle comme une panthère
Amour vos baisers florentins
Avaient une saveur amère
Qui a rebuté nos destins

Regret as in a harlot's face
And beauty like the panther's grace
Girded your kisses round,
Bitter and florentine to taste
Like our two destinies laid waste.

110

Apollinaire: Four

Ses regards laissaient une traîne
D'étoiles dans les soirs tremblants
Dans ses yeux nageaient les sirènes
Et nos baisers mordus sanglants
Faisaient pleurer nos fées marraines

Your eyes could strew a chain of stars
Across a trembling universe,
And sirens swam there too.
Our fairy-godmothers would weep
To see your kisses bite so deep.

Mais en vérité je l'attends
Avec mon cœur avec mon âme
Et sur le pont des Reviens-t'en
Si jamais revient cette femme
Je lui dirai Je suis content

But still I wait for you, I swear;
My heart and soul keep vigil there
On the bridge of Rendezvous.
And if you ever come that way
Again I won't begrudge my stay.

Mon cœur et ma tête se vident
Tout le ciel s'écoule par eux
O mes tonneaux des Danaïdes
Comment faire pour être heureux
Comme un petit enfant candide

Something has drained my heart and head
Like Zeus's sack when he had bled
His gold on Danæ.
After a child's delight is spent
What can you do to get innocent?

Je ne veux jamais l'oublier
Ma colombe ma blanche rade
O marguerite exfoliée
Mon île au loin ma Désirade
Ma rose mon giroflier

Oh, let me not be cured of her,
My pretty dove, my calm harbor,
Still let memory see
That argosy, that isle of spice,
The petalled flower of her face.

Les satyres et les pyraustes
Les égypans les feux follets
Et les destins damnés ou faustes
La corde au cou comme à Calais
Sur ma douleur quel holocauste

I am harassed by goats and satyrs
And filthy bugs that give off fire,
Whole holocausts of trouble.
I wear a noose around my neck
And sweat both good and evil luck.

Douleur qui doubles les destins
La licorne et le capricorne
Mon âme et mon corps incertain
Te fuient ô bûcher divin qu'ornent
Des astres des fleurs du matin

Sorrow, you've split my destiny
And made a poor forked thing of me,
Body and soul are double.
They scatter, seeing you torment
The morning stars for ornament.   III

Guillaume Apollinaire

Malheur dieu pâle aux yeux d'ivoire	Unhappiness, your ivory eyes
Tes prêtres fous t'ont-ils paré	Look palely on the sacrifice
Tes victimes en robe noire	Your crazy priests prepare.
Ont-elles vainement pleuré	In vain the black-robed victim strives,
Malheur dieu qu'il ne faut pas croire	His sentence is that he believes.
Et toi qui me suis en rampant	And you, old shadow on my trail,
Dieu de mes dieux morts en automne	God of my gods who died in fall,
Tu mesures combien d'empans	I know your niggard care—
J'ai droit que la terre me donne	Subtracting every breath I take
O mon ombre ô mon vieux serpent	From those allotted me, old snake.
Au soleil parce que tu l'aimes	Shadow-wife, I led you where
Je t'ai menée souviens-t'en bien	You like to walk, in sun and air.
Ténébreuse épouse que j'aime	In being nothing, you were mine.
Tu es à moi en n'étant rien	O my dear shadow, wearing black
O mon ombre en deuil de moi-même	You mourn for me behind my back.
L'hiver est mort tout enneigé	Now winter and all its snow is dead;
On a brûlé les ruches blanches	They've burned its white-tassled bed-spread
Dans les jardins et les vergers	That hung on tree and vine
Les oiseaux chantent sur les branches	And birds are saying in the trees,
Le printemps clair l'avril léger	What a fine spring, what a nice breeze.
Mort d'immortels argyraspides	The death of snow! Its silver shields
La neige aux boucliers d'argent	Like Alexander's quit the fields
Fuit les dendrophores livides	That time can never bleach.
Du printemps char aux pauvres gens	Tree-bearers come to cheer the poor
Qui resourient les yeux humides	Tired of winter's pompous war.
Et moi j'ai le cœur aussi gros	And I, I have a heart as fat
Qu'un cul de dame damascène	As some Damascan lady's prat—
O mon amour je t'aimais trop	I loved you much too much
Et maintenant j'ai trop de peine	And now I pay with too much grief:
Les sept épées hors du fourreau	The seven blades come from the sheath;

112

Apollinaire: Four

Sept épées de mélancolie
Sans morfil ô claires douleurs
Sont dans mon cœur et la folie
Veut raisonner pour mon malheur
Comment voulez-vous que j'oublie

LES SEPT ÉPÉES

La première est toute d'argent
Et son nom tremblant c'est Pâline
Sa lame un ciel d'hiver neigeant
Son destin sanglant gibeline
Vulcain mourut en la forgeant

La seconde nommée Noubosse
Est un bel arc-en-ciel joyeux
Les dieux s'en servent à leurs noces
Elle a tué trente Bé-Rieux
Et fut douée par Carabosse

La troisème bleu féminin
N'en est pas moins un chibriape
Appelé Lul de Faltenin
Et que porte sur une nappe
L'Hermès Ernest devenu nain

La quatrième Malourène
Est un fleuve vert et doré
C'est le soir quand les riveraines
Y baignent leurs corps adorés
Et des chants de rameurs s'y traînent

La cinquième Sainte-Fabeau
C'est la plus belle des quenouilles
C'est un cyprès sur un tombeau
Où les quatre vents s'agenouillent
Et chaque nuit c'est un flambeau

The seven swords of Love's dismay,
Unsharpened, as is sorrow's way,
Have entered my heart's breach.
And Folly offers his counsel yet,
Twisting a blade, "Try to forget."

THE SEVEN SWORDS

The first is a pure silver sword
It trembles with the name Paline
Its blade is made of winter sky
The blood it drinks is Ghibelline
When Vulcan finished it he died.

The second sword is called Noubosse
It has a pretty rainbow shape
Gods use it on their wedding night
It's killed some thirty foreigners
And bears the spell of Carabosse.

The third is femininely blue
But do not be deceived by that
Or other paradox of steel
This Hermes is a supple dwarf
Call him Lul de Faltenin

The fourth blade is named Malourine
It is a flood of gold and green
At night the river-girls come down
To bathe their precious bodies there
And songs of oarsmen stroke the shore.

A distaff is the fifth of them
A pretty blade called Saint Fabeau
It stands like cypress at the grave
The four winds genuflect like nuns
And every night it's like a torch 113

Guillaume Apollinaire

La sixième métal de gloire
C'est l'ami aux si douces mains
Dont chaque matin nous sépare
Adieu voilà votre chemin
Les coqs s'épuisaient en fanfares

Et la septième s'exténue
Une femme une rose morte
Merci que le dernier venu
Sur mon amour ferme la porte
Je ne vous ai jamais connue

Voie lactée ô sœur lumineuse
Des blancs ruisseaux de Chanaan
Et des corps blancs des amoureuses
Nageurs morts suivrons-nous d'ahan
Ton cours vers d'autres nébuleuses

Les démons du hasard selon
Le chant du firmament nous mènent
A sons perdus leurs violons
Font danser notre race humaine
Sur la descente à reculons

Destins destins impénétrables
Rois secoués par la folie
Et ces grelottantes étoiles
De fausses femmes dans vos lits
Aux déserts que l'histoire accable

Luitpold le vieux prince régent
Tuteur de deux royautés folles
Sanglote-t-il en y songeant
Quand vacillent les lucioles
Mouches dorées de la Saint-Jean

Apollinaire: Four

The sixth of these steel champions
Is nameless but has gentle hands
At sunrise, though, we have to part
Farewell farewell there lies your road
The cocks are weary who have crowed.

The final sword alone is weak
A woman merely, a limp rose
Be grateful that this seventh (who
Is also nameless) brings a close
To swords, love whom I never knew.

O Milky Way, white sister stream
To Canaan's brooks and the pale gleam
Of lovers' bodies drowned, can we
Go with you to new nebulæ?

The gods of hazard lead us down
The backstairs of the universe,
Dancing to fiddlestrings accurst
We go as other men have gone.

It is not to be understood,
This shivering of stars and kings
These women who are false in bed
And history pouring sand on things.

Did Leopold the regent prince,
Guarding the two mad royalties,
Weep to think of a royal dunce
As he watched the fickle fireflies?

Près d'un château sans châtelaine
La barque aux barcarols chantants
Sur un lac blanc et sous l'haleine
Des vents qui tremblent au printemps
Voguait cygne mourant sirène

By a chateau without chatelaine
The barque progressed, a dying swan,
A siren, singing barcaroles.
The light spring air breathed in the sails.

Un jour le roi dans l'eau d'argent
Se noya puis la bouche ouverte
Il s'en revint en surnageant
Sur la rive dormir inerte
Face tournée au ciel changeant

In the silver water the king drowned
One day. Later he floated by
Open-mouthed as if astounded,
His face fixed on the changing sky.

Juin ton soleil ardente lyre
Brûle mes doigts endoloris
Triste et mélodieux délire
J'erre à travers mon beau Paris
Sans avoir le cœur d'y mourir

My fingers blister but no tune
Comes from the burning lyre of June.
Anywhere but in Paris I
Would have the heart this month to die.

Les dimanches s'y éternisent
Et les orgues de Barbarie
Y sanglotent dans les cours grises
Les fleurs aux balcons de Paris
Penchent comme la tour de Pise

On Paris balconies the flowers
Lean like so many Pisan towers,
A barrel-organ sobs below.
Eternity, instead of hours
Is Sundays like this in a row.

Soirs de Paris ivres du gin
Flambant de l'électricité
Les tramways feux verts sur l'échine
Musiquent au long des portées
De rails leur folie de machines

The nights in Paris all drink gin
And fall asleep with their streetlights on.
Trolley-cars are mad machines
To make green sparks and scream like queens.

Les cafés gonflés de fumée
Crient tout l'amour de leurs tziganes
De tous leurs siphons enrhumés
De leurs garçons vêtus d'un pagne
Vers toi toi que j'ai tant aimée

Love weeps the band in the fat café
Love sighs the fizzy glass I clutch
Love, is that all they know how to say,
Your name that I have loved too much?

115

Guillaume Apollinaire

Moi qui sais des lais pour les reines	I've sung a song for the poorly-loved
Les complaintes de mes années	A song for everything I've grieved
Des hymnes d'esclave aux murènes	For unaccompanied slave and shark,
La romance du mal-aimé	For queens who've gone into the dark.
Et des chansons pour les sirènes	

Translated by William Meredith

"La Chanson du Mal-Aimé"[9] is a turning point in Apollinaire's development as a poet, perhaps *the* turning point: it marks his most concentrated use of the trappings of Symbolism, and at the same time the discovery of the poetic potentialities inherent in an area of experience hitherto ignored by poets. The archaic words, the references to occult sciences, the esoteric bits of information, the Zaporozhian Cossacks, Sakountala, and all the rest of the paraphernalia that make an encyclopedia necessary for a word-by-word reading of the poem are a culmination of the *"érudition amusante"* found in earlier poems like "Le Larron." In contrast, the "Aubade" is naive as the Rhine poems are naive—indeed it is thought to have been written while Apollinaire was in Germany—and the last stanzas, laid in Paris, are new and modern in their imagery. Everyday details of the contemporary scene are made to reveal their previously little-noticed poetic essence. They become full-fledged poetic objects. Here in the "Chanson" are these various modes in combination, producing a tension and a strangeness. Furthermore, there is a contrast between this complexity of form and the essential simplicity of the content, and it can be said, still further, that this contrast is itself a part of the content: apparently Apollinaire's feelings

[9] It has been characterized by Marcel Arland as "the testament of a gypsy Villon."

116

for Annie could be expressed in no other way. The complexity and the simplicity are equally full of the peculiar charm almost always present in Apollinaire's language, and the result is a very fascinating poem indeed.

The breaks and changes between moods, between the tones of stanzas and groups of stanzas, even the abrupt geographical jumps—from London to Ithaca to India to Germany to Canaan to Halicarnassus—all seem not only to follow the poet's association of ideas but also to echo the ebb and flow of a lover's emotions as he staggers under the loved one's rejection, wondering whether it is final.[10] "Am I to curse her? She *could* be as faithful as Penelope or Sakountala. Shall I go to a brothel? No. . . . Yes. . . . Love is dead. Is it? My soul, my body, are uncertain. . . ." Lovers in this situation are manic: their hope battles with their despair. The "Chanson" has the universality of their predicament.

Biographically, the title and certain absences are suggestive. The poet complains in the headline that he has been *mal aimé,* inadequately loved; the news that his own love has been unreciprocated is in smaller type. Throughout the long poem the image of the loved one is extremely vague, almost nonexistent. Physically we know nothing of her except that she has an inhuman glance and a scar on her neck; and nothing whatever is said about her mind or her soul. A love poem might be expected to have a double center: the "Chanson" is self-centered; it has nothing of Keats or Werther about it. Already some of the Rhine poems had suggested that for Apollinaire the affair with

[10] The careful architecture of the "Chanson" is well analyzed by LeRoy Breunig in *La Table Ronde*, September 1952.

Guillaume Apollinaire

L'Emigrant de Landor Road

A André Billy

Le chapeau à la main il entra du pied droit
Chez un tailleur très chic et fournisseur du roi
Ce commerçant venait de couper quelques têtes
De mannequins vêtus comme il faut qu'on se vête

La foule en tous les sens remuait en mêlant
Des ombres sans amour qui se traînaient par terre
Et des mains vers le ciel plein de lacs de lumière
S'envolaient quelquefois comme des oiseaux blancs

Mon bateau partira demain pour l'Amérique
Et je ne reviendrai jamais
Avec l'argent gagné dans les prairies lyriques
Guider mon ombre aveugle en ces rues que j'aimais

Car revenir c'est bon pour un soldat des Indes
Les boursiers ont vendu tous mes crachats d'or fin
Mais habillé de neuf je veux dormir enfin
Sous des arbres pleins d'oiseaux muets et de singes

Les mannequins pour lui s'étant déshabillés
Battirent leurs habits puis les lui essayèrent
Le vêtement d'un lord mort sans avoir payé
Au rabais l'habilla comme un millionnaire

Au dehors les années
Regardaient la vitrine
Les mannequins victimes
Et passaient enchaînées

118

Apollinaire: Four

The Emigrant of Landor Road

To André Billy

With his hat in his hand he stepped into the shop
Of the tailor who furnishes clothes to the king
And had recently cut off the heads of a ring
Of wax mannequins, every one dressed like a fop.

The herd in all quarters were milling around
And dragging their shadows unloved on the ground.
Sometimes their hands like white birds would take flight,
Pale waterfowl drawn to the sky-lakes of light.

I sail for America on the next tide
And I'll never come back bearing money I've saved,
Earned on those lyrical prairies, to lead
My shadow, blind shade, through these streets that I've loved.

It's all right for a man to come back from the Indies
But scalpers have sold all the medals I won.
I want to sleep once in new clothes of my own
Under trees full of mute birds, trees full of monkeys.

The mannequins having undressed were displaying
And beating the suits he was meant to try on;
The clothes of a peer who had died without paying
Made him look like a millionaire. They were marked down.

And the years looked in
Through the windowpane
At the doomed mannequins
And filed on in a chain.

119

Guillaume Apollinaire

Intercalées dans l'an c'étaient les journées veuves
Les vendredis sanglants et lents d'enterrements
De blancs et de tout noirs vaincus des cieux qui pleuvent
Quand la femme du diable a battu son amant

Puis dans un port d'automne aux feuilles indécises
Quand les mains de la foule y feuillolaient aussi
Sur le pont du vaisseau il posa sa valise
                    Et s'assit

Les vents de l'Océan en soufflant leurs menaces
Laissaient dans ses cheveux de longs baisers mouillés
Des émigrants tendaient vers le port leurs mains lasses
Et d'autres en pleurant s'étaient agenouillés

Il regarda longtemps les rives qui moururent
Seuls des bateaux d'enfant tremblaient à l'horizon
Un tout petit bouquet flottant à l'aventure
Couvrit l'Océan d'une immense floraison

Il aurait voulu ce bouquet comme la gloire
Jouer dans d'autres mers parmi tous les dauphins
              Et l'on tissait dans sa mémoire
              Une tapisserie sans fin
              Qui figurait son histoire

              Mais pour noyer changées en poux
Ces tisseuses têtues qui sans cesse interrogent
              Il se maria comme un doge
Aux cris d'une sirène moderne sans époux

Gonfle-toi vers la nuit O Mer Les yeux des squales
Jusqu'à l'aube ont guetté de loin avidement
Des cadavres de jours rongés par les étoiles
Parmi le bruit des flots et les derniers serments

120

Apollinaire: Four

The calendar told certain widow-days,
Slow and bloody Fridays at the sepulchre
Of whites and blacks overcome by rainy skies
When the devil's wife used to beat her lover.

Then in an autumn port with leaves afloat,
As the hands of the crowd scattered like leaves blown,
He put his suitcase down on the deck of the boat
And sat down.

Breathing their damp menace, the ocean winds
Kissed his hair. Some of the emigrants kept
Stretching out toward the harbor their weary hands,
Others fell to their knees and wept.

The dying shore still held his long glance.
On the horizon only some toy boats tossed
And a little bouquet covered with a vast
Flowering the ocean, by watery chance.

He wished those flowers could dally like a glory
In other seas, and crown the dolphinry.
And in his memory
An endless tapestry
Was being woven of his watery story.

But to drown those stubborn weavers, turned to lice,
Whose endless questions harried
Him, like a doge he took a wife, amid the cries
Of a siren, up-to-date, unmarried.

Swell toward the night, o sea. The eyes of dogfish gaze
Far off and ravenous, till dawn, on the corpses of days
Eaten away by stars, and there is moaning
Of the billows, and the last vows of the drowning. 121

Guillaume Apollinaire

Annie was a frustrating one, with Annie allowing certain exasperating liberties but puritanically guarding her jewel; the "Chanson" goes further, suggesting that Apollinaire's own objectives with the girl were limited, that what he was seeking was less romance than release. Luckily Annie, who didn't want him, or perhaps any man, as a lover, didn't want him, or perhaps any man, as a husband either: had she accepted him, it might well have been a case of the fleeing bridegroom. Little wonder that in attempting to elevate a calf affair into a universal image of disappointment in love itself, Apollinaire had to call on all the resources at his command, including all the ornamentations of Symbolism. The miracle is that the "Chanson" attains as high a place as it does in the roster of the world's great love poems.

With "L'Emigrant de Landor Road," Apollinaire has crossed a high pass; he is entering a new green country, that of truly Apollinarian poetry. The stanzas of the "Emigrant" contain no historical allusions, and their only literary echoes are faint strains of Kipling's "Mandalay" (recently printed in translation in *Le Festin d'Esope*) and perhaps some reminiscences of Rimbaud. The atmosphere surrounding the emigrant's departure is evoked in terms of precise personal experiences of a kind hitherto seldom charged with so much emotional tension—the sight of headless mannequins in a London shop (a very elegant shop, "by appointment to His Majesty the King"), the purchase of a suit at a reduced price, highly contemporary details like those which appear in the final stanzas of the "Chanson."

Taken together, these two poems that owe their inspiration to a puritanical English governess mark the be-

Apollinaire: Four

ginning of a new age in French poetry. It is as though Stendhal's despairing cry—"Who will deliver us from Louis XIV?" (by this time the king had donned the garb of the Symbolists)—was finally answered.

123

Guillaume Apollinaire

Five

Between Apollinaire's two visits to England his mother had rented a "villa" in the suburb of Le Vésinet. Pity the house owner whose tenant was Olga de Kostrowitzky! Such was the case of the luckless M. Charles André-Royer, a singer on the Paris stage. Years later he took what revenge he could in a letter to Marcel Adéma:

I owned a villa at Le Vésinet, 8 Boulevard Carnot (almost in Chatou). Since it was impossible for me to live in the suburbs, I had to rent the villa. Around 1904, for a period of three or four years, I had as tenant a certain Polish countess named Kostrowitzky. She lived with an Israelite named Weil, who was connected with the Stock Exchange and was somebody or something at the Banque de l'Ouest, located upstairs over a pastry shop in the Place du Havre, opposite the Gare Saint-Lazare.

When the couple rented my villa they owned no furniture. They had just come from Monte Carlo, where they had met. They furnished the place gradually. He was a great gambler, but a nice fellow. Short, shy, freckle-faced. She was tall, thin, hoarse-voiced, and drank her rum or whiskey straight, sometimes diluting it with a bit of tea, a very little bit. Poor Weil! She used to beat him up. One day when he came to pay the rent his freckles bore traces of nail-scratches. "I was playing with the monkey," he told me. (They had recently acquired one, which they kept in a cage.)

When Weil came to pay me he always took out of his pocket, quite openly, a wad of bank notes. I always wondered whether so much money was his own or the bank's. When she paid the rent there were always complaints. On several occasions she refused to pay, giving various reasons: a window stuck, one of the steps squeaked, a tree obstructed her view of the boulevard, etc.

Apollinaire: Five

One day when I went to inspect these excuses for not paying the rent and correct the situation, I found two panels of the dining-room door smashed in and two window panes broken in the bedroom—clearly a lovers' battle.

I remember that around 1905 or 1906 there was a question of installing a casino, first at Saint-Germain, then at Le Pecq. Le Pecq began to be referred to as "Little Spa"—the casino in the real Spa, in Belgium, had just been shut down because of roulette, like Monaco. Weil was to be in on the deal. . . . He showed me a huge billiard table that he had installed in the billiard room of my villa, and four folding card tables in the smoking room adjoining —a real gambling den. . . .

One summer Mme de Kostrowitzky had a huge oak tree cut down—she claimed it shaded the house too much. She used the oak wood, and also the wood from a small bridge on the property, which she also had demolished, to burn in the furnace. She dumped all the ashes in a small pool in the grounds. The furnace was not made to burn wood, and was ruined. The next winter she heated the house by means of a stove in the vestibule, and never paid to have the furnace repaired. The highway department told me that the retaining wall of the terrace giving on the Avenue du Lac needed repair. I took the proper steps, but Mme Kostrowitzky objected to the work being done and sent the workmen away. The highway department sent me a summons, and she finally let the work be done, but only when the police insisted. This all put me to extra expense, plus a fine! She let the water freeze in the wash tubs and the cistern: why should she pay any attention to them, she said, when she never used them? I was never allowed upstairs in the house. I saw only the diningroom (and the monkey) and the billiard room, the latter because Weil was so proud of it. Either she or he always brought the rent money to me, no doubt so that I wouldn't see the inside of the house. He was always polite, she always cranky. On my receipts I wrote Kostrowitzky with a *y*. She told me one day that Polish names ended in *i*, not in *y*. However, Weil always wrote *y*—the renting was done in her name. A queer household! How did they live? 125

Guillaume Apollinaire

They had no servant. Who did the shopping? The nearest stores were in Chatou, those in Le Vésinet being near the station, too far from the house. Who kept house? Who did the cooking? . . . .

It reminds one of André Salmon's wonder about who paid the printer's bills for *Le Festin d'Esope:* picturesque, bizarre existences with mysterious material underpinnings.

Not far from the villa in Le Vésinet there still existed, in 1904, the famous floating dance-hall in the Seine called La Grenouillère and the riverside restaurant Fournaise, both of them so often painted by the Impressionists and written about by Maupassant. Those two establishments, and the riverside suburban towns of Chatou and Bougival, were still, as they had been in Maupassant's day, boating, dancing, drinking, and lovemaking centers for Parisian clerks and Bohemians on week-end and summer holiday; and Olga de Kostrowitzky's landlord, M. André-Royer, includes in his reminiscences some scenes of Apollinaire's participation in rather boisterous Maupassantian festivities.

But in a train between Chatou and Paris there had taken place a few years earlier, about 1900, an encounter between two young men, both of them painters, that was to have decidedly post-Maupassantian and post-post-Impressionist consequences for the world. One, twenty-four years old, had spent his earliest years in a cottage in Le Vésinet with his grandmother, who had a vegetable stand in Les Halles, the central market in Paris, and with his parents—his mother was a piano teacher and his father gave violin lessons and sang tenor at marriages and funerals in the church of Saint-Merri in Paris. The young man himself, loud-voiced, muscular, athletic, but passionate, sensitive,

126

musical, anarchistic, became enraptured by the speed with which it was possible to fly across country on the still-young descendant of the velocipede, and became a professional bicycle racer before leaving for his military service at the prescribed age of twenty. On his return two years later he played the violin in Paris cafés and night clubs, but he detested such establishments and began, without instruction, to spend his daytime hours painting stretches of riverside landscape near his home—"to put some order into my thoughts, calm my desires, above all to purify myself a little." Soon he refused to have anything more to do with garish night life, earned what living he could by giving violin lessons like his father in Le Vésinet and neighboring suburbs, and painted more and more.

"My enthusiasm made me daring," he tells us, "and shameless in flouting the conventions of the painter's art."

I wanted to revolutionize life, show nature untrammeled, I wanted to free it from old theories, from classicism, whose authority I despised as much as I had despised that of my general or my colonel. There was neither jealousy nor hatred in me, but a wild desire to recreate a new world, the world my eyes were seeing, a world for myself alone. I was poor, but I knew that life was beautiful. And all I was asking was to discover, with the help of new methods, the deep ties that bound me to earth itself.

I brightened all the tones, I transposed all the emotions I could perceive into an orchestration of pure colors. I was a barbarian, gentle and full of violence. I translated, by instinct, without method, a truth that was not artistic but human. I didn't spare the ultramarines and the vermilions, expensive though they were, that I bought on credit from Père Jarry in his shop at the corner of the Pont de Chatou.

Fauvism was born of my chance meeting with André Derain.

127

Guillaume Apollinaire

That angry young man was Maurice de Vlaminck, the "de" being not the aristocratic particle but simply the word "the" in Flemish, "de Vlaminck" meaning "the Fleming," an accurate indication of the family's background. In saying "Fauvism was born of my chance meeting with André Derain," Vlaminck leaves unmentioned a third Fauve painter, named Henri Matisse, usually considered the first of them all both in time and in talent, but then artists have never been known for unswerving intragroup loyalty, and there are books of art history that put such matters right. "The very day after Derain and I became acquainted," Vlaminck says in another account, "we went out painting together for the first time, in the Ile de Chatou."

As for Derain, barely twenty at the time of their meeting, he too was a local boy, the son of a Chatou baker. He had gone to school in Le Vésinet and continued his formal education longer than had Vlaminck, with brief attendance at a Paris lycée and the Ecole des Mines—his parents hoped that he would be an engineer. But he preferred to read philosophy and to paint, and for a time he studied in a Montparnasse art school and did some painting in Brittany. Soon after their meeting in the train, the two young painters were sharing a studio—an old disused riverside restaurant in Chatou—and, as Derain later reminisced, they were continually "drunk with color, with words, which speak color, and with the sun, which imparts life to color."

Of the two spirited young men Derain was the more theoretical and reflective, although Vlaminck, for all his

128

lack of formal education, was far from illiterate: he was a great reader, contributed poems and articles to radical journals, and was even to write a novel or two. Before Derain's absence on military service between 1901 and 1903 they became enthusiastically acquainted with the paintings of Van Gogh and met the somewhat older Matisse, with whose ideas they were in sympathy. While Derain was in barracks they exchanged letters full of philosophical and artistic speculation. "I am aware," Derain wrote Vlaminck in one of them, "that the realist period in painting is over. We are about to embark on a new phase . . . on a great independent and unbounded existence."

In 1904 Vlaminck first exhibited some of his pictures, of the brilliantly colored kind today known as Fauve, in the Salon des Indépendants. That year, somewhere near Chatou or Le Vésinet, Apollinaire met both Vlaminck and Derain.

It was a fateful meeting for Apollinaire.

By now he was sabotaging the Soirées de *La Plume,* disappointed with most of the poets and artists who had impressed him when he had made his debut there. Between him and those last representatives of a dying Symbolism— whose approach to poetry can be sensed in Ernest Raynaud's chronicle of the soirées—was the gulf that always separates minds immersed in the past from those impatient for something new. With Jarry standing out as a near-genius eccentric, the general atmosphere among them was one of effete estheticism, poorly concealing a fundamental lack of substance, freshness, responsiveness to modern life. The contrast between Apollinaire's own contributions to *Le*

Festin d'Esope and the rest of its contents—representing, it must be supposed, the best he could find of the sort of thing he wanted—is eloquent in this regard. "La Chanson du Mal-Aimé" and "L'Emigrant de Landor Road" are clear evidence of the necessity he felt for a new, more direct expression. They also show that he was equipped with the necessary techniques for the purpose, and just now, in 1904, he must have been conscious of his power and aware that he was a twentieth-century original among a number of faded old copies. Vlaminck and Derain (the latter exactly Apollinaire's age), with their determination to break away from outworn esthetic patterns and create an art that would "recreate a new world, the world their eyes were seeing," their literacy, not to mention the undoubted congeniality of their company, must have dispelled any hesitation Apollinaire may have felt in pursuing his poetic progress—a progress whose landmarks so far had included "Clair de lune," "Le Larron," the Rhine poems, and now "La Chanson" and "L'Emigrant." The medium of his two new friends was different from his, but in them he found a kind of concrete encouragement and truly sympathetic understanding that had hitherto rarely if ever come his way. Here was objective confirmation of his ideas coming from artists whose vision was new and alive.

And then, almost immediately, he met other, still different, artists.

Apollinaire's "secretary," Baron Mollet, whose acquaintance among the more fantastic fauna of Paris was vast and varied, had a flair, in his never-ending search for amusing companions, for coming upon minor and even major geniuses: such things existed in Paris in 1904. Recently in Montmartre, through the Spanish sculptor Manolo, he had met a particularly fascinating pair of Bohemians, one of whom adored the other. Max Jacob, an enchanting, malicious, threadbare little Jewish poet from Brittany, twenty-eight years old, half mystic, half clown, who worked in a department store, had been earning an occasional few francs as part-time art critic a few years before and had seen some pictures in the gallery of Ambroise Vollard that had fascinated him. They were by a young Spaniard, living in Paris, named Pablo Picasso. He called on the artist. A sympathy was kindled, and before long Jacob was thinking of Picasso in a way that eventually found full expression: "You are what I love most in the world after God and the Saints, who already consider you as one of themselves. The world does not know your goodness and your qualities, but I know, and God too knows." Or, as he once put it: "The love-admiration (Madeleine-Christ) that I have for Picasso is an admirable love, a homage to God paid to his successful creations."

In 1904 both of them, Jacob, the minor genius who adored, and Picasso, the major genius who let himself be adored, were living in the Rue Ravignan, on the upper slopes of Montmartre. Picasso lived with a beautiful girl named Fernande Olivier in a wooden tenement-house at No. 13 that was to become celebrated under its nickname, "Le Bateau Lavoir," inspired by its fancied resemblance to one of the floating wooden washing-sheds built out from the banks of French rivers for the convenience of laundresses. Jacob had moved into No. 7 to be near his beloved.

131

Guillaume Apollinaire

At the time of their meeting, Jacob had thought of himself primarily as a painter, but when Picasso proclaimed "*Tu es le seul poète de l'époque*" he all but abandoned his brushes and concentrated on a special, very personal type of dream-like prose-poem, which he would read to friends at evening gatherings. Everyone was charmed by Jacob. He was always the life of the party, casting horoscopes, reading palms, producing one-man skits. "I have watched his imitation of the 'barefoot dancing girl' a hundred times," says Fernande Olivier, "each time with more pleasure than the last. His trousers, rolled up to his knees, showed his hairy legs; his shirt was wide open on a chest that was even hairier, a veritable curly black mattress; he was almost bald and he never took off his glasses, and he danced with airs and graces that made it impossible not to laugh and that were a perfect burlesque: his steps, his manipulations on tip-toe. . . !" Picasso "never tired," according to André Salmon, "of listening to Jacob sing songs like Offenbach's 'La Langouste atmosphérique.' " As for the twenty-three-year-old Picasso, with the famous wing of black hair falling down over his forehead, in the midst of his harlequin period and about to be taken up by the Steins—the vivid picture that Fernande Olivier gives of him in her memoirs, painting passionately in the bare, cold little studio in the Bateau Lavoir, has been reprinted in too many books to need repeating here.

Quite correctly, Baron Mollet thought that here were friends worthy of Apollinaire, who had so recently been excited—it is the proper word—by his meeting with Derain and Vlaminck.

Apollinaire: Five

Between the end of his day of clerking and the departure of the latest suburban train that would get him to Le Vésinet in time for dinner with his mother, Apollinaire was accustomed to seek relaxation (or, as some who knew his mother said, courage) in one or another of a series of English-style bars that existed in the Rue d'Amsterdam, opposite the Gare Saint-Lazare—English style because they catered to the jockeys, lads, and trainers, many of them British, who were constantly using the Gare Saint-Lazare on their way to and from the race track at Maisons-Laffitte. To one of these bars, either to the one called the Criterion, or to Austen's Railway Restaurant, Hotel and Bar, 26 Rue d'Amsterdam (variously referred to by French writers as Austen [or Austin] Fox's Bar, or Austin's Fox Bar, or L'Austin's Fox or Le Fox[1]), Baron Mollet one evening in the summer of 1904 or 1905 brought Picasso and introduced him to Apollinaire. And a week later Picasso, in turn, who knew when someone was worth his knowing, brought Max Jacob to meet Apollinaire in the same bar. Picasso, who has over the years observed a fairly complete autobiographical silence, has never described these meetings. The other three principals, however, have each of them made a few more or less reliable comments.

Baron Mollet:

[1] As simply "Fox" it figures as the title of a 1911 cubist etching by Georges Braque. The presence of the word "Fox" in connection with Austen's is a mystery as yet unclarified by research. The variety in the spelling and nomenclature of the place is as nothing compared with the disagreement in the writings of various members of the group around Picasso and Apollinaire as to where and when who first met whom. No one dealing with Apollinaire and his friends can hope for unanimity.

133

Guillaume Apollinaire

Our headquarters came to be a bar in the Rue d'Amsterdam that has since achieved fame—Austin's Fox. There Guillaume had made the acquaintance of an extraordinary man, a homeopathic medium, who had a cure for every sickness. One evening he introduced me to him: "Doctor Roussel, brother of the painter Roussel whom you've heard about." I must say that that evening the Doctor seemed to be dosing himself with absinthe. The bar became more and more heavily patronized, and it was there that I introduced Picasso to Apollinaire.

And to Mollet have also been attributed the further details that on that day Apollinaire was "in the company of a short, fat, red-headed man, an Englishman, flanked by two Negresses whose very bright costumes and gigantic feathered hats much impressed Picasso. Without interrupting a dissertation on the relative merits of English and German beer, Apollinaire gave Picasso a malicious wink."

However, one suspects that the bit about Apollinaire's uninterrupted dissertation may have been suggested to Mollet's later memory by the reminiscence of Max Jacob:

Apollinaire was smoking a short-stemmed pipe and expatiating on Petronius and Nero to some rather vulgar-looking people whom I took to be jobbers of some kind or traveling salesmen. He was wearing a stained light-colored suit, and a tiny straw hat was perched atop his famous pear-shaped head. He had hazel eyes, terrible and gleaming, a bit of curly blond hair fell over his forehead, his mouth looked like a little pimento, he had strong limbs, a broad chest looped across by a platinum watch-chain, and a ruby on his finger. The poor boy was always being taken for a rich man because his mother—an adventuress, to put it politely—clothed him from head to toe. She never gave him anything else. He was a clerk in a bank in the Rue Lepeletier. Without interrupting his talk he stretched out a hand that was like a tiger's paw over the marble-topped table. He stayed in his seat until he was finished. Then the three of us went out, and we began that life of three-cornered friendship which lasted almost until the war, never leaving one another whether for work, meals, or fun."

Apollinaire (writing from memory and hearsay in 1912 about all three of the painters whom he met in such rapid succession in 1904–05):

In 1902, early in the fall, a young painter, de Vlaminck, was painting the Pont de Chatou from La Grenouillère. He was painting fast, using pure colors, and his canvas was almost finished when he heard someone cough behind him. It was another painter, André Derain, who was looking at his work with interest. He apologized for his curiosity, saying that he too was a painter, and introduced himself. The ice was broken. They talked about painting. Maurice de Vlaminck was familiar with the works of the Impressionists, Manet, Monet, Sisley, Degas, Renoir, Cézanne, which Derain had not yet seen. They also talked about Van Gogh and Gauguin. Night came, and in the rising mist the two young artists kept on chatting and did not part until midnight.

This first meeting was the beginning of a close friendship.

Always on the lookout for esthetic curios, de Vlaminck had bought from junk dealers during his hikes through villages along the Seine, sculptures, masks, fetishes carved in wood by Negro artists of French Africa and brought to France by sailors or explorers. In these grotesque and crudely mystical works he no doubt saw similarities to the paintings, engravings, and sculptures that Gauguin had executed, inspired either by Breton religious images or by the primitive sculpture of Oceania where he had withdrawn to escape from European civilization.

However that may be, these singular African effigies made a deep impression on André Derain; he became very fond of them, admiring the art with which the image-makers of Guinea and the Congo succeeded in representing the human figure without using any elements borrowed from direct vision. Maurice de Vlaminck's taste for barbaric Negro sculpture and André Derain's meditations on these bizarre objects, at a time when the Impressionists

135

Guillaume Apollinaire

had at last freed painting from academic fetters, were greatly to influence the destinies of French art.

At about the same time there was living in Montmartre a youth with searching eyes whose face was reminiscent at once of Raphael and Forain. Pablo Picasso, who at the age of sixteen had achieved a kind of fame with canvases which were correctly regarded as somewhat akin to Forain's cruel paintings, had suddenly given up this manner to paint mysterious works in dark blue. He was living in that strange wooden house in the Rue Ravignan which was inhabited by so many artists famous today or in the way of becoming so. I met him there in 1905. His reputation had not yet spread beyond the boundaries of the Butte. His blue workman's blouse, his occasionally cruel quips, the strangeness of his art, were the talk of Montmartre. His studio, cluttered with canvases representing mystical harlequins and drawings on which people walked and which everyone was allowed to carry off with him, was the meeting place of all the young artists, all the young poets.

That year André Derain met Henri Matisse, and the meeting gave birth to that famous school of the Fauves to which belonged a large number of young artists who were later to become Cubists.

I mention that meeting because it may be useful to point out the part played by André Derain, a native of Picardy, in the evolution of French art.

Soon Apollinaire was frequenting the Bateau Lavoir. Like the bright landscapes of Derain and Vlaminck, Picasso's "mysterious works in dark blue" and "mystical harlequins" gave him new literary inspiration, as did the personalities and opinions of his new friends. "Still too Symbolist!" Max Jacob would sometimes cry, to Apollinaire's delight, before a new picture by Picasso. Apollinaire felt that he had moved into a world that was the best possible world for his own creation. In April, 1905 he made an attempt to revive *Le Festin d'Esope* under a more catchy title, *La Revue im-*

136

moraliste; and then, in May, after that single issue had attracted little attention, as the more respectable-sounding *Les Lettres modernes,* which died immediately. For *La Revue immoraliste* he wrote a defense of paintings and drawings by Picasso being shown along with works by Trachsel and Gérardin at the Galeries Serrurier: the critic Charles Morice had accused Picasso of harboring a "precocious disenchantment," and Apollinaire declared "I think the opposite. Everything enchants him, and his incontestable talent seems to me to be at the service of a fantasy that is a balanced combination of the delicious and the horrible, the abject and the delicate." In *Les Lettres modernes,* he printed four poems by Max Jacob, including "Le Cheval," dedicated to Picasso, and "Nombril dans le. brouillard," whose title reads just as prettily when translated into English. And the same month—May, 1905—he wrote for *La Plume* an article, very charming and sentimental, on Picasso's images of harlequins, beggars, and children, speaking of them as though they were human beings.

The poet was beginning a secondary career, which for some who know his name has tended to overshadow his poetry: a career as a writer about painters and paintings.

In 1907, two years after those first essays by Apollinaire about his new friend, Picasso painted "Les Demoiselles d'Avignon," Apollinaire met Braque and brought him to Picasso's studio, Braque and Picasso began to work together—"it was a little like rope-work in mountain-climbing," Braque has said of their collaboration after 1909, "both of us worked hard"—and with their joint work, infused by the sight of Cézanne, the much written-about

137

history of Cubism began. By 1912, when Apollinaire had been writing charmingly about exhibitions and painters in magazines and newspapers for a number of years (from 1910 to 1914 he was occasional art writer for the newspaper *L'Intransigeant*), this "new" movement of Cubism was considered worthy of an article in the authoritative newspaper *Le Temps*. On October 14 of that year *Le Temps* informed its readers:

Cubism is being much discussed. What does it mean? What are the cubists' theories, and under what conditions was the movement born? We addressed these questions to M. Guillaume Apollinaire, one of the earliest champions of cubism, who supplies the following interesting information.

Apollinaire's text, which follows, begins with the paragraphs quoted earlier in this chapter concerning Vlaminck, Derain, and Picasso, and then continues:

[In 1906 Derain] formed a friendship with Picasso, and the almost immediate effect of this friendship was the birth of Cubism, which was the art of creating new objects consisting not of visual but of conceptual elements. Everyone is capable of directly perceiving this inner reality. One does not have to be cultivated to grasp the fact, for instance, that a chair, no matter how you view it, will always have four legs, a seat, and a back. The Cubist paintings by Picasso, Braque, Metzinger, Gleizes, Léger, Jean [*sic*] Gris, etc. inspired Henri Matisse to coin the grotesque term 'Cubism,' which was destined to go so far so quickly: he had been greatly struck by the geometric appearance of these paintings in which the artists aimed at rendering essential reality with great purity. The young painters adopted Cubism at once because by representing conceptual reality the artist can suggest the three dimensions. He could not do this by rendering mere visual reality unless by resorting to illusionistic foreshortening or perspective, which would distort the quality of the conceptual form.

Soon new tendencies appeared within Cubism. Picabia, rejecting the conceptionist formula, practised with Marcel Duchamp an art no longer confined by any rules. Delaunay, for his part, quietly invented an art of pure color. Thus we are moving toward an entirely new art which will be to painting as it has been conceived of until now what music is to poetry. This will be pure painting. Whatever we may think of such a hazardous attempt, we are undeniably dealing with sincere artists, worthy of respect.

The following year, 1913, Apollinaire published something more elaborate than that bird's-eye view of Cubism and "pure painting" for newspaper readers: a volume of remarks on Cubism and on "Cubists," especially Braque and Picasso, which he entitled MEDITATIONS ESTHETIQUES: *Les Peintres cubistes*. (The volume is not a unity, but a patchwork of essays, prefaces to catalogues, and other art writings that Apollinaire had published here and there separately and often in somewhat different form.) The printer being careless with his capitals, however, the title page appeared as *Méditations Esthétiques:* LES PEINTRES CUBISTES, and it has been so reprinted ever since, or even with title and sub-title transposed, constituting a claim, never made by Apollinaire, that it is a unified work. It is a curious volume, much of it written in the turgid, pseudo-metaphysical style that Apollinaire seems to have been the first to consider essential to a discussion of *avant-garde* art but which has since become all too familiar to readers of prefaces to art books and introductions to exhibitions by contemporary artists. *Les Peintres cubistes* achieved a first, small reprinting only in 1922, and a second only in 1950, but it has always had a fame far greater than its sales. Widely referred to as "the first book on Cubism" (which it is not: Gleizes and Metzinger had published their

139

Du Cubisme a year earlier), it is chiefly *Les Peintres cubistes*—or, more precisely, its reputation—that has given Apollinaire himself a considerable reputation as an art critic, a reputation that has widened as the result of the publication in 1960 of LeRoy Breunig's collected edition of his other art writings. "*Chef d'école* of Cubism," and "Perhaps the greatest critic of our century" are only two of the *titres de noblesse* recently conferred on him by writers on modern art.

Vlaminck, who never recaptured, in his later painting, the freshness of his Fauve canvases, who never became a Cubist, and who spoke bitterly as he grew older of the acclaim given to the Cubists and the abstract artists, once said: "The abstract painters are the bigots of art." In the sense that there tends to exist a high degree of touchiness and churlish dogmatism among the often rather grim partisans of *avant-garde* art, Vlaminck is right: today Apollinaire's status as a poet, for example, can be discussed freely and without danger, whereas to question his competency to be "*chef d'école* of Cubism" is a perilous enterprise. It seems not to be widely known that several of the very painters about whom Apollinaire wrote in *Les Peintres cubistes* are, to put it mildly, skeptical on this point.

When an exhibition of Braque's graphic work, for example, was held at the Bibliothèque Nationale in Paris in 1960, Braque approved the catalogue, which contained the following remarks on his Cubist etching of 1911 entitled "Fox":

Fox is the name of a bar near the Gare Saint-Lazare, where Apollinaire and his friends used to meet. "It should not be forgotten," said Apollinaire (*Anecdotiques,* 1912), "that . . . most of the

Cubist painters lived in the company of poets." But the painters, Braque, Villon, Picasso, have often said that Apollinaire and the poets were inspired by them, rather than the other way round.

In a conversation with the author, Braque expressed himself as follows:

Apollinaire's art writings are those of a poet, attracted to the new painting by sympathy for Picasso, myself and other personalities; also, he was a little proud to be part of something new. He never wrote penetratingly about our art, as did for example Reverdy. I'm afraid we kept encouraging Apollinaire to write about us as he did so that our names would be kept before at least part of the public.

Jacques Villon, mentioned in *Les Peintres cubistes* as a "new adherent to scientific Cubism," was at the time of its publication painting, or had painted, such Cubist pictures as "La Table servie," "Instruments de musique," and "Soldats en marche," and had exhibited at the Section d'Or exhibition of 1912 at the Galerie de la Boétie. In connection with this exhibition (which was also the occasion for *Le Temps* asking Apollinaire for his article, quoted above) Apollinaire delivered a lecture on the "new" painting. In conversations with the author, Jacques Villon has several times expressed an opinion of Apollinaire's lecture, and of Apollinaire's art writings in general, always in the same few words: "Nothing whatever to do with painting!" Beginning in 1911 Villon, together with his brothers Raymond Duchamp-Villon and Marcel Duchamp, was often host, in his Puteaux studio, to a number of painters who became known as the "Puteaux group" and later as the "Section d'Or"—Gleizes, LaFresnaye, Léger, Delaunay, Metzinger, Picabia, and Kupka among them. Their paint- 141 ing was "very different from that of the Montmartre group; some of it was more Cézannesque, some more abstract." Apollinaire, who was closely in touch with the Puteaux group and wrote admiringly of their work, nevertheless remained apparently unaware of the esthetic nature of these painters' link with Cézanne, and scolded them privately for being "too learned," precisely the same remark that was to be leveled at Apollinaire himself when his volume of poetry, *Alcools,* was published in 1913. In effect, he was employing in a derogatory way Bernini's famous compliment concerning Poussin, a compliment uttered with forefinger pointed to head: *"Egli lavora di là!"*

Picasso is no less outspoken than Braque and Villon on Apollinaire the art "critic." The following is a paragraph recently composed after consultation with him, and bearing, especially in its reference to other painters, the master's unmistakable *griffe:*

As for Picasso, he has often said to friends that there is a great distinction to be made between the three aspects of Apollinaire: the poet, the man, and the journalist art critic. Picasso has never questioned, then or now, the greatness of Apollinaire the poet. On a personal plane, too, he greatly enjoyed Apollinaire's company, was stimulated by his constant flow of exciting ideas, shared many of his sentiments, and derived much encouragement from discovering the similarity of their esthetic outlook. But Picasso's attitude to Apollinaire in his role as art critic is less uncritical. For while Picasso was—and still is—deeply grateful to Apollinaire for the material help which his journalistic writings brought him in the early stages of his career through making his name known and building up his reputation,[2] yet Picasso knew at

[2] It is easy to forget how little known Picasso was in those early years, despite his work of the period that is now so loved and his being taken up by

the time that Apollinaire was writing about things which he could not really understand. Of all Apollinaire's friends Picasso was probably the first to realize—as Braque also did later—that Apollinaire's powers of visual comprehension were limited, and therefore he was not in the least surprised to find him enthusiastically supporting Gleizes, Delaunay, and Villon and switching his allegiance from pure Cubism to the Section d'Or, Futurism, and Orphism. Discussing Apollinaire's collected art writings recently with Douglas Cooper, Picasso commented that it was sad to find how shallow they were, how little good sense they contained, when one remembered how important they had seemed to be at the time of publication.

Finally there is the testimony of Daniel-Henry Kahnweiler, the impresario of the Cubists:

It pains me to have to say once again that I do not highly value Apollinaire's writings on painting. I was Apollinaire's friend, I had a great liking for him as a man. As for the great poet, let me recall that I was his first publisher. What vitiated his writings on esthetic matters was his complete lack of plastic sensibility. We, his friends, were well aware of this. For this reason he could not depend on his instinct for guidance. What unleashed his enthusiasm was novelty, true or false. His work on the Cubist painters is a conglomeration of passages written under the dictation of the painters themselves (sometimes altered at the last moment as the result of quarrels), magnificent lyric flights, and a number of purely pataphysical elucubrations, for instance the classification of the painters into "physical," "scientific," "instinctive," and "Orphic" Cubists.

One thing about *Les Peintres cubistes* that arouses the mirth of the survivors of the epoch is its inclusion of the painter Marie Laurencin as an exponent of "scientific Cubism." Marie Laurencin has written about her own painting: "The little I learned was taught me by the men

the Steins. (See LeRoy C. Breunig, "Apollinaire as an Early Apologist for Picasso," *Harvard Library Bulletin,* Vol. VII, No. 3, Autumn 1953.)

whom I call the great painters, my contemporaries: Matisse, Derain, Picasso, Braque. They will be furious at me for naming them—that is the way they are. They make me think of the song from *Carmen: 'Si tu ne m'aimes pas, je t'aime. . . !'* If I never became a Cubist painter it was because I never could. I wasn't capable of it, but their experiments fascinated me." At the time when Apollinaire's article mentioning Marie Laurencin as a Cubist appeared in the *Soirées de Paris* the painter had separated from the poet after being his intimate for several years; in his loneliness he had written "Le Pont Mirabeau" (also published in that magazine), and friends had recently tried to bring about a reconciliation, but Marie would have none of it. Some of Apollinaire's old friends suspect that his inclusion of her as a Cubist painter in the article, and his subsequent allowing her to remain as one in the volume, were, in part, favors that he did her in including her among such high artistic company, and, in part, a kind of wooing, an attempt to persuade her to return. Others wonder whether he really thought she was a Cubist painter. Were Apollinaire's "powers of visual comprehension" as "limited" as that?

As we have seen, the extreme vagueness of the figure of the loved one in "La Chanson du Mal-Aimé," the striking, almost complete absence from the poem of the figure whom one might think central, seems to reflect Apollinaire's lack of deep feeling for Annie Playden; and similarly striking to anyone who has seen Neuglück, the witch-countess's house in the Rhineland where Apollinaire lived as tutor, is the poet's failure ever to describe it even in a phrase or two, whether in poem or letter. Neuglück is a

144

construction of no ordinary ugliness. The meanness of all its dimensions and proportions is exacerbating in the extreme, and equally outrageous is the relentless, crawling proliferation of lamentable carvings, mouldings, paintings, and appliqués: the place is a uniquely irritating and depressing conglomeration of hideosities. And yet there is no indication that Apollinaire was impressed by this masterpiece of Rhenish carpentry in which he lived, off and on, during the year when he was showing himself highly sensitive to Rhenish landscape and legend.

Then there is one of his poems of that year in Germany: "La Vierge à la fleur de haricot à Cologne," the only Rhenish poem whose subject is a picture.

Actually the title of that fifteenth century madonna in the Wallraf-Richartz Museum at Cologne is and always has been "The Virgin with the Pea Blossom," and the young mother is clearly holding leaves, pods, and blossoms of the wild pea, not of any kind of bean. Modern art historians speak of the picture merely as being the work of "a northwest-German painter, active in Cologne, Westphalia and Lower Saxony about 1410–40," but at the time Apollinaire saw it, it was attributed to a certain Meister Wilhelm of Cologne, the "maître Guillaume" of the poem's next-to-the-last line. "The description of the famous picture," says the editor of the most complete edition of Apollinaire's poems, "is the occasion for a discreet madrigal to Annie, who could recognize herself in this Virgin with blue eyes, painted by Maître Guillaume." Apollinaire's interest in this picture, singled out by him from several galleries of old masters, was certainly due to the magic that   145

La Vierge à la fleur de haricot à Cologne

La Vierge au brin fleuri est une Vierge blonde
Et son petit Jésus est blond comme elle l'est
Ses yeux sont bleus et purs comme le ciel ou l'onde
Et l'on conçoit qu'elle ait conçu du Paraclet

Deux Saintes veillant dans les volets du triptyque
Pensent béatement aux martyres passés
Et s'extasient d'ouïr le plain-chant des cantiques
Des petits anges blancs dans le ciel entassés

Les trois dames et l'enfant vivaient à Cologne
Le haricot poussait dans un jardin rhénan
Et le peintre ayant vu de hauts vols de cigognes
Peignit les séraphins qui chantent maintenant

Et c'est la Vierge la plus douce du royaume
Elle vécut au bord du Rhin pieusement
Priant devant son portrait que maître Guillaume
Peignit par piété de chrétien ou d'amant

his own name always had for this multi-named yet name-less child of Trastevere; but if he recognized himself in "Maître Guillaume" Annie Playden could scarcely have recognized herself in this Virgin, for Annie's eyes were blue, whereas the eyes of the Virgin are, and always have been, olive-green. "Still," writes a generous gentleman from the Wallraf-Richartz Museum, "Apollinaire *may* have seen blue eyes. The daylight is very deceptive at times in old-fashioned galleries. The Wallraf-Richartz in his days looked rather gloomy." And defenders of Apollinaire the art "critic," quoting Baudelaire's remark that "the best *compte-rendu* of a picture can well be a sonnet or an elegy,"

146

The Virgin With the Bean Flower at Cologne

The Virgin with the flowering sprig is a blond Virgin
And her little Jesus is blond as she is
Her eyes are blue and pure as the sky or the sea
And it is conceivable that she conceived by the Paraclete

Two saints watching in the wings of the triptych
Think blissfully of ancient martyrdoms
And listen enraptured to the plain-chant of the canticles
Sung by little white angels huddled in the sky

The three ladies and the baby lived in Cologne
The bean grew in a Rhenish garden
And the painter, having seen high flights of storks
Painted the seraphim who are singing now

She is the sweetest Virgin in the realm
She lived beside the Rhine piously
Praying before her portrait that Maître Guillaume
Painted with the piety of a Christian or a lover

retort with asperity to such pedantic remarks as the above
concerning their hero that, clearly, this new Maître Guillaume *re*-painted, in his poem, the picture on the museum
wall, to do honor to Annie. But surely the substitution of
blue eyes for green can be welcomed as deliberate homage
to Annie only if the substitution of bean blossoms for peas
can be shown to be similarly complimentary? Is a bean a
more seemly feminine attribute than a pea? Isn't it more
probable, after all, that Apollinaire looked at, but simply
did not see very well, this picture that so impressed him?

Indeed, it is difficult to discover, in all of Apollinaire's
art writings, a mention of a picture that sounds as though   147

Guillaume Apollinaire

the picture has been seen—let alone seen as an artist's image. His prose and verse writings on paintings by Delaunay are probably the most convincing in this respect.

As to Apollinaire's degree of art *knowledge* at the time of his meeting with the painters, in his gossip column, "Notes du mois," in the issue of *Le Festin d'Esope* for July, 1904, he mockingly says:

> In the *Mercure de France,* June issue, there is a curious article by Charles Morice about Claude Monet's series of paintings, "Scenes on the Thames." Never does the painter of the "Déjeuner sur l'herbe . . ." says Morice, in speaking of Monet. The painter Diriks is right in finding French art criticism very bizarre.

In other words, the painter Edward Diriks (a friend of Apollinaire's), who probably brought the item in the *Mercure de France* to Apollinaire's attention, and Apollinaire himself, thought that the critic Charles Morice was confusing Monet with Manet in attributing to the former a canvas called "Déjeuner sur l'herbe," and probably in part because Morice was known as a Symbolist, Apollinaire was delighted to catch him out. Ignorance has seldom been more blissfully expressed. Claude Monet did indeed paint several versions of a "Déjeuner sur l'herbe," and in 1904 one version was still in the possession of the artist at Giverny, where Charles Morice had doubtless seen it.

And as late as *Les Peintres cubistes* Apollinaire was capable of writing, apparently unaware of the centuries-old pictorial role played by letters in Islamic art, "It is perfectly legitimate to use numbers and printed letters as pictorial elements; new in art, they are already soaked with humanity."

That statement is one of several by Apollinaire seri-

148

ously quoted in a book recently published under the auspices of a well-known American museum—typical of the obeisance often paid to even his most naive art pronouncements. "Apollinaire sanctioned the use of numbers and letters as pictorial elements," says the author of this work, introducing Apollinaire's gracious permission to artists to do what artists had been doing for hundreds of years. And he includes, apparently with respect, a perfect example of Apollinaire's bland double-talk that has since become the *lingua franca* of "the art world" (I shall mercifully leave it in the original French): "*l'objet réel ou en trompe-l'œil est appelé sans doute à jouer un rôle de plus en plus important. Il est le cadre intérieur du tableau et en marque les limites profondes, de même que le cadre en marque les limites extérieures.*"

Let us be thankful that Apollinaire devoted much of his time to other things than that. Almost any line or group of lines of his poetry

As-tu connu Guy au galop. . . ?

Une femme qui pleurait
Eh! Oh! Ha!
Des soldats qui passaient
Eh! Oh! Ha!

stands out brightly against all the pages of his art writings.

No, it is not in the pages of Apollinaire's so-called art criticism, whether in the portentous pseudo-analysis of *Les Peintres cubistes,* or even in his easier, often spirited and charming accounts of exhibitions and salons, that we find the most significant results of his association with the artists. He is no Reverdy, as Braque said. Nor is he a Diderot, applying profound philosophical insights to the field of art criticism. He is no Baudelaire, revealing to the dazzled reader the secrets of Delacroix's discoveries in the realm of color: indeed he might be considered a triumphant refutation of Baudelaire's: "I consider the poet the best of critics. . . . All great poets naturally become critics." For innovation in art Apollinaire had an erratic flair, like that of a hound who picks up too many scents, and he did a good deal of happy, excited barking about it. All the painters agree with Picasso that he was a loyal promoter, championing them against a thousand hostilities: for them he was "a man of good will, who saw himself as the herald of the great new art with which the great new century was destined to be rewarded, [and] was prepared to write what would prove most helpful to his artist friends provided they would guide his pen." (Indeed, in his art writings Apollinaire is often at his best when one senses that he is parroting his artist friends. On the other hand, some of his most embarrassing passages are also obvious parrotings, as when he gives himself connoisseur–like airs concerning the masters, passing judgments on the authenticity of a Chardin or a Goya, and declaring that a so-called Gros was probably painted by an Englishman!)

His efficacy as a promoter, the extent of his role in the snowballing success of the Cubists and their successors, is of course impossible to gauge.

How was Apollinaire most marked by his association with the painters? Did he—as has sometimes been said—become a "Cubist poet?" What is a Cubist poet?

"Would you say that Apollinaire sometimes wrote 'Cubist poetry' after associating with the Cubists?" Georges

Braque was asked by the present writer.

"I suppose that when he printed some of his poems in the shape of guitars and other objects that we used to use in our canvases, that could be called 'Cubist poetry,'" was Braque's answer, "though personally I should prefer to call it 'Cubist typography!'"

Others have not hesitated to speak of "Cubist poetry." Apollinaire's "Lundi Rue Christine,"[3] for example (a poem written in 1913, its scene apparently laid in the same "*sinistre brasserie*" where in 1904 he had announced to his friends the birth of *Le Festin d'Esope*), has been called "literary Cubism," a "description of a bar done in the taste of a Cubist picture, like Braque's etchings 'Fox' and 'Bass.'" Not that there is any question here of Cubist typography: "Lundi Rue Christine" is printed in conventional verse lines. The analogy is more remote, based on the simultaneity of points of view that a Cubist picture is apt to present: "Lundi Rue Christine" is made up of simultaneous snatches of conversation, overheard, or invented, by the poet in the little Left Bank bar. It is a poem with the true Apollinairian magic; the poet might or might not have written it had he not seen Cubist pictures; but—"Cubist poetry?" Some of us will always prefer Braque's more seemly and elegant, more strictly pictorial, use of the word "Cubism," and will agree with Pierre Reverdy: "*La 'poésie cubiste'? Terme ridicule!*"

No: if what the painters found in Apollinaire was a friend and a poet doubling as a promoter, what he found in them was what Braque has said—a group of sympathetic

[3] See p. 268.

151

Guillaume Apollinaire

personalities: artists of his own age, with talent or genius, who gave him stimulus and the courage to recognize in himself the only living poet he knew with a vision as fresh as theirs. The two who became his particular friends were Picasso and Marie Laurencin. Later he grew close to Delaunay.

That Picasso recognized Apollinaire as someone of value was apparent in his rapid return to Austen's Bar to present Max Jacob; and his esteem can be chronicled, if only ·in the number of portrait-drawings, often good-natured caricatures, that he did of the poet. The first of these is a bookplate—"Guillaume Apollinaire, Ex-Libris, Picasso fecit"—that he drew and presented to his new friend in 1905, showing a huge Gargantuan king at table, holding a wine-glass. (Apollinaire was growing no slenderer, and his feats at table were considerable—he was capable of eating two entire meals in rapid succession. In a recently published French treatise which purports to discover the "basic theme" expressed in the work of each of a number of poets, Apollinaire's theme is isolated as "Food.") The figure resembles that of the paunchy jester in the painting called "Family of Saltimbanques" in the National Gallery, Washington, and Picasso once told Douglas Cooper, who formerly owned the bookplate, that he had come to think of it as representing Apollinaire as king among poets and as jester—i.e. amuser of painters—among art critics. There is an amusing series of drawings depicting the poet in various guises—as pope, as academician, as duelist, as sailor, as gymnast; Picasso's little Catalan notebook of 1906 contains two others, and there are several showing Apollinaire

Apollinaire: Five

153

Picasso, "Ex-Libris: Guillaume Apollinaire," 1905

in the uniform of the French army. Finally, in 1959, one of Picasso's sculptures—a woman's head—presented by Picasso, was placed as a memorial to Apollinaire in the little garden just north of the main portal of the church of Saint-Germain-des-Prés, near the street behind the Café des Deux Magots which had recently been rechristened the Rue Guillaume Apollinaire.

Apollinaire's admiration of Picasso fills many a page in *Les Peintres cubistes* and the *Chroniques d'art;* he dedicated to him the poem "Les Fiançailles," in which he intensely describes the difference his friendship with the artists had made in his life; harlequins and saltimbanques appear here and there in his verse, and in a calligrammatic poem which spells out the word "Montparnasse" the letter *N* is filigreed into a thumb-like shape outlined by the words *"Noble pouce à la main droite du peintre sculpteur bien connu Pablo Picasso."* But the most characteristic, and the most prophetic, of the poet's tributes to the painter is contained in one of the strangest of his works, *Le Poète assassiné,* the fantastic prose novelette that abounds in poetically-licensed (and poetically licentious) autobiographical references.

One of the characters in *Le Poète assassiné* is a painter-sculptor, first shown working in his bare studio on Montmartre, "dressed in blue, barefoot," and called merely *"l'oiseau du Bénin,"* "the Benin bird." After the assassination of the book's hero, Croniamantal (who was in the habit of referring to himself as "the greatest living poet"), his former mistress Tristouse Ballerinette (read Marie Laurencin) "went into mourning for him and went up to Montmartre, to the house of the Benin bird, who began

154

by paying court to her and when he had had what he wanted they began to speak of Croniamantal."

"I must make a statue of him," said the Benin bird. "For I am not only a painter, but a sculptor as well."

"That's the thing," said Tristouse. "We must put up a statue to him."

"But where?" asked the Benin bird. "The government won't grant us a plot of ground. Times are bad for poets."

"So they say," replied Tristouse, "but perhaps it isn't true. What do you think about the woods of Meudon, Monsieur the bird of Benin?"

"That's just what I was thinking, but I didn't dare say it. The woods of Meudon will do very well."

"What kind of a statue?" asked Tristouse. "Marble? Bronze?"

"No, that's all too old-fashioned," replied the Benin bird. "I must make something really deep, a statue out of nothing material, like poetry and like fame."

"Bravo! Bravo!" said Tristouse, clapping her hands. "A statue made of nothing at all, a void! That's marvelous! When will you carve it?"

"Tomorrow, if you like. We'll go to dinner, we'll spend the night together, and the first thing in the morning we'll go to the woods of Meudon and I'll carve that deep statue."

No sooner said than done. They went out to dinner with the elite of Montmartre society, returned home to bed toward midnight, and the next morning at nine, after equipping themselves with a pick, a shovel, a spade, and chisels, they set out for the pretty woods of Meudon . . . .

In a clearing the Benin bird set to work. In a few hours he dug a hole about half a meter wide and two meters deep.

Then they had a picnic.

The afternoon was given over by the Benin bird to carving the inside of the monument in the likeness of Croniamantal.

The next day the sculptor returned with workmen who lined the well with a concrete wall eight centimeters thick, all

155

Guillaume Apollinaire

except the bottom, which was thirty-eight centimeters thick, so that the empty space had the form of Croniamantal—the hole was filled with his ghost . . . .

Le Poète assassiné was published in 1916, two years before Apollinaire's death, forty-two years before Picasso's memorial to him was unveiled in the garden beside Saint-Germain-des-Prés. The poet's vision that the Montmartre painter who was also a sculptor would some day provide his memorial, his oracular evocation of the most unpredictable artistic genius of our age as a mythological bronze bird from Africa, the replacement of a possible actual statue by the mere definition of its form, the substitution of void for matter—could there be a more striking, a more poetic, a more suggestive anticipation of the new art, so paradoxically combining intellectual refinement and direct appeal to the most primitive instincts, heralded by the friends Apollinaire and Picasso?

It was Picasso who brought Apollinaire together with Marie Laurencin. *Le Poète assassiné* tells us how the great poet Croniamantal first heard of the charming young woman Tristouse Ballerinette:

[The bird of Benin] turned toward Croniamantal and said: "I saw your wife last night."
"Who is she?" asked Croniamantal.
"I don't know. I saw her but I don't know her. She's a nice young girl, the way you like them. She has the somber and childlike face of those destined to make men suffer. She has a graceful way of holding out her hands to keep you off, and she has none of the nobility that repels poets because it would deprive them of their sufferings. I have seen your wife, I tell you; she is ugliness and

Marie Laurencin

beauty, like everything else we love today; she must taste like fame."

It is only in the definitive edition of *Le Poète assassiné*, published after Apollinaire and Marie Laurencin had separated, that the words "destined to make men suffer" appear: in an earlier manuscript, apparently written the year of their meeting, Tristouse Ballerinette is said, rather, to be "made for eternal loves." Apollinaire might have written "destined to make men suffer" from the beginning had he seen at that time some candid passages that Marie was to write about herself in future years. "If I feel so far removed

157

Guillaume Apollinaire

from painters," she tells us, "it is because they are men, and in my view men are difficult problems to solve. Their discussions, their researches, their genius, have always been too much for me. . . . But if the genius of men intimidates me, I feel perfectly at ease with everything that is feminine. . . . My happiest days were when I used to be taken as a girl to a little community of nuns: the sisters took me in their arms, showed me picture books and let me play on the harmonium. . . ."

Such was the young woman concerning whom Picasso is supposed to have said to Apollinaire, one day, "I have a fiancée for you," after meeting Marie Laurencin in an art gallery. He introduced them, it "took," and before long Apollinaire moved away from his mother for the first time since returning from Germany. He rented a flat in the present Rue Henner on the lower slopes of Montmartre, where Marie Laurencin visited him; and when she and her mother moved to Auteuil he followed them. "She is bright, witty, kind-hearted, and very talented," are his best-known words about his new mistress. "She's like a little sun—a feminine version of myself. She's a true Parisian, with all the adorable little ways of a Paris child. Just think—when she came to see me in the Rue Gros she would skip rope all the way across the garden."

"A feminine version of myself. . . ." There were dangers in that. "[In Marie Laurencin] he had acquired a graceful mistress, as original and unconventional as he was himself: not that the similarity was conducive to continual peace and harmony," one of his friends later commented. Fernande Olivier, who like many people disliked Marie,

158

Marie Laurencin, self-portrait, 1906

159

Guillaume Apollinaire

described her as having "the air of a little girl who was naive and a little vicious, too naive to be simple." "The living room [in the flat in the Rue Henner]," says Fernande, "was too small for guests. It opened into a bedroom, where we would go to be a little more comfortable. We would sit down in there, being very careful not to disarrange anything—Guillaume wouldn't have liked that. We had to be especially careful never to touch the bed. The slightest wrinkle, the slightest sign of its having been sat on, made him frown and look irritated. I was a friend of his mistress, who told me that their love-frolics were restricted to an armchair: his bed was sacred."

The accommodating mistress, a homely yet piquante-looking creature in those days, tall and thin, with almond eyes and frizzy hair that caused some to say that she must have "Creole" blood, had attended the Lycée Lamartine and studied at the Académie Humbert with Braque. Laurencin was her mother's name: like Apollinaire, she was illegitimate. All that seems to be known about her father is that she once inscribed a book *"Marie Laurencin, née d'une mère normande et savoyarde et d'un père picard,"* and that in another of her autobiographical fragments she wrote: "Marie was nine years old, with an aloof, charming mother who spoke little and sang very well, and a father who from time to time for his own amusement liked to teach his daughter and look after her studies. Marie had a horror of all these masculine episodes—the louder voice, the kisses on the forehead, even the words of praise, and a certain crudeness in this man's pride in his daughter."

160 Marie seemed to be rather afraid of her mother, as

Apollinaire was of his: Madame Laurencin's equivalent of Olga de Kostrowitzky's *hauteur* and high style, in her irregular situation, was a grim, resolutely quiet respectability. Apollinaire and Marie knew better than to bring their two unmarried mothers together: Olga would at best have grandly condescended to the concierge-like little woman who spent her days at home embroidering, whereas Madame Laurencin, just as Olga de Kostrowitzky had instantly scented the policeman in the poet who had called on her son, would have recoiled from Olga as from the whore of Babylon. Both ladies detested the Bohemian friends their children had chosen. Olga, when Apollinaire hesitantly brought Montmartre or Left-Bank acquaintances to the villa in Le Vésinet on Sundays, tended to be upstage, to introduce all of them to "my other son, the banker" (Albert, whom we last saw as a boy picking mushrooms in the Ardennes, had become a far more respectable bank employee than his brother), or, alternatively, she would vanish into the kitchen and emerge with a superb meal for them all that she had prepared with the splendid casualness of a *grande dame,* the remnants of which she would order them to take home to their garrets. Olga was well known as a terror among Apollinaire's friends. They had a song, containing a scabrous pun, that they sang about her when Apollinaire was not present:

> *Épouser la mèr' d'Apollinaire*
> *La mèr' d'Apollinaire,*
> *La mèr' d'Apollinaire,*
> *De quoi qu'on aurait l'air?*
> *De quoi qu'on aurait l'air?*

161

Guillaume Apollinaire

Madame Laurencin sat severe beside her fire while the artists romped around her; her only recorded comment is her embroidery of Apollinaire's face in black thread on a firescreen.

Before long Apollinaire was promoting Marie:

I cannot find words to describe the typically French grace of Mademoiselle Marie Laurencin. Though she has masculine defects she has every conceivable feminine quality. The greatest error of most women artists is that they try to surpass men, losing in the process their taste and their charm. Mademoiselle Laurencin is very different. She is aware of the deep differences that separate men from women—essential, ideal differences. Mademoiselle

Apollinaire: Five

*"Group of Artists," painting by Marie Laurencin (1908);
self-portrait with Apollinaire, Picasso, and Fernande Olivier*

163

Guillaume Apollinaire

Laurencin's personality is vibrant and joyful. Purity is her very element.

After their rupture, Apollinaire was to take a certain ungentlemanly revenge by inserting into *Le Poète assassiné* a passage concerning the role he had played in Marie Laurencin's life, and the form her gratitude took:

Six months went by. For five months now Tristouse Ballerinette had been the mistress of Croniamantal, whom she loved passionately for exactly one week. In return for this love the lyrical young man made her famous and immortal forever by celebrating her in marvelous poems. "I was unknown," she thought, "and now he has made me illustrious among all the living. Everybody thought I was an ugly duckling, with my skinniness, my big mouth and bad teeth, my assymetrical face, my crooked nose— and now I am a beauty and all the men tell me so. Everyone poked fun at the jerky, mannish way I walked, at my pointed elbows that swung like the legs of a chicken. Now they think I'm so graceful that other women imitate me. There are no miracles that a poet's love cannot work. But how heavily it weighs on me, the love of poets! So many moments of sadness, of silence! And yet now the miracle has come to pass, I am beautiful and famous. Croniamantal is ugly, he has gone through his money in no time, he is poor and inelegant besides. He is humorless, the slightest thing he does makes a hundred enemies. I don't love him, I don't love him any more! I don't need him now. My adorers are enough for me. I'm going to break away from him slowly. But the delay won't be pleasant. Either I must go or he must disappear—I can't have him bothering me and scolding me." A week later Tristouse became the mistress of Paponat.

Marie Laurencin is not known ever to have said that *Le Poète assassiné* was among her favorite books, but in her autobiographical writings she confirms parts of that soliloquy by Tristouse. "As a girl I was dreary and homely, and there seemed to be no future for me. My only pleasure was

164

watching my mother," she writes of herself as she was before she and Apollinaire met. And although Apollinaire's promotion brought her to the attention of art dealers, she does seem to have felt, at least in later years, that she paid a high price for success.

Apollinaire usually spent the evening at Picasso's with Max Jacob, at 13 Rue Ravignan, and the three of them did nothing but quarrel, catch each other up, glower at one another and above all exchange curses— this last they were very good at; and the next minute they would be adoring one another. They seldom drank— maybe once every two months they would get drunk and act with excessive politeness. I never paid any attention to them; I would read love stories, Marivaux's *Marianne,* and felt nothing but hatred for those men for being so unlike myself. Especially their Negro sculpture! It set my nerves on edge.

"Those were the best days of my life," Max Jacob once said about the years following the three-cornered meeting of Jacob—Picasso—Apollinaire in Austen's Bar, and the words are equally applicable to Apollinaire himself. The seven years, from 1904 to 1911, that began with the writing of "La Chanson du Mal-Aimé" and saw its publication in the *Mercure de France* in 1909—the first evidence a wider public had that a poet with a new voice was writing in France—were not only the years of his liaison with Marie Laurencin but also the period during which he achieved one of his great self-liberations: he freed himself from clerking. One has only to read two poems, "La Porte" and "Les Fiançailles," to sense what this meant to him.

He accomplished his escape chiefly by means of erotica. In 1906, to increase his earnings, he wrote two 165 pornographic novels, *Les Onze mille verges* and *Les Exploits d'un jeune don Juan.*

Les Onze mille verges can best be described as a high-spirited parody of a holocaust by the Marquis de Sade; as such it is a *tour de force,* and indeed Picasso once owlishly pronounced it Apollinaire's masterpiece. Although it was published anonymously, it bears the author's signature in several places: bottles of Apollinaris water make their appearance during a scabrous lunch in a dining-car, two Symbolist poets are portrayed as brothel-keepers spouting priapic verse, and a French journalist-sculptor named Genmolay (pronounced Jean Mollet) displays his artistry with the whip. Despite these and other clues, *Les Onze mille verges* has not always been recognized for the romp that it is, and it continues to be sold under the counter as a "serious" work of pornography. As for *Les Exploits d'un jeune don Juan,* it is so limpidly perverse, so fragrant with young private perfumes, that one wonders whether it may not be another of Apollinaire's anti-Symbolist sallies: this time the work parodied might be Henri de Regnier's tender novel of adolescence, *Les Vacances d'un jeune homme sage,* in which the charming teen-age hero is *dépucelé* (in this case, off-stage) by a member of his mother's generation. Frenchmen are apt to speak of *Les Exploits* in tones of affection: *"C'est de la pornographie innocente, ça!"*

It was apparently Apollinaire's authorship of those two books that brought him to the attention of the publisher Briffault in the Rue de Furstenberg who was planning a series of erotica to be called *Les Maîtres de l'amour.* Apollinaire was put in charge, and for a number of years he was

166

periodically engaged in such modestly profitable tasks as editing an anthology of writings by the Marquis de Sade, translating Aretino's sonnets, prefacing *Les Mémoires de Fanny Hill,* and writing, for the same publisher, a number of pulp-like "historical" novels entitled *La Rome des Borgia, La Fin de Babylone,* etc. With his easy flow of language and his facility with plot, this was an easy source of income. With two literary friends, Fernand Fleuret and Louis Perceau, who shared some of his labors, he compiled a catalogue of the so-called "Enfer," the locked collection of erotica and sexology in the Bibliothèque Nationale. This was a strictly unauthorized enterprise. The daring trio, needy writers all, obtained access to the forbidden books by tipping an employee; three by three he would bring the volumes to them at their desks, and there, in full view of the staff and officials of the library, the clandestine list of nine hundred books was compiled. The Bibliothèque Nationale expressed pained surprise on receiving a printed copy, dutifully presented by its publisher, the Mercure de France (French publishers are required by law to present a copy of each of their books to the Bibliothèque Nationale); however—one is reminded of the plaque commemorating Apollinaire's stay in the Stavelot hotel from which he skipped—the catalogue by Apollinaire, Fleuret, and Perceau was promptly recognized as invaluable by the custodians of l'Enfer, and it is in use at the Bibliothèque Nationale to this day.

Apollinaire also wrote a certain amount of "libertine" verse. He has often been unfavorably viewed because of his willingness to be immersed to such a degree in a kind of   167 literature that even in France is apt to be sold under the counter. This no doubt reflects a certain aspect of his personality and interests. However, the reader of Apollinaire never feels that this is the area of his greatest artistic concentration: rather, he seems to have practiced the genre as a sideline, not scorning it, but well aware of its limitations.

He added to his income by his art "criticism" and by reviewing novels, and early in 1911 he was given a department in the bimonthly *Mercure de France,* a kind of literary and artistic gossip column that he baptized *"La Vie anecdotique."* These contributions have been collected in the volume *Anecdotiques,* with a preface by Marcel Adéma (Gallimard, 1955). To sustain such a column, consisting only of anecdotes, single-handed over a long period of time, even irregularly, and at a consistently high level, is a rare accomplishment. The comparable regular department in *The New Yorker,* "Talk of the Town," is the work of many contributors and is considerably more inhibited in content. Apollinaire's best known anecdote appeared in the *Mercure* for April 1, 1913—a divertingly scabrous reportage on the funeral of Walt Whitman. Several indignant Americans, apparently oblivious of the significant date of the issue, wrote letters of protest to the magazine. Apollinaire blandly replied that the story had been told him "in the presence of a young poet of talent, M. Blaise Cendrars," who had visited the United States, and that he would never have printed it had he not supposed that the facts it contained were "indisputably known in America."

During these years were published the first three of Apollinaire's "serious" books. On November 28, 1909, ap-

Apollinaire in 1909

peared *L'Enchanteur pourrissant,* the dreamlike scenario that had been printed in *Le Festin d'Esope,* now enlarged by a later-written section explicitly entitled "Onirocritique" ("Interpretation of Dreams"), in which is embedded the exquisite short poem "Par les portes d'Orkenise," one of a number of Apollinaire's poems later set to music by Francis Poulenc.[4] In her *Carnet des Nuits* Marie Laurencin mentions a resemblance: "Apollinaire had a way of reciting his poems in a low, chanting voice which is almost like the music of Poulenc. And yet Poulenc never knew Apollinaire, unless I am mistaken." *L'Enchanteur* was the first book published by a young German named Daniel-Henry Kahnweiler who had recently opened an art gallery in Paris and who was to

[4] Columbia LP ML 4484 and ML 4333.

169

Guillaume Apollinaire

play a celebrated role as artists' impresario and publisher of books illustrated by modern artists: "What would have become of us if Kahnweiler hadn't been a good business man?" Picasso once exclaimed. *L'Enchanteur* was the first book ever illustrated by the artist chosen by Apollinaire and Kahnweiler to do the woodcuts—André Derain. That Apollinaire regarded *L'Enchanteur* as his first book is shown by a quatrain he wrote to Kahnweiler to celebrate the first anniversary of publication:

A Henry Kahnweiler

Vous êtes le premier, Henry, qui m'éditâtes;
Il faut qu'il m'en souvienne, en chantant votre los.
Que vous célèbrent donc les vers et les tableaux
Au triple étage habité par les trois Hécates!

Guillaume Apollinaire

28 novembre 1910

170

Apollinaire: Five

The author, whose talents as a publicist were at his own disposal as well as at that of his artist friends, wrote the blurb for *L'Enchanteur* himself:

> Full of completely new and striking ideas whose philosophical background is unique in any literature, *L'Enchanteur pourrissant* by Guillaume Apollinaire is one of the most mysterious and most lyrical books of the new literary generation. Its roots reach down to the Celtic depths of our tradition. This book is illustrated by André Derain, the most rigorous regenerator of plastic esthetics. The pictures, lettering, and ornaments that he has engraved on wood make this book a pure artistic marvel. . . . There are few books in which the genius of the author and the artist are more harmoniously combined than in *L'Enchanteur pourrissant*. . . . The taste for beautiful editions seems to be reviving. Today the publisher-bibliophile, Henry Kahnweiler, offers to lovers of art and letters a book which combines with its literary and artistic attraction that of a typography which all concerned have endeavored to make flawless.

Although there is no way of computing Apollinaire's effectiveness as a promoter of his artist friends, over the years, in the face of a hostile or indifferent public, records are available to show the results of that blurb for *L'Enchanteur:* only one hundred copies were printed, and five years later fifty-eight remained unsold.[5]

In 1910 appeared *L'Hérésiarque et Cie.,* a collection of short stories. "L'Hérésiarque," the title story, which had appeared in the *Revue blanche* in March, 1902, while Apollinaire was still in Germany, was the first piece of writing that he had signed with his new name, and now he dedi-

[5] The current price (1962) for a copy of this first edition of *l'Enchanteur pourrissant* in wrappers, on ordinary paper, is approximately $1,500. It was reprinted in 1921 by the NRF in two-thirds its original size.

Guillaume Apollinaire

cated the volume containing it and its "company" to Thadée Natanson, the editor of the *Revue blanche* who had given him his start and in whose magazine several others of the company had also first been printed. None of these stories, some of which Apollinaire had written even before going to Germany, and which he had been publishing in magazines since his return to Paris, has ever been put into English, and a translation of the volume as a whole would make an interesting project for a Francophile with a flair and a fondness for language. "The author of all these inventions," Apollinaire says in his own blurb for *L'Hérésiarque et Cie.,* "is intoxicated by a charming erudition, which he makes use of to intoxicate his readers, as well." Apollinaire had originally intended to entitle the volume *Phantasmes;* indeed the dedication reads "*A Thadée Natanson ces philtres de phantase";* and perhaps the best indication of the mood of the volume is conveyed by the definition, by Larousse, of the word "*phantasme*": ". . . *du gr. phantasma, fantôme. Pathol. Images et croyances imaginaires, distinctes des hallucinations, qui se produisent chez les névropathes ou chez les femmes nerveuses, et les jeunes filles au moment de leur formation.*" A definition much to Apollinaire's taste, one feels, and one that could well have determined him in his original choice of title. When *L'Hérésiarque et Cie.* was reviewed in the *Mercure de France,* the reviewer, Lucien Maury, mentioned certain "influences" that he felt were apparent in the stories, and Apollinaire immediately wrote a letter to Maury making the improbable denial that he had ever read anything by Hoffman, Poe, Nerval, Baudelaire, or Barbey d'Aurevilly. In conversation with friends, he later amplified this

172

list of unread writers to include Zola, Maupassant, Mirbeau, Whitman, Claudel, and Francis Jammes. *Les phantasmes volontaires du poète! L'Hérésiarque et Cie.* was among the books voted on for the Prix Goncourt the year of its publication. It was far too "special" for any such popular award, and received few votes: this was the only time a book by Apollinaire was considered by a prize committee. That year Colette's *La Vagabonde* was voted down, too: the prize was awarded to Louis Pergaud for a novel called *De Goupil à Margot*.

And then in 1911 came the third book in three years—Apollinaire's first volume of poetry, *Le Bestiaire, ou Cortège d'Orphée*. Apollinaire's charming idea of portraying in verse the procession of animals following Orpheus and his lyre took the form of a parade of four-line allegorical poems, each about a different beast, each printed separately on its page; and each beast was accompanied by its image in a woodcut. This time the artist was another young friend of Apollinaire's, Raoul Dufy. Everything about *Le Bestiaire* is graceful. Under the first woodcut, of Orpheus, is a compliment by the poet to the artist:

> *Admirez le pouvoir insigne*
> *Et la noblesse de la ligne...*

In the octopus, portrayed by Dufy as rotund and swollen, like Picasso's jester-king, Apollinaire sees himself, and in Apollinaire's octopus every other writer who reads the *Bestiaire* sees *himself*:

> *Jetant son encre vers les cieux,*
> *Suçant le sang de ce qu'il aime*
> *Et le trouvant délicieux,*
> *Ce monstre inhumain, c'est moi-même.*

173

Guillaume Apollinaire

Once again Apollinaire wrote his own blurb:

The sober poems of *Le Bestiaire, ou Cortège d'Orphée* by Guillaume Apollinaire are one of the most varied, seductive and accomplished poetical works of the new lyric generation. This collection, very modern in sensibility, is closely akin in inspiration to the works of the highest humanist culture. The same spirit that animated the poet has animated the illustrator, Raoul Dufy, who is known as one of the most original and talented innovators who are the pride of contemporary French art.

Printing by hand-presses is a very slow operation, requiring great care. Only in this way can perfect results be obtained. Bibliophiles who are lovers of letters and the arts will be grateful to the publisher Deplanche for giving them this product of the printing firm of Gaulthier-Villars, famous for beautiful typography.

Le Bestiaire, ou Cortège d'Orphée will merit being considered one of the rarest and most beautiful books of our day.

"Apollinaire was right," says Marcel Adéma. "*Le Bestiaire* is now one of the most sought-after modern books. And yet, as in the case of *L'Enchanteur,* it was a failure. Of the 120 copies printed, only about fifty were sold. Deplanche was long put off by the printing costs; he had kept making and breaking appointments, and only Dufy's determination had got him finally to make up his mind. This edition—so perfect a production that it is difficult to know whether Apollinaire's verses are a poetic commentary on Dufy's woodcuts or vice versa—was remaindered to the antique dealer and bookseller Chevrel, who sold them at forty francs apiece—a price calculated to make today's bibliophiles tremble with envy."[6]

[6] Today a first edition of *Le Bestiaire, ou Cortège d'Orphée,* in wrappers, on ordinary paper, fetches several thousand dollars. Both the text and the woodcuts have been reprinted in the Pléiade edition of Apollinaire's verse. A copy of the work was sold in Paris in May 1963 for 23,900 francs (almost $5000).

174

These were the years when Apollinaire emerges in his full self-created image—if the singular of the word can be applied to one so curiously proteiform, who impressed so many people so differently. "Guillaume Apollinaire never gave me the impression of being completely natural," one of his friends records. "As I remember him, he seemed always to be playing the parts of several characters simultaneously. Even his handwriting was affected by this, and his bank required him to supply five or six specimens of his signature." And Marcel Adéma tells us: "Apollinaire had been described to P.V. Stock [the publisher of *L'Hérésiarque et Cie.*] as mysterious, unfathomable, a mixture of madness and good sense, a mystifier, crammed full of old anecdotes, extravagant, disorderly, etc. However, from the outset he showed himself to be charming, well balanced, extremely sensible and acute, and almost shy. Here too Apollinaire gives evidence of his adaptability, his ability to modify his behavior according to the place and the company. He often took a malicious pleasure in giving a false impression of extravagance if he felt this to be advantageous, or, similarly, he would display deference, courtesy, and reserve."

"The shape of Apollinaire's head reminded you a little of a pear," Fernande Olivier says of him.

He was pleasant-looking, distinguished, with sharp features, small eyes rather close together, a long, thin Roman nose, and eyebrows like commas. A little mouth, which he often seemed to make deliberately smaller when he spoke, as though to give more bite to what he was saying. He was a mixture of distinction and a certain vulgarity, the latter coming out in his loud, childish laugh. His hands and his unctuous gestures made you think of a priest. (In fact there were rumors that he was the son of a Vatican prelate.

175

His mother was Russian or Polish.) What struck you above all was his evident good nature. He was calm and gentle, serious, affectionate, inspiring confidence the moment he spoke—and he spoke a great deal.

Charming, well read, an artist, and what a poet! Perhaps not of the most refined sensibility, yet with a child-like sentimentality that was enchanting. He was paradoxical, theatrical, rhetorical and at the same time simple and naive.

Like Picasso, he smoked a pipe, and it was always with a pipe in his mouth or in his hand that he told his stories, always with a very serious air even when they were trivial or rollicking.

He loved to recite his own poems, but he was very bad at it. He swallowed most of the lines. Nevertheless he managed to stir us.

I can see him now. He would arrive, always in a hurry, laden down with old books and engravings that he had unearthed and bought for a few sous all over Paris. He was always sure that he had got extraordinary bargains. Sometimes he would absentmindedly leave a newly bought book in the subway or the bus.

"He loved fruit," Marie Laurencin offers, as an additional touch to the portrait, "especially melons, oranges, and grapes, and he loved the sun before the sun became fashionable. He took a passionate interest in everything that was done at home, writing, painting, lace-making; he had a horror of working at a table, and his great joy was to take walks, look at shops, and have a companion with whom he could argue, almost come to blows. At thirty he was very handsome, with large dark eyes that were incredibly expressive, eyebrows like those on the masks of Greek tragedy, a tiny mouth, and his voice was like Poulenc's music for the *Bestiaire*."

Louise Faure-Favier speaks of his "excellent manners." Others tell of his love of walking through the city: "Apolli-

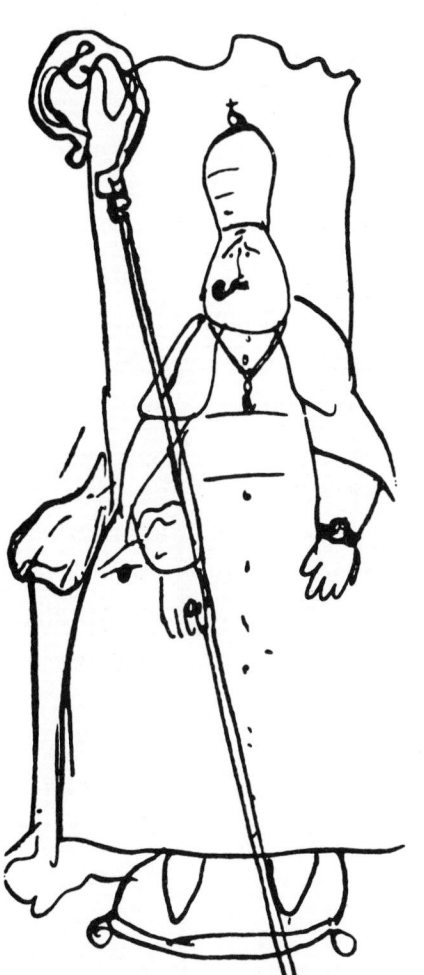

Drawings of Apollinaire by Picasso

177

Guillaume Apollinaire

naire knew all the cafés chosen as meeting places by certain categories of craftsmen—gem-cutters, etc. He knew something about each place: one of them was where Moréas had told him about his father and his little house in Greece, surrounded by olive trees; another was where Jarry had pulled out his revolver, or poured ink into his Pernod." Like Jarry, Apollinaire himself "did not hesitate to try daring food mixtures, like adding snuff to veal to give it the taste of venison. Next day, even if the result had been inedible, he would go everywhere telling everybody who would listen about his marvelous recipe."

These were the years of Paul Fort's Tuesday night poetry readings at the Closerie des Lilas and Apollinaire's contributions to Fort's magazine, *Vers et Prose*—"L'Emigrant de Landor Road" among them; of his contributions also to Jean Royère's neo-Symbolist *La Phalange;* of Apollinaire's own Wednesday night gatherings in Montmartre and later in Auteuil, artists' dinners in cheap Montmartre and Left Bank restaurants, nights of song and recitation at the Lapin Agile, the "banquet years," as Roger Shattuck has called them, the most famous banquet—we would call it a party—being the one for the Douanier Rousseau in Picasso's studio in the Bateau Lavoir, at which Braque played his guitar, Marie Laurencin sang songs her mother had taught her, and Apollinaire read a eulogy. After first having reviewed Rousseau's pictures unfavorably, Apollinaire added him to his list of promotees. In the Douanier's *simpliste* treatment of subjects both exotic and everyday, some have seen one of Apollinaire's sources of poetic inspiration, but it has to be pointed out that Apollinaire achieved simplicity after proving his ability to handle the most intricate poetic techniques, whereas Rousseau all his life aspired in vain to equal the academic perfection of a Meissonier.[7]

The farcical treatment accorded Rousseau by the writers and painters around him points to one of the defects of the brilliant, amusing group. "There was communion of mind, of art, often of ideas," says Fernande Olivier. "Rarely communion of heart, of generosity. And so many protestations of admiration, of friendship, in which sincerity played so small a part. . . . Few of the friends in the group stood up for any who were not present; on the contrary, I often noticed that despite their seeming ties of affection, no sooner did one of them leave the house than the others would begin to speak ill of him."

During these years Apollinaire experimented with

[7] Rousseau's earliest promoter was the farceur Jarry. The story of his more or less farcical promotion by other artists has never been treated quite candidly by historians of modern art. Minority opinions concerning this very popular painter have seldom been expressed in print. In conversation with the author, Lionello Venturi has said "I never understood why mere failure to become academic, through technical incompetence, should be considered a virtue." Jacques Villon: "*Ce qu'il y a de bien chez Rousseau, c'est le feuillage.*" Fernand Fleuret tells an anecdote about Rousseau visiting the Louvre with Raoul Dufy:

"I thought," Dufy told us, "that seeing the Primitives, Rousseau would be beside himself with admiration and utter inspired words. But the old idiot said to me: "Young man, those people in the dark ages simply didn't know how to draw. I like their color well enough, but it's not the real thing." I thought I would go down through the Chauchard collection, where there are pictures by Neuville and Meissonnier, and get rid of Rousseau by walking fast. But he kept up with me, making ridiculous remarks that I stopped listening to. Suddenly he caught hold of my coat and pulled me to a stop in front of a Meissonier: "Look at that, my friend; *that's* beautiful. Everything is there—the buttons on the gaiters and the coats, the gold braid on the epaulettes—he even tells you the number of the regiment."

179

opium-smoking, pretended for more than a year to be a woman poet named Louise Lalanne, reviewing the work of "her sister poets" in *Les Marges,* posed for his portrait by Jean Metzinger (the "first Cubist portrait," exhibited at the Salon des Indépendants in the spring of 1910), wrote and lectured on poetry (he defined his own goal as a "new and humanistic lyricism"), and severely described this period as "a moment at which poetry in France seems to have as its only aim a pleasure adapted to the feelings and language suitable to the middle class of Society." Every Tuesday he "spent a few hours in Briffault's office . . . correcting proofs of the *Maîtres de l'amour* series, lunched generously in the Rue de Seine, occupied his customary table in the Café de Flore, and attended the weekly afternoon reception of the *Mercure* in the Rue de Condé." "He was always busy at his daily rounds, a pile of magazines or books under his arm, shuttling between lectures, poetry readings, articles, banquets, appointments." His mother complained that he visited Le Vésinet only to pick up his laundry—"he only comes to see me when he wants to change his shirt." His life was with his friends, with journalism that was literary, artistic and "special," and above all with poetry. "Les Fiançailles," "Le Voyageur," "Saltimbanques," "Crépuscule," "Poème lu au mariage d'André Salmon," "1909"— all these poems familiar to readers of Apollinaire's *Alcools* were written at this time.

He had the moodiness of any artist, and when his spirits were high they were infectious. He won the hearts of the editors of the little magazine *Isis* by his answers to the first and last items in a literary questionnaire they had submitted to a number of writers:

QUESTION: Do you believe in the existence of Homer?

ANSWER: Certainly I believe in the historical reality of Homer. Let me add that in the more or less distant future I intend to take the initiative in launching a subscription for the erection in Paris of a monument to the glory of Adam and Eve.

QUESTION: Do you approve of the abandonment of the study of Greek?

ANSWER: My incompetence in pedagogical matters should keep me from replying to your last question. However, I will not conceal from you that if I had my way, not only would the study of Greek not be abandoned, but young Frenchmen would also be inculcated with the rudiments of Sanskrit.

He summed himself up in a letter mailed November 9, 1910, to Thadée Natanson, his old editor on the *Revue blanche*, who had written to ask for something about his "history"—biographical details to be included in a review that Natanson was to write of *L'Hérésiarque et Cie.*:

> . . . I don't know what to say. I have no past, and for that reason I should be happy, like peoples without history. A few travels in Europe, *La Revue blanche, Le Festin d'Esope,* defending painters I like, literature, poetry—that is all there is on the credit side of my ledger. I am writing a novel and a play and am preparing a collection of my poems. That is my entire personal history. My assets consist of a total lack of money, a knowledge of literature that I believe extensive, a few languages living and dead, and a rather varied experience of life. . . .

The "rather varied experience of life" was now to be considerably added to.

181

Guillaume Apollinaire

Six

From the newspaper *Paris-Journal,* Wednesday, August 23, 1911:[1]

IS ARSÈNE LUPIN ALIVE?

MONA LISA GONE FROM THE LOUVRE!

The Police, Late on the Scene, Surround the Museum—
Investigation Leads Nowhere—Robbery, or Practical Joke?

The news of a theft from the Louvre (as happened now and then) usually evoked the remark: "One of these days they'll take the Mona Lisa." This was always said with ironic emphasis, the implication being that such a hypothesis was an absurdity.

The fact is, in the eyes of the public, even the uneducated, the Mona Lisa occupies a privileged position that is not to be accounted for by its value alone. For many, the Mona Lisa is the Louvre. The Mona Lisa is always referred to as the very model of beauty; it is the Mona Lisa that the high school boy goes to see on Sunday; it is she, also on Sunday, who is the goal of the young intellectual from the provinces doing his military service in Paris; finally, ordinary folk choose the Mona Lisa to give a kind of blessing to their wedding parties—as we know from *L'Assommoir.*

No wonder everyone was dumbfounded yesterday afternoon when the city, until then engrossed in the palavers of our politicians, suddenly heard the incredible news: "The Mona Lisa has disappeared! The Mona Lisa has been stolen!"

IN THE LOUVRE

In the Louvre, as is easily imaginable, there was considerable excitement—indeed, near-panic.

It was about noon, so we are told, that the disappearance

[1] *Paris-Journal* was an evening newspaper, bearing the date of the next day. This issue was on sale the afternoon of Tuesday, August 22.

Apollinaire: Six

of Leonardo's masterpiece was discovered. A captain of the guards, suddenly noticing that the wall space in the Salon Carré ordinarily occupied by the Mona Lisa was vacant, gave the alarm. What had happened to the picture?

There was great commotion, great bustle, but to no avail. All curators and department heads who happened to be in Paris were hastily summoned. What could they do? Notify the Under-secretary for the Beaux Arts? They reluctantly agreed that there was no other course. But M. Dujardin-Beaumetz [the Under-secretary] was not in Paris. A desperate telegram was sent to him at once. The Prefect of Police was also alerted, and he immedi-ately ordered M. Hamard to go to the Louvre, taking with him sixty inspectors and a number of regular police.

M. Hamard's first step was to order all the doors of the Louvre palace to be locked, and to evacuate all the galleries of the museum. At the same time he stationed policemen on the roof, to intercept the thief should he attempt to use that route to escape to the building formerly occupied by the Ministry of Colonies.

As for M. Lepine [the Prefect of Police], after he had person-ally delivered the news to the Ministry of the Interior, he went to the Louvre and took charge of operations. On his order the palace was searched from cellar to attic. The sole result was the discovery, on the grand staircase, at the feet of the Victory of Samothrace, of the Mona Lisa's frame, together with the sheet of glass that had protected the picture.

The frame, by the way, was absolutely intact. Obviously the thief had carefully removed the linden-wood panel on which Mona Lisa smiles her eternal smile. It is thought that he performed the operation on a landing of the small staircase that opens into the gallery of primitive paintings by a door that is always kept locked. He must have been working there a good half hour.

THE INVESTIGATION

M. Lepine then left the Louvre and went to the Ministry of Justice, where he informed the Minister of the disappearance of

Guillaume Apollinaire

the Mona Lisa and of the futile preliminary search. M. Cruppi, with whom the Beaux Arts had already registered a complaint against person or persons unknown, immediately informed the Public Prosecutor. The latter appointed M. Drioux, investigating magistrate, who went to work at once.

It must be admitted that the magistrate's task is far from an easy one. Everything about this strange story is weird: it is not possible even to establish on what *day* Vinci's masterpiece disappeared.

Was it yesterday, or the day before yesterday, that the Mona Lisa was carried off? Mondays, as everyone knows, the Louvre is closed: Monday is cleaning day. Only a few privileged visitors are allowed in the galleries. Presumably, the thief took advantage of that circumstance.

Another circumstance that perhaps facilitated the theft was the presence, in a gallery contiguous to the Salon Carré, of a scaffolding built against a wall that is under repair. It is even reported that a mason, on his way to work on the scaffold, pointed out the Mona Lisa to another workman as they passed it, saying: "Look, that is the most beautiful picture in the Louvre."

An hour later—according to those who believe that the theft took place on Monday—the picture was gone.

As stated above, a few privileged visitors have access to the museum on Mondays. By a strange coincidence, it happens that last Monday M. Granié, assistant prosecutor for the Département of the Seine, was among these visitors, when all of them were, on a vague pretext, forbidden access to the Salon Carré. M. Granié protested, but in vain. He had to turn back. Why should this order have been given?

However, if the theft was discovered on Monday, what is the explanation of the police department's being alerted only yesterday, and rather late in the day at that? And how to explain the sudden mobilization of the police force, if the news had been known the day before?

Still, this fact remains: visitors to the Louvre yesterday morning were astonished not to see the Mona Lisa, and the guards replied to their inquiries with the explanation that the picture was

Apollinaire: Six

merely in the photographic studio—until, as we said above, the captain of the guard gave the alarm.

THE HYPOTHESES

Are we dealing with a real theft, or a practical joke? It would not be the first time that the wish to write a sensational newspaper story has turned one of our fellow-reporters into a temporary burglar. There have been other happenings in the Louvre that remind us of this disappearance of the Mona Lisa.

If Vinci's masterpiece has been whisked away by a sensation-seeking journalist, all that is needed is a little, a very little, patience: the Mona Lisa will be returned to the Louvre with a maximum of publicity.

The hypothesis of the practical joke is the most commonly accepted. How can a real thief hope to profit financially from a picture so universally known? There remains the hypothesis of a fanatical collector, absolutely determined to possess the masterpiece and planning to keep it hidden from every gaze but his own. However, this is most unlikely.

In short, for the public and the magistrates alike everything about this extraordinary event remains mysterious, and only the person guilty of the theft—or of the practical joke—knows exactly how and why the Mona Lisa has disappeared.

AN INTERPELLATION?

M. Delaroche-Vernet, deputy from the Loire-Inférieure, has just notified M. Steeg, Minister of Public Instruction, that he will raise certain questions, when the Chamber of Deputies reconvenes, concerning the conditions under which the Mona Lisa disappeared from the Louvre, and concerning measures which the Minister plans to take to safeguard the masterpieces in our national museums.

One more detail: M. Dujardin-Beaumetz returns to Paris today.

Was the writer of that article André Salmon, Apolli-   185

Guillaume Apollinaire

naire's friend and fellow-poet, now art critic on *Paris-Journal?* Much in the article bespeaks his authorship. The lightness of the grief displayed at the theft of a national treasure, for one thing: Salmon, Apollinaire, and others of the *bande Picasso* were accustomed to proclaim that museums and their contents were nothing but the dead hand of the past, holding down a struggling new art. And the touch about the curators of the Louvre "reluctantly" deciding that they had better inform their superiors in the government that the Mona Lisa was not where she should be, the elaborate bureaucratic minuet begun by the stunned officials in the various departments, the policemen prowling the roofs of the Louvre, the thief calmly spending a half-hour removing the frame and then placing it as a kind of tribute "at the feet of the Victory of Samothrace," the hurried return to Paris of the Undersecretary—M. Dujardin-Beaumetz[2]—(for the robber had inconsiderately robbed in August, when important people were away on holiday): it was a gleeful moment for *Paris-Journal's* reporter, whether it was Salmon himself or a newsman assigned to cover the theft.

Apollinaire was writing occasional articles on art at this time for *L'Intransigeant,* another evening newspaper. *L'Intransigeant* had announced the theft of the Mona Lisa in

[2] Henri-Charles-Etienne Dujardin-Beaumetz, who in the Larousse encyclopedia is given the unusual tag of "French painter and politician," was not unknown to Apollinaire, Salmon, and the others. As the highest government official connected with the arts, he was a target for their gibes; and on the occasion of a fake reception they staged for the Douanier Rousseau, one of them, dressed in formal clothes, had pretended to be M. Dujardin-Beaumetz, on hand to offer the painter his official congratulations.

Apollinaire: Six

a news story in its second edition of the evening before, the same evening as *Paris-Journal;* and the next day there appeared an odd little article by Apollinaire himself.

AND THE GUARD THAT WATCHES THE GATES OF THE LOUVRE. . . .
THE ABDUCTION OF THE MONA LISA

The Mona Lisa was so beautiful that her perfection has come to be taken for granted.

There are not many works of which this can be said.

The Apollo Belvedere, the Venus de Milo, the Mona Lisa, the Sistine Madonna, the Last Judgment, the Embarcation for Cytherea, the Angelus, the Island of the Dead—those, with perhaps a few others, have been singled out by humanity among the artistic production of all ages. Those are the most famous art treasures in the world.

This is not to say, however, that the reputation of some of these works is not higher than their artistic value. Boecklin's Island of the Dead and Millet's Angelus are unquestionably prized above their merits, but the fame of the Mona Lisa was on a par with her beauty, if not, indeed, below it.

But what shall we say of "The guard that watches the gates of the Louvre?"

There is not even one guard per gallery; the small pictures in the Dutch rooms running along the Rubens gallery are literally abandoned to thieves.

The pictures, even the smallest, are not padlocked to the wall, as they are in most museums abroad. Furthermore, it is a fact that the guards have never been drilled in how to rescue pictures in case of a fire.

The situation is one of carelessness, negligence, indifference.

The Louvre is less well protected than a Spanish museum.

Still, if we need to console ourselves at all costs for the disappearance of a masterpiece, we might recall that in Germany during the nineteenth century curators and restorers scraped away and repainted all the old pictures confided to their care. As a result, in German museums there is no more old painting to be seen, but 187

Guillaume Apollinaire

only the strident productions of Herr Professor so and so—a man as guilty in his way as the ravisher of the Mona Lisa.

That same day *Paris-Journal* printed two articles about the theft, one an editorial scolding the government for fostering the system of *"fonctionnairisme"*—the system under which minor state employees, *"fonctionnaires,"* such as museum guards, are paid tiny salaries and are not expected to be alert[3]—and the other a news article as chatty and nonchalant as the first, offering readers such assorted bits of information as the fact that a certain toilet in the Louvre, where it was thought the thief might have spent the night, was known as *"les W.C. de la cour du Sphinx,"* and the further news that the Louvre had recently received a postcard addressed to "Mona Lisa, Louvre Museum, Paris," and bearing as a message a "red-hot love declaration, peppered with 'I love you's' and 'I adore you's,'" leading certain officials to wonder whether the theft might not be the work of an *erotomane*. It also reported the opinions of two clairvoyants (both of them probably inventions), a Madame Albane de Siva, who, after "ascertaining at the Central Astronomical Office the position of the planets at the time of the theft, deduced that the picture was still hidden some-

---

[3] *Paris-Journal* later proposed that the following notice be posted in all French museums:

In the Interest of Art
And For the Safeguarding of the Precious Objects
THE PUBLIC
Is Requested to be Good Enough to
WAKE THE GUARDS
If They are Found to be Asleep

Another day the newspaper printed a trick photograph of the cathedral of Notre-Dame with one of its towers missing, captioned: "Couldn't this happen, too?"

Apollinaire: Six

where in the Louvre, and that the thief was "a young man with thick hair, a long neck and a hoarse voice, who had a passion for rejuvenating old things," and a Madame Elise, who pronounced sadly: "The Mona Lisa has been destroyed." During the days that followed, *Paris-Journal* kept its readers regularly amused in this fashion. But *L'Intransigeant* contained no more articles by Apollinaire about the theft of the Mona Lisa. Why was he silent? Why had his first and only article about it been so strangely jerky-sounding, so much duller than those in *Paris-Journal?* Praise of the Mona Lisa's beauty comes oddly from the pen of Apollinaire, who had recently been heard to agree with the Italian Futurist Marinetti, at one of Paul Fort's Tuesday evening poetry readings at the Closerie des Lilas, that "all museums should be destroyed because they paralyzed the imagination."

The explanation is to be found in the personality and exploits of a young Belgian named Gery Pieret, who had acted for a time, like Baron Mollet, as Apollinaire's "secretary": in Pieret, the poet's fondness for the odd fauna of Paris had got the better of him.

Apollinaire had met the young man back in 1907, when they were both working for one of the vague financial institutions that had paid the poet a weekly wage: Apollinaire's salary from this one, called *le Guide des Rentiers* ("Investors' Guide"), had ceased abruptly when the *Guide* was closed by the police because of the more than dubious nature of some of its guidance, and Pieret's had apparently ceased equally abruptly, and earlier, when he had tried to blackmail his employers. Pieret, who claimed to be the son of a Belgian government official and to have deserted from the Belgian army, appealed to Apollinaire's fancy as a refugee from the establishment; he had been a boxer and a stoker, and on first coming to Paris he had been sheltered by the Salvation Army. Apollinaire had embroidered on him, calling him "Baron Ignace d'Ormesan",[4] in one of the tales in *L'Hérésiarque et Cie*. Pieret's Latin was excellent, and his wit was diverting and original.

For example, one day he said to Marie Laurencin: "Madame Marie, this afternoon I am going to the Louvre: can I bring you anything you need?" Given the question, everyone assumed that he was offering to shop for Marie in the Magasins du Louvre, a department store on the Rue de Rivoli often referred to by Parisians as "the Louvre"; but that evening he turned up at Apollinaire's apartment bearing two Iberian stone sculptured heads, which he gleefully announced had indeed come from the Louvre—the museum.

This *coup* must have aroused much mirth among the artistic revolutionaries in Montmartre, and when Pieret announced that he was, as usual, in need of cash, and offered the statues for sale, they were recommended to Picasso, who bought them and who subsequently, with his usual flair, found a new inspiration in these antiquities from his native Spain. Indeed, in 1907 Picasso had reached one of his many turning-points and was just beginning a new canvas, which was later to be entitled "Les Demoiselles d'Avignon" and to

[4] It is the first version of this name, "Ormespant," found in one of Apollinaire's manuscripts, that is thought to be a clue to the poet's paternity, "Ormespant" being an anagram of "Aspermont."

Apollinaire: Six

be known in art history as "the first Cubist picture." Anyone who looks at the Demoiselles can see Pieret's stolen heads—or at least their ears—in the two central figures. (Picasso later repainted the remaining heads under the inspiration of Negro sculpture, previously "discovered" by Derain and Vlaminck.)

Apollinaire himself later wrote his own version of the story that has become known as *"l'affaire des statuettes"*:

In 1911 I gave shelter to a young fellow who was intelligent but crazy and unscrupulous—unfortunate rather than wicked—who knows what has become of him? In 1907 he had stolen from the Louvre two Hispano-Roman statues, which he had sold to X——, whose name, thanks to me, was never mentioned in this affair. I tried, long before 1911—still back in 1907 or 1908—to persuade X—— to give the statues back to the Louvre, but he was absorbed in his esthetic studies, and indeed from them Cubism was born. He told me that he had damaged the statues in an attempt to discover certain secrets of the classic yet barbaric art to which they belonged. The method I had found for returning them would have been perfectly safe and honorable for him. My friend Louis Lumet, an official at the Beaux-Arts, to whom I had told the story, proposed combining this worthy action with an amusing fake journalistic *coup*. We would have suggested to the newspaper *Le Matin* that it demonstrate publicly that the treasures in the Louvre were poorly guarded—by stealing first one statue (sensation!) and then another (second sensation!). If this had been done there would have been no trouble. But X—— wanted to keep the statues. . . . In 1911 the fellow who had stolen them turned up again. He came to see me, arriving from America, his pockets full of money which he proceeded to lose at the races. Penniless, he stole another statue. I had to help him—he was down and out—so I took him into my flat and tried to get him to return the statue; he refused, so I had to put him out, along with the statue. A few days later the Mona Lisa was stolen. I thought, as the

191

Guillaume Apollinaire

police later thought, that he was the thief. . . .

So it becomes apparent why Apollinaire was nervous, and not writing at his best, and why he was so obsessed by the scarcity of guards in the Louvre, when he dutifully turned in that article about the Mona Lisa for *L'Intransigeant*. Actually, as we shall see later, Apollinaire knew quite well in 1911 that Pieret could not have stolen the picture; but the subject of museum thefts was not one that he could write serenely about.

For the following week the Louvre closed its doors while further vain internal search was made. M. Drioux, the investigating magistrate put in charge of the case, set up headquarters in a curator's office in the museum and questioned employees and others; two "suspicious" young Germans were arrested in Paris and quickly released; M. Théophile Homolle, an esteemed archeologist who was Director of National Museums, was dismissed from his post by the Minister of the Interior, eager to find a scapegoat. The magazine *L'Illustration* offered a reward of 40,000 francs, no questions asked, to anyone who would deliver the Mona Lisa to its offices, and another 10,000 to anyone who would reveal to the magazine information leading to its return; *Paris-Journal* offered 50,000 francs and anonymity, and published an article by the critic Camille de Sainte-Croix denying that the Mona Lisa had ever been "the Louvre's masterpiece," and stating that "it charms some and irritates others, for sexual reasons."

Then came news scarcely calculated to calm Apollinaire.

192 From *Paris-Journal,* August 29, 1911:

Apollinaire: Six

Curator Admits the Piece is from the Museum.
An edifying story—Our Museum is a supply center for
unscrupulous individuals. . . .

Yesterday morning's mail brought *Paris-Journal* a rather strange letter, addressed to the director.

"Monsieur"—it ran, in substance—"On the 7th of May, 1911, I stole a Phoenician statuette from one of the galleries of the Louvre. I am holding this at your disposition, in return for the sum of ———— francs. Trusting that you will respect my confidence, I shall be glad to meet you at such and such a place between ———— and ———— o'clock."

Now, *Paris-Journal,* even though it has offered 50,000 francs to anyone who will bring in the Mona Lisa, has never undertaken to ransom *all* the works of art stolen from the Louvre.

Still, since this was an opportunity to check a detail that would be interesting if proven genuine, one of our reporters went to the appointed place at the appointed time. There he met a young man, aged somewhere between twenty and twenty-five, very well-mannered, with a certain *chic américain,* whose face and look and behavior bespoke at once a kind heart and a certain lack of scruple. This was "The Thief"—since so he must be called.

The thief confirmed to our reporter the contents of his letter. He showed him the object that he claimed to have taken from the Louvre. It is a rather crude bust, an example of the somewhat rudimentary art of the Phoenicians, 28 centimeters high, 22 wide, and weighing no less than 6 kilos, 750 grammes!

He consented to put into writing, for *Paris-Journal,* the story of his theft, which we herewith reproduce without altering a word:

"It was in March, 1907 that I entered the Louvre for the first time—a young man with time to kill and no money to spend. At that time I had no idea of ever 'working' in the museum. I was born in Belgium, where every museum picture is padlocked to the wall and every museum statue firmly fastened to its pedestal, and my travels in the United States, Canada, and almost every country of Europe except France had done nothing to change my idea that

193

Guillaume Apollinaire

a museum was an impregnable fortress of art.

"It was about one o'clock. I found myself in the gallery of Asiatic antiquities. A single guard was sitting motionless. I was about to climb the stairs leading to the floor above when I noticed a half-open door on my left. I had only to push it, and found myself in a room filled with hieroglyphs and Egyptian statues, I believe—in any case, the place impressed me profoundly because of the deep silence and the absence of any human being. I walked through several adjoining rooms, stopping now and again in a dim corner to caress an ample neck or a well-turned cheek.

"It was at that moment that I suddenly realized how easy it would be to pick up and take away almost any object of moderate size.

"I was wearing a box-type overcoat, and my natural slimness made it quite possible for me to add a little to my dimensions without attracting the attention of any of the Cerberi (?), who have no idea of anatomy anyway. I was just then in a small room, about two meters by two, in the 'Gallery of Phoenician Antiquities.'

"Being absolutely alone, and hearing no sounds whatever, I took the time to examine about fifty heads that were there, and I chose one of a woman, with, as I recall, twisted, conical forms on each side. I put the statue under my arm, pulled up the collar of my overcoat with my left hand, and calmly walked out, asking my way of the guard, who was still completely motionless.

"I sold the statue to a Parisian painter friend of mine. He gave me a little money—fifty francs, I think, which I lost the same night in a billiard parlor.

"'What of it?' I said to myself. 'All Phoenicia is there for the taking.'

"The very next day I took a man's head with enormous ears—a detail that fascinated me. And three days later a plaster fragment covered with hieroglyphs. A friend gave me twenty francs for this last: I stole it from the large room adjoining the Phoenician room.

"Then I emigrated.

"I made a little money in Mexico, and decided to return to

194

France and form an art collection at very little expense. Last May 7 I went to my Phoenician room, and was surprised to find it very much changed. The arrangement of the heads had been altered, and although there had been more than forty when I left, I now found only twenty or twenty-five. The thought that the others had probably been removed by imitators of mine made me indignant. I took the head of a woman, and stuffed it into my trousers. The suit I was wearing was of heavy material and very ample, but the statue was outsized for me, and even though I was wearing a raincoat it was obvious despite my sex that I was pregnant with something.

"It took me at least twenty minutes to leave the museum. The statue kept shifting considerably from left to right, and I was afraid that it would drop out and break to pieces on the floor. This did not happen, but it put quite a strain on my clothes, and I decided to postpone my series of burglaries for a few weeks until I could provide myself with a pair of leather cowboy trousers and some special suspenders. Unfortunately, being fickle-minded I turned my attention to other things, necessitating a delay of several months in my antiquarian projects.

"And now one of my colleagues has spoiled all my plans for a collection by making this hullabaloo in the paintings department! I regret this exceedingly, for there is a strange, an almost voluptuous charm about stealing works of art, and I shall probably have to wait several years before resuming my activities. . . ."

The reporter from *Paris-Journal* who had interviewed the thief took the stolen head to the office of the newspaper —the article went on to say—where it was examined by a Louvre curator and identified as belonging to the museum's collection not of Phoenician, but of Iberian antiquities. The curator confessed that the museum had not even noticed its absence. "The person who turned the statuette over to us," *Paris-Journal* concluded, "is requested to come to our office, 195

Guillaume Apollinaire

where he will receive the sum of money agreed upon. As for the statuette itself, our readers can see it on exhibition today, in our window."

From *Paris-Journal,* August 30, 1911:

FIRST RESTITUTION

THE PHOENICIAN BUST

M. Dujardin-Beaumetz registers a complaint against
Person or Persons Unknown–He thanks Paris-Journal—
A Plea by the Thief.

No sooner did *Paris-Journal* announce, yesterday, the other theft perpetrated in the Louvre, than crowds began to visit our display window, to see the bust formerly part of, and soon to return to, the Museum collections. There were many initial expressions of disbelief, but the facts were irrefutable, and the realization that organized pillage of our museums indeed exists, as revealed with such perverse ingenuity by our thief, caused general stupefaction.

The visitors to our windows exchanged many comments, and we shall spare the officials of the French government any repetition of the litany of vigorous remarks addressed in their direction. So many cameras, both still and motion-picture, were aimed at the bust that the enigmatic Mona Lisa might almost have been jealous.

We had a visit—a business visit, this time—from "The Thief" who, after pocketing the agreed ransom, handed us a sheet of paper on which he had written this amusing protest:

"To the Editor-in-chief:

"In an age when the right of REPLY is universally recognized by the press, you will allow me a few words of protest against certain terms of abuse leveled at me in your issue of yesterday, relative to the theft of the Phoenician statuette. A professional thief, lacking all moral sense, would remain unaffected by them; but I am not without sensitivity, and the few pilferings I have

Apollinaire: Six

engaged in have been caused by momentary 'difficulties.' Bourgeois society, which makes life so hard for anyone without funds, whatever his intellectual qualities, is responsible for these wanderings from the straight and narrow. . . ."

That article continued with the news that M. Dujardin-Beaumetz was registering, with the Public Prosecutor, a complaint against person or persons unknown.

Does the word "first" in the top headline hint that André Salmon, the art critic of *Paris-Journal,* had already learned from his friends Apollinaire and Picasso that the two heads stolen from the Louvre in 1907 were still in existence, in Picasso's possession, and that the frightened poet and equally frightened painter had decided to return these heads, too, via *Paris-Journal?* Apollinaire, in his version of the affair, continues his narrative as follows:

I thought, as the police later thought, that he [Pieret] was the thief. He was not, but he sold his statue to *Paris-Journal,* which returned it to the Louvre. I went to see X——, to tell him how unfortunate it was that he had damaged the other two heads, and in what a dangerous position this placed him. I found him terrified. He confessed that he had lied to me, and that the statues were intact. I told him to turn them in, under pledge of secrecy, to *Paris-Journal,* which he did. *Grande scandale!*"

Many aspects of the "affair of the statuettes" are not clear, among them André Salmon's degree of knowledge and his attitude toward his friends Apollinaire, Picasso, and Pieret. In his memoirs he qualifies Pieret as a *"demi-fou"* and a *"vilain singe,"* and says that at this time he himself and Apollinaire had not seen each other for three months because of a "foolish quarrel"; but quite possibly he, like   197 many another who visited Apollinaire and Picasso, had already known about the provenance of the stolen heads. It is also possible that Pieret had not approached *Paris-Journal* by letter, as the newspaper informed its readers, but through personal contact with Salmon. Did Salmon know what dread was struck into the hearts of Apollinaire and Picasso by the announcement that M. Dujardin-Beaumetz was registering a complaint against person or persons unknown? Especially when *Paris-Journal* explained, a few days later: "This 'Unknown' is the same mysterious, anonymous person who recently delivered to the offices of *Paris-Journal* the Phoenician statuette that he had stolen from the Louvre."

Continued concealment of Pieret's identity from the forces of the law depended entirely on the dubious discretion of a newspaper office. Revelation would lead straight to those who had sheltered him and bought his stolen objects.

Fernande Olivier, Picasso's mistress at the time, has written an account of the state of mind in which Picasso and Apollinaire found themselves:

> I remember perfectly that Apollinaire and Picasso had a miserable time for a few days. . . . I see them both now, a pair of contrite children, terrified and thinking of fleeing abroad. It was thanks to me that they did not give in to their panic; they decided to stay in Paris and get rid of the compromising sculptures as quickly as possible. But how? Finally they decided to put the statues in a suitcase and throw it into the Seine at night. After a hastily swallowed dinner and a long evening of waiting, they set out on foot about midnight with the suitcase and came back at two in the morning, worn out and still carrying the suitcase with

the statues inside. They had wandered through the streets, never finding the right moment, never daring to get rid of their suitcase. They thought they were being followed, and their imagination conjured up a thousand possibilities, each more fantastic than the last. I must say that although I shared their fears I had been watching them rather carefully that night. I am sure that perhaps involuntarily they had been play-acting a little—to such a point that although neither of them knew anything about cards, while they had sat waiting for the fatal moment when they would set out for the Seine—"the moment of the crime"—they had pretended to play cards all evening, doubtless in imitation of certain bandits they had read about. In the end, Apollinaire spent the night at Picasso's, and went the next morning to *Paris-Journal,* where he turned in the undesirable statues under pledge of secrecy. This was a windfall for *Paris-Journal,* which enthusiastically accepted this unhoped-for bit of publicity.

Was it Picasso (as Apollinaire wrote), or was it Apollinaire (as Fernande Olivier wrote), who turned in the two heads to *Paris-Journal?* In any case:

From *Paris-Journal,* September 6, 1911:

WHILE AWAITING MONA LISA
THE LOUVRE RECOVERS ITS TREASURES
Two New Restitutions are made to Paris-Journal—
The Possessor of the two other stolen statuettes mentioned by "Our Thief" turns them in to us. The stone man and the stone woman are identified by the administration.

Paris-Journal recently restored to the Louvre an antique bust, an example of Iberian art but now famous under the incorrect designation of "Phoenician statuette" employed by the thief, whose curious account of the affair we printed without change.

Our readers will not have forgotten that in this account he mentioned other statues stolen from the Louvre a few years ago and sold to an art-lover. It was not specified whether the sculptures had been bought in good faith or whether the art-lover knew their provenance.

199

Guillaume Apollinaire

Yesterday our mail contained a letter written on a typewriter. This document emanated from the mysterious art-lover whose identity neither the sagacity of our fellow newspapermen nor the professional skill of the police had as yet been able to discover.

He asked us, of course, to promise discretion, and offered to come in person in the event that we cared to take the responsibility of returning the stolen statues to the Louvre without involving him.

Naturally we accepted, our prime consideration being that our national collections be complete.

A VISIT

At the appointed time, the mysterious visitor was announced. Our editor-in-chief received him.

The statement by the possessor of the sculptures can be summed up in a few words:

An amateur artist, fairly well-to-do, his greatest pleasure is in collecting works of art.

The sculptures in question were offered to him a few years ago.

Seeing these examples of a rather crude artistic style, he had no idea that they might have come from the Louvre, and attracted by the relatively low price asked for them, he purchased them.

But recently his attention was drawn to the thief's story as published in *Paris-Journal,* a story that has had wide repercussions.

The reproduction in our pages of a "Phoenician statuette" caused him to realize that he possessed pieces that were very similar, and the thief's mention of two other objects quickly convinced him that he had them in his collection.

His dismay is easy to imagine. At first he did not know how to proceed, and then it occurred to him that he might have recourse to *Paris-Journal.*

Apollinaire: Six

Our visitor had brought with him the sculptures in question. They correspond to the summary description provided by the thief. One is a man's head with an enormous ear, and the other the head of a woman whose hair is rolled into a kind of twist. The dimensions are approximately those of the statue which we previously restored to the Louvre. . . .

YES, THESE ARE BOTH OBJECTS STOLEN FROM THE LOUVRE!

At the Louvre . . . the curator in charge of these antiquities, M. Pottier, declared: "Yes, these are the two objects. . . . They are two fine works from the period corresponding to the end of the Roman Republic. . . ."

There was silence on September 7, except, in *Paris-Journal*:

A PLEA FROM OUR THIEF TO HIS "COLLEAGUE"

"Our Thief" has sent us the following letter:

"I do not want to leave France without once again sending you my thanks for the chivalrous manner in which you handled the little matter in which I was concerned. And I hope with all my heart that the Mona Lisa will be returned to you. I am not counting very heavily on such an event. However, let us hope that if its present possessor allows himself to be seduced by the thought of lucre, he will confide in your newspaper, whose staff has displayed toward me such a praiseworthy degree of discretion and honor. I can only urge the person at present holding Vinci's masterpiece to place himself entirely in your hands. He has a colleague's word for it that your good faith is above all suspicion.

"Adieu. I am about to leave France, to finish my novel. . . ."

It was probably during the day of the 7th that some-body talked, or that an anonymous letter was received by the police. That evening Apollinaire was visited in his apartment in the Rue Gros in Auteuil by a celebrated police detective named Robert and an assistant. The two police-

201

Guillaume Apollinaire

men proceeded to search the premises, and among Apollinaire's papers they found letters from Gery Pieret. It was the morning papers of the 9th that carried the news:

From *Le Matin,* September 9, 1911:

ARREST

Judge Drioux arrests an art critic, M. Guillaume Apollinaire,
in connection with the Egyptian statuettes stolen from the Louvre.

It was not without emotion and surprise that Paris learned last night of the arrest made by the Sureté in connection with the recent restitution of Phoenician statuettes stolen from the Louvre in 1907.

The mere name of the person arrested is enough to account for this reaction. He is M. Guillaume Kostrowky [*sic*], known in literature and art as Guillaume Apollinaire.

M. Guillaume Apollinaire, of Russian-Polish origin, is thirty years of age and lives in Auteuil, at 37 Rue Gros.

He is secretary of a literary review, *Les Marges,* and the author of a book entitled *L'Hérésiarque et Cie.,* which was a candidate for the last Prix Goncourt. He writes for numerous other magazines and reviews; indeed the readers of *Le Matin* have seen short stories by him in our department "Tales of a Thousand and One Mornings."

Such is the man who was arrested the night before last on the order of M. Drioux, on the charge of "harboring a criminal." What exactly are the charges against him? Both the Public Prosecutor and the police are making a considerable mystery of the affair.

"Without endangering progress already made," *Le Matin* was informed, "we can say nothing except that we are on the trail of a gang of international thieves who came to France for the purpose of despoiling our museums. M. Guillaume Apollinaire committed the error of giving shelter to one of these criminals. Was he aware of what he was doing? That is what we are to determine. In any case, we feel sure that we shall shortly be in possession of all

202

Apollinaire: Six

the secrets of the international gang, the name of one member of which has already been revealed to us."

In artistic and literary circles, however, where M. Guillaume Apollinaire is very well known and highly thought of, it is generally believed that the authorities may have been overhasty, and that before long the ex-Goncourt candidate will be exonerated.

The following is what we have been able to ascertain concerning M. Apollinaire's arrest.

THE ARREST

The afternoon of the day before yesterday, two persons presented themselves at 37 Rue Gros in Auteuil. They asked to be directed to the apartment of M. Guillaume Apollinaire, where they remained approximately an hour with the occupant, and then left. A few minutes later, M. Apollinaire joined the mysterious visitors in the street after handing his keys to the concierge of the building. The three men entered a taxi, which drove rapidly away in the direction of the Department of Justice.

The gentlemen who had conversed with M. Apollinaire were none other than two inspectors attached to the office of M. Hamard, assigned to take the writer to the Sureté for questioning.

M. Apollinaire was first received by M. Jouin, assistant chief of the Sureté, and was then soon brought before M. Drioux, the investigating magistrate.

BEFORE THE JUDGE

The interrogation of M. Apollinaire lasted well into the night. After the writer had provided the usual personal details, M. Drioux informed him that anonymous denunciations had been received by the Public Prosecutor's Office, stating that he had been in contact with the thief of the Phoenician statuettes, and also that he was a receiver of stolen goods, having recently returned, via *Paris-Journal,* two other busts belonging to the same collection.

On hearing these charges, M. Apollinaire protested vigorously, but shortly admitted that he was acquainted with the person who had committed the robbery.

203

Guillaume Apollinaire

"But," he added, "there is nothing in the law that forces me to reveal his name to the authorities."

"In that case," replied M. Drioux, "I charge you with complicity in harboring a criminal."

And the investigating magistrate immediately signed a warrant of arrest.

At that moment, M. Guillaume Apollinaire, aghast at the measure taken against him, exclaimed:

"All I can tell you is that I knew the thief of the statuettes. He is a young Belgian. I employed him as secretary for a few weeks. But when I learned that he was a thief I discharged him, and took it on myself to return, via *Paris-Journal,* the things he had stolen. What have I done wrong?"

And M. Apollinaire finally consented to reveal the name of his robber-secretary.

Nevertheless M. Drioux affirmed the warrant of arrest that he had just signed, and M. Apollinaire was forthwith placed in a cell.

With Apollinaire behind bars, where he had been kept for twenty-four hours before his arrest was even announced (M. Drioux later told reporters that this had been at Apollinaire's own request, "in order that the affair not be talked about"), the police revealed additional details. The detectives who had searched the flat in the Rue Gros had found a letter or letters written to Apollinaire by Gery Pieret which apparently confirmed the anonymous accusations that Pieret had stolen the statues and that Apollinaire had long been aware of his misdeeds. Furthermore: "The Sureté announced yesterday morning," said *Le Matin* of the 10th, "that new charges have been brought against M. Apollinaire. He has confessed that on Sunday he helped Gery Pieret flee from Paris. He went with him to the sta-

204

tion, bought him a railway ticket to Marseilles, and gave him 160 francs in cash. . . ." *Paris-Journal* printed an acid editorial entitled "La Gaffe":

> The police, doubtless to avenge themselves for certain all too justified sarcasms aimed in their direction for some time past, have, with their usual ineptitude, thrown their hooks into "someone who knew the thief" and who—a supreme boon for the officers of the law—happens to be a man of letters and a foreigner.

Pieret, claiming to be in Frankfurt and signing himself with the name under which Apollinaire had portrayed him in *L'Hérésiarque et Cie.*, wrote *Paris-Journal:*

> It is deeply regrettable, it is indeed sad, that a kindly, honest, and scrupulous man like M. Guillaume Apollinaire should be made to suffer a single moment because of the personal affairs of someone who was for him only a literary "subject."
> Baron Ignace d'Ormesan.

But the police persisted in believing, or in claiming to believe, that the vanished Gery Pieret belonged to an international band of crooks, whose purpose in coming to France had been to strip the country's museums, and who might have taken the Mona Lisa: it was because of his possible knowledge of this gang that Apollinaire was held for further questioning. Petitions protesting his arrest, signed by many artists and writers, were delivered to the police and the investigating magistrate. (Frantz Jourdain, an architect who was chairman of the Salon d'Automne and whom Apollinaire had treated rather roughly in his art writings, replied when asked to sign the petition: "What? My signature to get Apollinaire released? Never! To get him hanged, any time you like.") The prisoner's brother Albert visited him at the Santé Prison, spoke with him through a grille,   205 and told reporters about "the bare cell, No. 15, Section 11 in the new building," in which the poet was confined "like a big boy punished for being too charitable." "It is probably today," said *Le Matin* in its article of the tenth, "that M. Apollinaire will be questioned again by M. Drioux, this time in the presence of Maître José Théry, the attorney chosen by the writer. Will this be followed by M. Apollinaire's release? Who can tell. . . . ?"

There was a delay of one more day, and then,

From *Paris-Journal,* September 13, 1911:

THE THEFTS IN THE LOUVRE
RELEASE OF M. G. APOLLINAIRE

The Public Prosecutor realizes that the charges made against the author of L'Hérésiarque et Cie. *are without basis.*

. . . M. Guillaume Apollinaire's bad dream is ended. Yesterday M. Drioux, the investigating magistrate, finally . . . restored him to his mother and his innumerable friends.

THE INTERROGATION

It was at three o'clock that Apollinaire, pushing through the crowd of reporters, photographers, and friends from the worlds of journalism, letters, and the arts, come to bring him the comfort of their sympathy, entered the magistrate's office. A policeman accompanied him. Apollinaire—we deplore this inadmissable harshness on the part of the prison authorities—was handcuffed. Nor had the authorities thought of providing a taxi for his trip from the Santé to the Palais de Justice—taxis, apparently, are reserved for bigger game. . . . Apollinaire is penniless: he had stolen nothing, and lives solely by his pen.

Maître José Théry was present to defend his client. Two other attorneys, Maîtres Arthur Fraysse and Toussaint Luca, personal friends of the "accused," were also there, and shook hands with the individual described by the Sureté as "chief of an inter-

Apollinaire: Six

national gang come to France to despoil our museums." Even in the Sureté they write novels—very bad ones!

Apollinaire replied candidly and with good grace to the magistrate's questions. Now and again he smiled at the memory of the erratic and extraordinary Gery Pieret—the kindly, indulgent smile that his friends know so well.

The magistrate, fingering the meager dossier so laboriously compiled by the Sureté, first questioned him about the origin of his acquaintance with the famous "Baron d'Ormesan". . . .

The interrogation continued for about an hour and a half.

"You admit that even though you knew it was stolen, you kept that third statue, stolen in 1911, in your house from June 14 to August 21?"

"Certainly. It was in Pieret's suitcase. I kept everything— the man, the suitcase, and the statue in the suitcase. I assure you that I wasn't very happy about it, but I did not think that I was committing a serious sin". . . .

"Such a degree of indulgence surprises me," said M. Drioux, who had been following M. Apollinaire with interest.

"Here is part of my reason," said M. Apollinaire. "Pieret is a little bit my creation. He is very queer, very strange, and after studying him I made him the hero of one of the last short stories in my *L'Hérésiarque et Cie.* So it would have been a kind of literary ingratitude to let him starve. . . ."

Certain of the accusations brought forward by M. Drioux, some of them anonymous, were of a lunatic or would-be humorous type: he seemed to enjoy prolonging the questioning.

"You bought, very recently, it has been alleged, a castle in the *département* of the Drôme?"

"You must be referring to a castle in Spain. I have seen many of those evaporate."

"I have a letter here from someone who says that you borrowed two books from him, and that one of them, *La Cité gauloise,* you never returned."

"I imagine his reason for lending them to me was that I might read them. I haven't read them yet. I will return them to him as soon as I can."

Maître José Théry (he was a lawyer who wrote on legal subjects in the *Mercure de France*) had petitioned that his client be provisionally released, and M. Drioux finally announced that the interrogation was over and that the petition was granted. It was necessary, however, that Apollinaire return from the Palais de Justice to the Santé for the formalities of release. "It was not until five o'clock that Guillaume Apollinaire left the investigating magistrate's office," said *Paris-Journal.* "The crowd of sympathetic onlookers surged forward. As photographers, those slaves of the news, clicked their cameras, friendly hands were stretched out toward the man whom a policeman was leading away. There was consternation at the sight of Apollinaire being led handcuffed to the Souricière. [Literally 'Mousetrap'—the cell-block in the Palais de Justice.] Since he was to be released, could he not have been spared that useless humiliation?"

At the Santé, where this time Apollinaire was taken by taxi, it was learned that the messenger bearing the magistrate's order of release must, by law, cover the distance between the Palais de Justice and the prison on foot. After that final delay Apollinaire was released—granted provisional freedom—about seven o'clock. "The hour was growing late," said *Paris-Journal,* "and his mother was waiting."

One wonders what sort of a reception Apollinaire's mother gave him, in the suburbs. She had moved out of the

208

villa in Le Vésinet. "You know that I sold my house," she wrote in a letter of thanks to the lawyer Toussaint Luca, Apollinaire's old school friend from Nice who had attended the interrogation out of loyalty. "I now live in Chatou, not far from the station." As usual, Olga de Kostrowitzky poses a mystery: she had rented her earlier house from the landlord whose account of his tenants we quoted earlier—how could she have sold it? "You know," she wrote to Luca, "Wilhelm doesn't listen to me very much now that he is a man. Perhaps you have more influence on him than I. So scold him for seeing the kind of people he does. . . . Albert told me that you don't think much of his friends, and I think you are right." Gery Pieret, Picasso, Braque, Marie Laurencin—they were all the same to Olga, all riffraff. Little though her son might listen to her, there was certainly a tongue-lashing that night when he got home from the Santé. Did Olga de Kostrowitzky remember that her son Wilhelm had appeared before a magistrate on an earlier occasion? The "affair of the statuettes" was his second offense, his first having been the skip from the Stavelot hotel, undertaken at her command. Was it because he was a second offender, perhaps, that the police had been so severe? Was it to her, rather than to his "*mauvaises fréquentations*," that he owed his five days in the Santé?

Apollinaire's testimony at the interrogation brought about the collapse of the case which the police had been trying to build up against Gery Pieret as the possible thief who had taken the Mona Lisa on August 21 and against Apollinaire as accomplice or accessory. *Le Matin* for Sep-   209 tember 13 published an interview with Apollinaire in which he underlined that fact:

On August 21 I had definitely decided to ask Gery Pieret to leave my house. This fatal date had a great deal to do with my arrest. The police saw a connection between the theft of the Mona Lisa and the time that Pieret left my flat. Those two events took place on the 21st—a very disturbing coincidence, of which I am the victim. However, I can state that on the 21st Pieret was not absent from the Rue Gros. At the moment of getting rid of him I decided to make him a gift of a few engravings. "You can sell them," I told him. "That way you'll have a little money." We spent the morning selecting the engravings and at two o'clock Gery went out to a shop and bought some eggs and fruit which we ate for lunch. He was gone only a quarter of an hour, scarcely long enough to steal the Mona Lisa. . . .

Pieret, the rolling stone, disappeared from public notice. "He was arrested in Cairo at the end of 1913," Apollinaire wrote in his later account of the affair, "and the courts acquitted him. I was glad of this. The poor fellow was crazy rather than a criminal; the courts must have thought so, too."

As for the Mona Lisa, it was recovered in Florence in December, 1913. The thief proved to be a mad Italian housepainter named Vincenzo Peruggia, formerly employed in the Louvre, who had conceived it as his mission to return the picture to its native land. He had walked into the Louvre that Monday morning of August 21, 1911, chatted with workmen on duty whom he knew, found the Mona Lisa unguarded; he took it down, removed the frame on a staircase, and walked out of the museum with the picture under his blouse. After keeping it hidden for two years in his flat in Paris he carried it across the Franco-Italian border without difficulty in a suitcase "along with some old shoes" and offered it for sale to a Florentine picture dealer.

Before the picture was returned to France it was exhibited in Italy. It is said that, when the official appointed to take it from Rome to Milan was ensconced with it in his railway carriage, a colleague on hand at the station to see him off cried out: "Keep your eyes on that woman. I don't trust her an inch."

What was the effect of it all on Apollinaire? Something, perhaps, can be gathered from an article which he wrote the day after his release and which appeared in *Paris-Journal* on the 14th, its title borrowed from Silvio Pellico and from Alfred de Musset, another poet who had spent a few days in prison:

MES PRISONS

What are the impressions that a man can have when, knowing that he has never harbored a reprehensible thought, he nevertheless finds himself arrested and kept four days in prison?
It occurred to us that it would be interesting to ask this question of M. Guillaume Apollinaire, who as our readers know has just undergone this ordeal.

As soon as the heavy door of the Santé closed behind me, I had an impression of death. However, it was a bright night, and I could see that the walls of the courtyard in which I found myself were covered with climbing plants. Then I went through a second door; and when that closed I knew that the zone of vegetation was behind me, and I felt that I was now in some place beyond the bounds of the earth, where I would be utterly lost.

I was questioned several times, and a guard ordered me to

211

Guillaume Apollinaire

take my "kit": a coarse shirt, a towel, a pair of sheets, and a woolen blanket; and then I was taken through interminable corridors to my cell, No. 15, Section 11. There I had to strip naked in the corridor and was searched. I was then locked up. I slept very little, because of the electric light that is kept on all night in the cells.

Everybody knows what prison life is like: a purgatory of boredom, where you are alone and yet constantly spied on.

The food given by the state to its prisoners is not very abundant, but it is good.

Every morning there is bread, and, after the daily walk, broth with a few vegetables swimming in it.

At three in the afternoon there is a dish either of beans or potatoes; and on Sundays there is a piece of meat to vary the menu—a rather lean menu, perhaps, but of excellent quality.

At noon, instead of a meal there is served a strange drink called a *"tisane."*

I have tried in vain to identify the ingredients composing this drink. Its taste is reminiscent of copper, and its bitterness of the aloe, while in color it resembles white wine.

As reading matter they gave me a French translation of of *The Quadroon,* by Captain Mayne Reid, whose adventure novels I remember reading as a schoolboy. During my confinement I read *The Quadroon* twice, and despite certain shocking improbabilities I found it a book not to be dismissed contemptuously.

The first jolt that I experienced in the Santé came from an inscription scratched in the paint on the metal bed: "Dédé de Ménilmontant, in for murder."

I experienced a much more agreeable sensation when I read a few naive verses left in my cell by a former inmate who signed them "Myriès le chanteur."

I wrote some verses too, and poetry almost consoled me for the absence of liberty.

The special delivery letters and telegrams from my attorneys, Maîtres José Théry and Arthur Fraysse, lifted my spirits.

I learned that the Press was defending me, that writers who are the honor of France had spoken in my favor, and I felt less alone.

212

Apollinaire: Six

But all my misery came back on Tuesday, when I was "extracted" to be taken to the investigating magistrate.

The ride in the police car seemed extremely long. I was locked in a kind of cage where it was very hot. The guard told me that I would do well to take off my collar and put it in my pocket.

At the Palais de Justice they locked me in one of the narrow, stinking cells of the "Mousetrap," where I waited from eleven in the morning until three in the afternoon, my face glued to the bars, to see who passed by in the corridor. Four mortal hours: how they dragged! Eventually the long wait ended, and a guard led me, handcuffed, to the magistrate's office.

What a surprise to find myself suddenly stared at like a strange beast! All at once fifty cameras were aimed at me; the magnesium flashes gave a dramatic aspect to this scene in which I was playing a role. I soon recognized a few friends and acquaintances: Maître Toussaint Luca, André Salmon, René Bizet; and there were my attorneys beside me; I think that I must have laughed and wept at the same time.

During my wait in the "Mousetrap" I had put on my collar. But my regulation tie would not stay in place, probably because I didn't know how to fasten it. Finally I put it back in my pocket, after I had been photographed and when the guard had begun to move on, forcing me to follow him (since I was handcuffed to him).

There remains one obligation for me to fulfill: let me express here my thanks to all the newspapers, all the writers, all the artists who have given me such touching evidence of solidarity and esteem.

I hope that I may be forgiven for not yet having thanked each person separately. But that will be done, by letter or by personal call. However, mere observation of the simple rules of politeness will not make me consider that I have paid my debt of gratitude.

—*Guillaume Apollinaire.*

213

Guillaume Apollinaire

That concern about his tie. . . . It is an allusion to a photograph of himself, handcuffed and tieless, which the *Paris-Journal* photographer had unexpectedly snapped after the other photographers had finished, and which the paper had cruelly published the day before. One feels that he went further than merely observing "the simple rules of politeness" in alluding to it so obliquely. How happy was he to write his article for the newspaper which, behind the double façade of "wishing above all to restore the national treasures to the Louvre" and pouring scorn on Apollinaire's accusers, had nevertheless made such a mint of light-hearted publicity for itself out of his scare? He was, as always, short of cash. The day before, *Paris-Journal* had printed a rather poor short story of his, "La Favorite"; let us hope that for that and for "Mes Prisons" they temporarily filled his pockets. To give them credit, in their accounts of the affair they had mentioned *L'Hérésiarque et Cie.,* as often as they could, but there was never any hope that even such publicity would enable that very special collection of tales to sell widely.

But there was more to the story than that. As usual, not everything had appeared in the papers.

Fernande Olivier's account of the affair continues as follows:

The next day [the day following the turning-in of the statuettes to *Paris-Journal*] Apollinaire was wakened in his flat in the Rue Gros by the police. . . . No one told us anything. We had no news of him, and were worried, but we didn't dare call on him; and then one morning, about seven o'clock, someone rang Picasso's doorbell. . . . I went to the door. It was a policeman in plain clothes: he displayed a card from the Prefecture, introduced

M. APOLLINAIRE SORTANT DU CABINET DU JUGE

mis lui connais- | la! de restituer. Il n'en voulut rien fai
| Cependant, il ne cessait de me harceler
t le maigre dos- | questions, me demandant si je ne conna
ar la Sûreté, lui | sais pas un antiquaire qui pût lui ache
de ses relations | les objets d'art. Je refusai de lui indiqu

Apollinaire in Handcuffs, September 12, 1911

Guillaume Apollinaire

himself, and told Picasso that he was under orders to take him to appear at nine o'clock before the investigating magistrate. The trembling Picasso hastily dressed; I had to help him—he was beside himself with fear. The policeman was nice enough, smiling, wily, trying to find out what he could, but we were on our guard and said nothing. Picasso went with him to the Prefecture, not very clear as to what was wanted of him. He long remembered that awful ride in the Pigalle—Halle-aux-Vins bus; it was against regulations for a policeman to take a taxi at his client's expense.

When they arrived at the depot there was a long wait, and then Picasso was ushered into the office of the investigating magistrate, where he saw Apollinaire—pale, disheveled, unshaven, his collar torn, his shirt open at the neck, no tie, haggard, a sad sight. After two days of arrest, subjected to long grillings like a criminal, he had confessed everything they asked him to. The truth was the least part of his admissions. What wouldn't he have admitted in order to be left in peace!

Picasso was so affected by the sight of him that he became distracted; he was even more terrified than he had been earlier, when he had been unable to dress himself for trembling. The scene that he later recounted to me passes description. He too said everything the examiner wanted him to say. Besides, Guillaume had admitted so many things, both true and false, that he had irretrievably implicated his friend. Whom would he not have implicated, in his confusion? They both wept, it seems, in the presence of the fatherly judge, who was hard put to it to keep a stern countenance in the face of their childish sorrow.

It was said at the time that Picasso had denied his friend, pretended not to know him. That is entirely false. He did not let him down—on the contrary; and his friendship for Apollinaire showed itself at that moment stronger than ever.

It was indeed commonly recounted in Apollinaire's circle that in addition to his terror, and his "impression of death" when the prison door closed behind him, he had had to experience the peculiarly bitter despair that comes

Apollinaire: Six

from the defection of a close friend. Despite Fernande Olivier's loyal denial, the story gradually found its way into print. The painter Albert Gleizes, who was able the following January, because of his friendship with an assistant prosecutor, to have Apollinaire's provisional release turned into a dismissal of the indictment, wrote in 1946: "Guillaume had suffered very much in the course of the interrogations that the investigating magistrate had subjected him to. Especially in his affections. Didn't one of his dearest friends deny him when they were brought face to face, losing his head so completely as to declare that he did not know him? Apollinaire spoke to me about this with bitterness, and without hiding his dismay."

In 1952 was printed Apollinaire's version of the whole affair, written to a friend in 1915. "They arrested me," it goes on (after the sections quoted earlier), "thinking that I knew the whereabouts of the Mona Lisa because I had had a 'secretary' who stole statues from the Louvre. I admitted having had the 'secretary,' but refused to betray him; they grilled me and threatened to search the homes of all persons close to me. Eventually the situation became exhausting and terrible. Finally, in order to avoid causing great trouble to my *amie* and to my mother and brother, I was compelled to tell about X——: I did not describe his actual part in the affair, I merely said that he had been taken advantage of, and that he had never known that the antiquities he bought came from the Louvre. Next day, confrontation with X——, who denied knowing anything whatever about the affair. I thought I was lost, but the investigating magistrate saw that I had done nothing, and was simply being victim-

217

ized by the police because I had refused to betray the fugitive to them, and he authorized me to question the witness; and using the maieutics dear to Socrates I quickly forced X——to admit that everything I had said was true."

Years after the "confrontation," Picasso himself was finally quoted about it.

From *Paris-Presse*, June 20, 1959:

PICASSO NOW CONFESSES

Gilbert Prouteau is preparing an art film in which the great contemporary painters will play themselves. Last week he went to solicit the participation of Picasso.

"I know you," the Seigneur of Vauvenargues said to him. "You are the one who taught me that there is such a thing as remorse, when I saw your film on Apollinaire last year. During the hour I spent watching it, I was thirty years old again. And I think I shed a tear or two. . . ."

"Memories, Maître?"

"Yes, but not the kind you are thinking of. I can admit it now. I did not behave very well with 'Apo' on one occasion. It was after the affair of the theft of the Mona Lisa. Guillaume had returned the picture in care of a newspaper, but despite that precaution our little group was being watched rather carefully. We wanted above all to repeat our offense. We were at the age of the gratuitous act. Such childishness amused us, and the idea of owning a series of little statues for a few days delighted me. It wasn't robbery, just a good joke. No sooner said than done. But this time the police were ready. I took fright and wanted to throw the package into the Seine. 'Apo' was against it.

" 'They don't belong to us,' he said.

"And he got himself arrested. Naturally, they confronted us. I can see him there now, with his handcuffs and his look of a big placid boy. He smiled at me as I came in, but I made no sign.

"When the judge asked me: 'Do you know this gentleman?'

218

I was suddenly terribly frightened, and without knowing what I was saying, I answered: 'I have never seen this man.'

"I saw Guillaume's expression change. The blood ebbed from his face. I am still ashamed...."

An odd bit of reporting! Apollinaire had in his youth been called "Kostro," but did Picasso or anyone else ever call him "Apo"? And could Picasso have said that "Guillaume had returned the *picture* by way of a newspaper"? Of course this was forty-eight years later; Picasso was now seventy-eight; allowance has to be made for the passage of so long a time. Or is the error an unconscious attempt to confuse the facts and thus weaken the impact of the episode that is the story's point? Be that as it may, M. Gilbert Prouteau, the producer who made the documentary film on Apollinaire, tells the story a little differently. In his version, he was running the film off for Picasso; as the moment of the "affair of the statuettes" approached, the Master became tense; when the commentary passed over it tactfully, without mention of the famous "confrontation," there was a visible relaxing, and at the end of the screening a cordial smile, and a handshake, and: "Come and see me some time; I'd like to give you a picture."

At the very least, it makes one remember Fernande's words about the *"bande Picasso"*: "Communion of mind, of art, often of ideas. Rarely communion of the heart, of generosity. And so many protestations of admiration, of friendship, in which sincerity played so small a part...." The poem "Les Fiançailles," written about 1908, testifies to the "communion of mind, of art, often of ideas," that existed between Apollinaire and Picasso, and the two men

219

remained "friends" for the rest of Apollinaire's life; but one suspects that the "friendship" was subject to the conditions mentioned by Fernande.

"At the time, the affair made a lot of noise," Apollinaire wrote in 1915.

All the newspapers printed my picture. But I could very well have done without that publicity. Because, although I was passionately defended by most of the newspapers, at the beginning I was attacked, sometimes ignobly, by the anti-Semites, who cannot imagine a Pole not being a Jew. Léon Daudet went so far as to deny having voted for me for the Prix Goncourt. . . .

Such is the story, strange, incredible, tragic, and amusing all at once, the upshot of which is that I was the only person arrested in France for the theft of the Mona Lisa. The police did everything they could to justify their action; they grilled my concierge and my neighbors, asking whether I brought home little girls or little boys or whatever. If my life had been the slightest bit questionable they wouldn't have let me go, the honor of the corporation being at stake. It made me understand the man who said that if he were accused of stealing the bells of Notre Dame he would take to his heels immediately. I will add that no apology was ever extended to me, but that most of the newspapers held me up as a model of hospitality. . . .

Such is the background of the six little poems written in the Santé. . . .

He was referring to the six short pieces that he wrote in prison and published in the collected volume, *Alcools,* under the title "A la Santé"—the sparse and poignant wreckage that the three-week storm of the affair had cast up on the shore. The Santé poems are favorites with readers who prefer Apollinaire at his most direct; and even those who try to harden their hearts to the self-pity and appeals

220

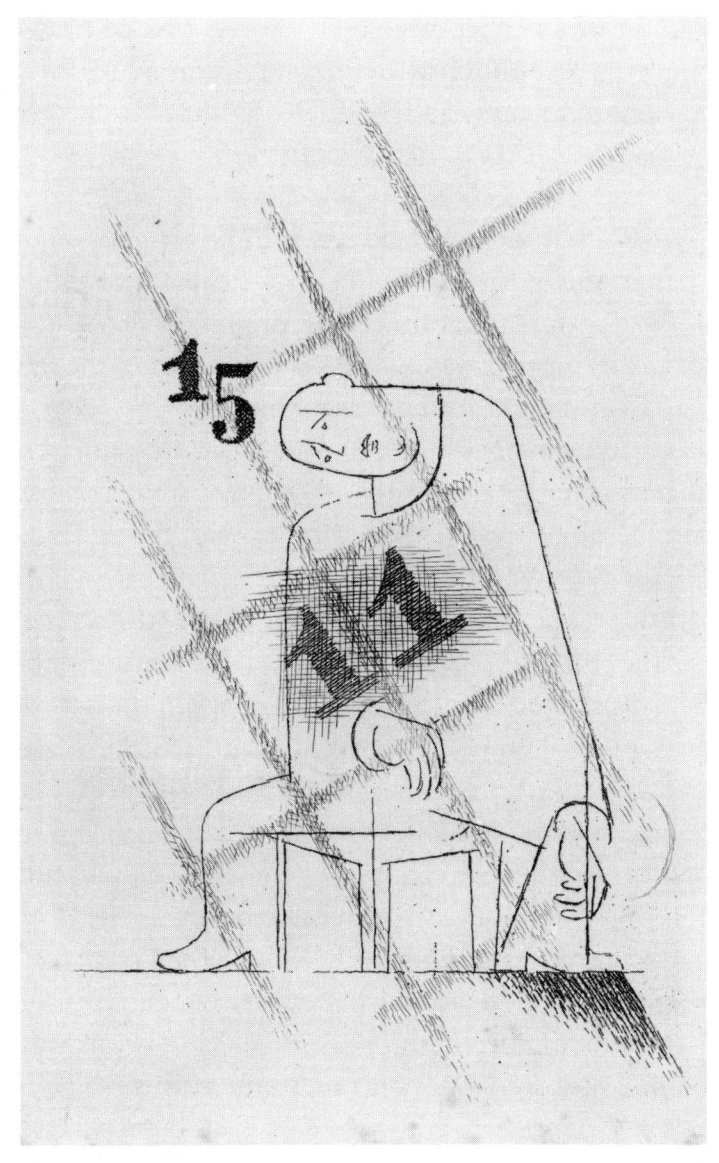

Illustration for "La Santé" (Alcools)*, etching by Marcoussis*

221

Guillaume Apollinaire

to God of an irresponsible Bohemian whose near-criminal prank had caught up with him are disarmed by the suffering obvious in the lines and especially by the closing apostrophe:

Nous sommes seuls dans ma cellule
Belle clarté Chère raison

One of the Santé poems is linked to two slightly later poems, one of them more famous than any of those written in the prison, and commemorating another event that was also, in its way, a consequence of the "affair of the statuettes."

During the months that followed his provisional release, Apollinaire's life was badly out of joint. His subsequent career in the war was to show him as possessed of considerable courage both physical and moral; but nothing bites more savagely into the personality—especially that of a man whose position in society is as equivocal as Apollinaire's: bastard, foreigner, writer of erotica, poet—than first-hand evidence and public proclamation that society does indeed consider one contemptible and expendable. *"Monsieur Apollinaire, vous êtes une canaille!"* one of the police officials is said to have shouted at him; and for someone of Apollinaire's carefully built-up name and personality this is to be made to tremble on the brink of the abyss. In his anecdotal column in the *Mercure de France* for October 16 he referred wryly to "the events which recently obliged a resident of the Right Bank to take a room on the Left Bank;" and someone who met him at this time wrote that he was "depressed, considered himself deserted by all, irretrievably ruined; he had been much affected by his incarceration in the Santé and the unconcealed pleasure that certain malicious fellow-writers had taken in his plight."

222

Apollinaire: Six

In October he moved out of the flat in the Rue Gros that had been searched by the police, into another in the nearby Rue LaFontaine, Marie Laurencin's street, still in Auteuil; and it was Marie Laurencin, that autumn, "one late afternoon, as a few young painters were chatting, leaving a poetry recital at the Salon d'Automne," who urged the painter Albert Gleizes to do what he could with his friends in the Department of Justice to have Apollinaire's indictment dismissed—"because Guillaume is worried sick about it." One of the reasons for his being "worried sick" was that he feared being expelled from France as an undesirable foreigner. No sooner was Gleizes successful, in January, 1912, than Apollinaire was threatened again: the police seemed to be about to prosecute, on grounds of immorality, the publisher Briffault and everyone else connected with the series *Les Maîtres de l'amour,* for which Apollinaire had long been doing translations and prefaces. Gleizes's friend the assistant prosecutor had to bring his influence to bear once more.

But even though doubly rescued from the hands of the law, Apollinaire was not destined to enjoy for long his greater nearness to Marie Laurencin in Auteuil. Almost immediately after his move their intimacy ended. It had been a stormy liaison: the chronicles of their friends abound in anecdotes of discord. But apparently it was Marie's ultra-respectable mother who hastened the end. Her health was declining, she was aging rapidly, her scorn for Apollinaire as one of the ne'er-do-wells with whom she hated to see her daughter associated had been triumphantly justified by his imprisonment. Probably a certain quality of brusqueness

223

and brutality that Apollinaire seems to have displayed toward women—the testimony is unanimous that women did not, in general, find him sexually sympathetic—was exacerbated by his recent trials; at the end he seems to have given Marie no good reason to remain.

"Why, Marie, didn't you marry Guillaume?" her friend Louise Faure-Favier asked her thirty years later. "You knew him how long?"

"Since 1907. At the beginning, there was a question of marriage. But Madame de Kostrowitzky, his mother, thought I wasn't rich enough. And after 1911 it was my mother who wouldn't hear of Guillaume. They took turns."

The former lovers did not immediately stop seeing one another, and following their break love poetry poured from Apollinaire as it had during the years of his involvement with Annie Playden. With a difference, however: now the poet laments not that he has been *mal-aimé*—inadequately loved—but that his beloved, with whom he has tasted love to the full, has left him. Four of these love poems about Marie Laurencin are in *Alcools*. Apollinaire himself enumerates them in a letter to Madeleine Pagès in 1915:

"Cors de chasse" evokes the same agonizing memories as "Zone," "Le Pont Mirabeau," and "Marie" the most agonizing of all, I think.

If "Marie" is the most agonizing, "Le Pont Mirabeau" is the most famous, printed in all the anthologies, and it is those two that form the most direct link between Apollinaire's days in prison and his loss of Marie Laurencin. For in a manuscript in Apollinaire's hand, written in the Santé itself, the draft of the third Santé poem, beginning

Le Pont Mirabeau

Sous le pont Mirabeau coule la Seine
Et nos amours
Faut-il qu'il m'en souvienne
La joie venait toujours après la peine

Vienne la nuit sonne l'heure
Les jours s'en vont je demeure

Les mains dans les mains restons face à face
Tandis que sous
Le pont de nos bras passe
Des éternels regards l'onde si lasse

Vienne la nuit sonne l'heure
Les jours s'en vont je demeure

L'amour s'en va comme cette eau courante
L'amour s'en va
Comme la vie est lente
Et comme l'Espérance est violente

Vienne la nuit sonne l'heure
Les jours s'en vont je demeure

Passent les jours et passent les semaines
Ni temps passé
Ni les amours reviennent
Sous le pont Mirabeau coule la Seine

Vienne la nuit sonne l'heure
Les jours s'en vont je demeure

Mirabeau Bridge

Under Mirabeau Bridge flows the Seine.
Why must I be reminded again
Of our love?
Doesn't happiness issue from pain?

Bring on the night, ring out the hour.
The days wear on but I endure.

Face to face, hand in hand, so
That beneath
The bridge our arms make the slow
Wave of our looking can flow.

Then call the night, bell the day.
Time runs off but I must stay.

And love runs down like this
Water, love runs down.
How slow life is,
How violent hope is.

Come night, strike hour.
Days go, I endure.

Nor days nor any time detain.
Time past or love
Can not come again.
Under Mirabeau Bridge flows the Seine.

Bring on the night, ring out the hour.
Days wear away I endure.

Translated by William Meredith

225

Guillaume Apollinaire

Dans une fosse comme un ours
Chaque matin je me promène

contains the line

Quand donc finira la semaine

that appears in "Marie"; and it ends with two lines that are, with one syllable omitted, the refrain in "Le Pont Mirabeau".

The "affair of the statuettes" was a background to a good deal more than "the six little poems written in the Santé." As we shall see, it is scarcely too much to say that it was a background to everything that happened to Apollinaire during the seven more years he had to live.

To quote Fernande Olivier for a last time—to quote her this time *de travers,* as someone who though she often gets things triumphantly right, sometimes puts things quite hopelessly wrong:

Picasso and Apollinaire . . . had acted like children. Like children they quickly forgot all their anguish as soon as the indictment was dismissed and they felt themselves safe. They remembered only the humorous side of that eventful episode.

One doubts that that was true of Picasso; certainly it was far from true of Apollinaire.

226

Apollinaire: Six

Seven

Everybody wrote or talked about the Mona Lisa at the time of its theft: all kinds of contemporary references to it keep turning up in places both likely and unlikely. In the midst of Odilon Redon's journal, *A Soi-Même,* for example, sandwiched in between paragraphs concerning the loss of a family property and a letter to a Monsieur X—— on the meaninglessness of the word "humanism" as applied to a work of art, one suddenly comes upon a paean to the stolen masterpiece:

1911, September. The Mona Lisa is a consecrated thing. By this I mean that in the course of time, over four centuries, she has received the tribute or the admiration of the masters. This is not because of her smile; but if painting in the strictest sense of the word, in its essence, aims at producing, on a plane surface, with the help of lights and shadows, one of the elements of nature, even a human face with spiritual radiance, in the greatest possible relief, this aim is achieved by Leonardo—sublimely, powerfully, miraculously.

The episode inspired the German writer Georg Heym to quite a different performance—the long short story "Der Dieb," in which the thief who steals the Mona Lisa begs her to stop smiling at him. Max Jacob wrote a characteristic prose-poem, entitled "L'Ame de la Joconde," about an alarm clock called "le Jocond" (grammatically the masculine form of "la Joconde"). The clock "has the soul of La

227

Guillaume Apollinaire

Joconde, and stops or goes in accordance with the adventures of that unhappy painting." Mona Lisa's "mysterious smile keeps watch at night" at the bedside of the baroness who owns the clock. Newspapers all over the world carried their more or less accurate accounts of the theft. Apollinaire was mentioned in many of them. *The New York Times* on September 17, 1911, let its readers know that "M. Apollinaire, a well known Russian literary man living in Paris, was recently arrested and underwent searching examination." The Parisian press did so thorough a job of attaching his name to the robbery that Louise Faure-Favier, writing in 1945, could still say: "Guillaume Apollinaire abruptly became famous throughout the entire world. He was thought of as the man who had stolen the Mona Lisa. Even today there are Parisians who believe it, and who are a little disappointed to learn that Apollinaire had nothing to do with the theft."

He was also attacked in print by xenophobes and anti-Semites. Many people supposed him to be a Jew. When his brother Albert had visited him in the Santé, he had given a reporter from *L'Aurore* an account of the Kostrowitzky family's great respectability:

Many inaccurate reports have recently been published following my brother's arrest. It is a sad business having to correct them. For example, it has been claimed that he comes of a Jewish family. Nothing could be more false: we are Roman Catholics. My brother and I made our first communion; we were educated in France by the Marianists, the same order that used to be in charge of the Collège Stanislas in Paris. My mother was a pupil of the Dames du Sacré Coeur, a French order, in the convent of Trinità dei Monti in Rome, which admitted only young ladies of noble family. Our family comes from Minsk, in Lithuania. Several among our ancestors served in the Russian army. One of our great-uncles died during the Sebastopol campaign. Our father distinguished himself during the Crimean War. Later, having retired to Rome, he became *cameriere segreto* to Pope Pius IX.

Such was Albert's "correction" of earlier inaccuracies. Was it he, or the reporter, who placed Minsk in Lithuania? For "father," of course, read "grandfather": perhaps that error, too, was the reporter's. Throughout Apollinaire's life he was constantly spoken of as being Jewish. The mistake probably had its principal source in his mother's continued liaison with Jules Weil, but it was given currency by anti-Semites who, as Apollinaire put it, "couldn't imagine a Pole not being a Jew," and also by someone who knew the truth: Max Jacob, who had been converted to Roman Catholicism after seeing a vision of the Virgin in his room in Montmartre, took an odd delight in spreading the rumor of his Catholic friend's Jewishness.

Many in Apollinaire's circle of "friends" apparently could not let the subject of his arrest alone. Paul Léautaud, one day, greeted him with the seemingly innocuous words: "*Comment va la santé?*" And André Salmon, with a transparent pretence of regret, tells us in his memoirs what *he* said:

Guillaume had been released, but there was still much talk about the affair of the Phoenician statuettes. A man of his distinction could not help being bitter at the thought that he had been questioned at length by the magistrate: it choked him—he was like a man who had swallowed a fishbone. I called on him: he asked me to admire his monkey, a fine specimen he had recently acquired. This tame macaque was merrily eating an apple, playfully jumping from one piece of furniture to another. His master, praising its gentleness, observed: "You see, he doesn't really have to stay in his cage." Some devil prompted me to reply: "Well, at least he can be *provisionally* released." Whereupon Picasso, who was present, angrily grabbed the animal by its blue behind and thrust it back into its cage. People sometimes react in strange ways.

Exploited by the press, deserted by his mistress, plagued by wits, Apollinaire was in a depressed state that caused concern to those who were his true friends; and one of these, André Billy (who at the time of the present writing is the literary critic of the newspaper *Le Figaro*), thought of a device that might restore the poet's enthusiasm: the establishment of a magazine of which he might be editor, a recapturing, perhaps, of the amusing days of *Le Festin d'Esope*. In his account of the founding of this magazine, whose first number appeared quite promptly, in February, 1912, with the title *Les Soirées de Paris,* André Billy generously gives partial credit to others:

> Apollinaire's stay in prison left him for a long time with a feeling of terror, and we did our best as friends to help him get over it. He had become a public figure, but he had reached that position via the door that bears the inscription "All hope abandon, ye who enter here." He was marked for life, and even the war, his courage, and his wound would never succeed in silencing certain persons who, out of ignorance, envy, stupidity, or self-interest, banded against him and continually attacked him as an artist and as a man. He was harassed by slanders to the end of his days, but was too proud to complain.
>
> To a certain secret extent, the *Soirées de Paris* was founded by Guillaume's closest friends with a view to helping him at this time of crisis. There were four of us in addition to him—André Salmon, René Dupuy (Dalize), André Tudesq, and myself. Our

230

first conference took place at the Café Flore. I suggested the title, the financial arrangements, and the make-up, and these were accepted. Dupuy, who had great hopes of financial success from the enterprise . . . was appointed managing editor. He was not naturally qualified for this position, but he had more free time than the rest of us and was more zealous, and he was determined to get the best possible return for his efforts. He was confident that sooner or later the *Soirées de Paris* would be a paying proposition, and he continually reminded us that the very successful *Mercure de France* had also been founded by a group of writers. Salmon, Tudesq, and I thought of our activity in connection with the *Soirées* simply as a temporary diversion, and Dupuy's long-range plans made us smile. But when we saw that our skepticism annoyed him we straightened our faces. I remember how upset our managing editor was by Guillaume's first article, entitled "The Subject in Modern Painting." "It's stupid, it's absurd," he cried indignantly—of all of us he was the one who spoke most bluntly to Apollinaire. "You'll ruin us with your Cubism. The *Soirées* was not founded to support the ignorant and pretentious painters you like to be with because they flatter you. Except for four or five, they're completely worthless."

I confess that I shared Dupuy's opinion of Cubism, and I had frequent arguments with Apollinaire. He displayed an extraordinary talent for splitting hairs, but when pushed to the wall he would agree that many of the painters he praised were undeserving. "But," he added, "when you support a revolutionary movement in art you would hamper its development if you were to distinguish between the various artists belonging to it, in the name of good taste. It is my duty to praise them all, without distinction. Posterity will know how to separate the good from the bad." However, concerning certain painters he would never yield an inch, even though the sole merit of their works consisted in a kind of offensive incongruousness—I am thinking particularly of the lugubriously Germanic nightmares painted with maniacal meticulousness by the Italian Chirico. Apollinaire would burst into laughter when he looked at them, but he consistently refused,

231

Guillaume Apollinaire

to my great exasperation, to admit that these productions of a hypochondriacal furniture-mover were devoid of any truly artistic quality.[1]

Apollinaire, with his somewhat dim perception of painting, nonetheless differed from most of the literary men around him in having any interest in art at all. According to one experienced observer, artistic perception and interest in the arts are generally at their dullest and lowest in two groups: theologians, and those professionally concerned with literature (as distinct from "creative writers")—especially, in the United States, professors of English. André Billy was, and remains, a man of the pen. With him and others as co-editors of the *Soirées de Paris,* Apollinaire stood little chance of stimulating any intra-magazine enthusiasm for Chirico's "nightmares" and other contemporary works; it was only later, when the magazine changed ownership, that he was free to devote most of the magazine to promotion of modern art. As we have seen, Apollinaire's early championing of his artist friends, which has brought him so much fame, reflected his excitement over the bold novelty [2] of it all and his pleasure in their company, rather than any acuteness of eye; but whatever its source, this

[1] Apropos of Apollinaire's "duty" to praise all the "revolutionary" painters, "without distinction," he actually wrote to Ardengo Soffici in 1912: "Don't you think that to make it possible for a new conception of art to assert itself, mediocre works must appear along with the sublime? It is for that reason, and for the sake of great artists like Picasso, that I champion Braque and the Cubists in my writings."

[2] He comes closest to seeing, or admitting, this in an essay on "The New Painting," in the *Soirées:* "For my part I admire extremely the modern school of painting because it seems to me the most daring that has ever existed."

Apollinaire: Seven

championing was to make the later issues of the magazine much more distinguished than their predecessors.

Still, any issue of any magazine that contains a poem by Apollinaire can scarcely be said to be without distinction, and, as had been the case with the *Festin d'Esope,* it was the frequent appearance of Apollinaire's verse that shed the greatest luster on those early numbers of the *Soirées.* The first issue was irradiated by the beauty of "Le Pont Mirabeau," that haunting lament for the lost Marie Laurencin, which here made its original appearance, accompanied by another, lesser poem, "Per te praesentit aruspex," of which a manuscript copy has been found inscribed to quite a different lady, one who still basks, in Paris, in the memory of her brief romance with Apollinaire in 1912 when he was on the rebound from Marie. "Le Pont Mirabeau" contrasts strikingly with the miscellaneous remainder of the contributions, including Apollinaire's own jejune essay "The Subject in Modern Painting"—"The subject no longer counts, or, if it counts, it counts for little. . . . A Picasso studies an object as a surgeon dissects a cadaver"; and throughout the next sixteen issues a similar contrast makes itself felt whenever verses by Apollinaire appear.

The monthly requirements of the magazine fulfilled André Billy's hopes: Apollinaire became busy and regained some of his normal cheerfulness of manner. Billy attributes the rise in his spirits partly to the editorial habit of eating and drinking together:

The editors of the *Soirées de Paris* had several Bacchic meetings *chez* Baty [a restaurant in Montparnasse], at which Apollinaire played a leading role, and we would forgather also at Billancourt and Ville d'Avray. There was also a dinner at Tudesq's flat in the Rue Bonaparte, and I remember that on that occasion Apollinaire forbade us to address even the slightest word to the lady of the house, lest we distract her from her saucepans. It might be hard to believe that he would go to such a length, were his passion for culinary matters not so well known. I wonder whether he was perhaps not more brilliantly competent in this field than in the plastic arts. He was versed in the cooking of every nation— Provençal, Chinese, Jewish, Spanish, Russian, Arab, Serbian, Greek, Polish, and Turkish. He placed Italian and French cooking above the rest, and condemned British cuisine. He classified me as an advocate of the latter because of my deplorable liking for red meat. When he was present, table talk was confined to culinary matters; when he was a guest, his criticism of the various dishes would be given politely, but he never compromised in his opinions, and always found a way to suggest, in the midst of his praise, that something might have been done better. He did this so charmingly, he was so inventive in finding ways to criticize without offending, that one could not help thinking him a born diplomat. He was really wonderfully delightful on such occasions.

In October, 1911, he had moved to the Rue Lafontaine, Marie Laurencin's street; and now, less than a year later, he found this new house intolerable in his loneliness. Making a radical change of neighborhood, he signed a lease on a small top-floor flat at 202 Boulevard Saint-Germain. Not very surprisingly, perhaps, No. 202 happens to be on the corner of a street called the Rue Saint-Guillaume; it is only a hundred yards or so from the church of Saint-Germain-des-Prés and two literary cafés, the Deux Magots and the Flore. The new flat was not to be available until January, and in the interim he avoided the Rue Lafontaine, and lived for weeks at a time with friends.

234

Apollinaire: Seven

One of these, Robert Delaunay, had been described by Apollinaire barely two years before in *L'Intransigeant* as the painter of "canvases which unfortunately look as though they commemorated an earthquake"—a phrase that referred to Delaunay's now-famous series of paintings of the Eiffel Tower and the church of Saint-Séverin. Since then, however, the two had become friendly; and now, in 1912, when Delaunay was on his way to developing "a much more purely abstract kind of painting with color as its principal element," Apollinaire wrote of his large canvas, "La Ville de Paris," as "the most important picture in the Salon [d'Automne]." He was so impressed that he added: "No longer is there any question of experimentation, archaism, or Cubism." Shortly before, he had written: "Possibly it is too late to speak of Cubism. The time for experimentation is passed. Our young artists are interested now in creating definitive works." This qualification of Cubism as old-fashioned and nondefinitive, one of the many weird formations that dot the moonscape of Apollinaire's art criticism, he was to repeat yet once again this same year. Apparently finding it necessary to invent a name for Delaunay's kind of painting, he performed the baptism in a lecture given at the largest Cubist exhibition, the Section d'Or, in October, 1912. Coolly announcing his subject as "The Dismemberment of Cubism," the lecturer declared to the assembled artists and their friends that Cubism was "dismembered" because of a new art invented by Robert Delaunay and practiced also by Fernand Léger, Francis Picabia, and Marcel Duchamp; Picasso, too, had a place in it, "because of the luminosity of his works." This is the

235

lecture that Jacques Villon quite accurately remembers as having had "nothing whatever to do with painting." Marcel Duchamp, who knew Apollinaire at this time, puts it more generally: "Apollinaire was a very charming man. Of course he was always sounding off on all kinds of subjects he knew nothing about."

In the December 1912 issue of the *Soirées* Apollinaire printed some of Delaunay's notes on painting that have since become well known especially for their use of the phrase "simultaneous contrast of colors" ("Simultaneism" is another name sometimes given to Delaunay's "Orphic" style of 1912). The same month, as a poem-preface to the catalogue of Delaunay's exhibition at the gallery Der Sturm in Berlin, Apollinaire wrote a poem, "Les Fenêtres," the title being that of one of the pictures.

André Billy writes as follows about the composition of "Les Fenêtres":

Let me quote another example of [Apollinaire's] way of working. One day he and Dupuy sat with me *chez* Crucifix, Rue Daunou, drinking vermouth. Suddenly Guillaume burst out laughing: he had completely forgotten to write the preface to Robert Delaunay's catalogue, which he had promised to mail that very day at the latest. "Waiter, quick, paper, pen, ink!" The three of us got the job done in no time. Guillaume began at once:
Du rouge et vert tout le jaune se meurt
and stopped there. Then Dupuy dictated:
Quand chantent les aras dans les forêts natales
Apollinaire transcribed that faithfully, and added:
Abatis de pihis
And once again he stopped.
Then I dictated:
Il y a un poème à faire sur l'oiseau qui n'a qu'une aile

236

"Windows" ("Les Fenêtres simultanées"), painting by Delaunay, 1912

237

Guillaume Apollinaire

That was close to something I remembered from *Alcools,* but Apollinaire wrote it down without hesitation.

"It would be a good idea," I said, "since the matter is urgent, to send your preface as a *message "téléphonique."* [3]

And that is why the following line reads:

Nous l'enverrons en message téléphonique

I no longer remember all the details of this strange collaboration, but I cay say with certainty that a great part of the preface for Delaunay's catalogue was composed that way. Guillaume called compositions of this kind "conversation poems."

Robert Delaunay and his wife Sonia, also a painter, promptly challenged that account by Billy when it appeared in print, claiming that "Les Fenêtres" had been written in their studio one day when they were eating sea urchins *(oursins)* and pointing to the inclusion of the word *oursin* in the poem as proof, along with mention of other remarkable features of the studio—a curtain, a window, and an old pair of tan shoes. Probably the Delaunays showed a certain lack of understanding here. They apparently failed to realize how wildly and casually any poet may set down a first draft of any poem: Billy's remark that "Les Fenêtres" came "in large part" out of that "strange collaboration" in the restaurant allows for a great deal of revision, some of it perhaps done in the Delaunays' studio—revision that made

[3] Let no one think that a "message téléphonique" is an ordinary telephone call. It is a means of communicating with people who have no telephone. "Something like a telegram," a friend obligingly informs me, "but cheaper when done within Paris. You ask the telephone operator to connect you with the post office nearest the person you wish to get in touch with. You dictate your message to the postal clerk, who sees to it that it is delivered within the hour"—one of the blessings of the national ministry of the "PTT" (Postes, Télégraphes, et Téléphones, recently rechristened Postes et Télécommunications.)

Apollinaire: Seven

the poem finally into the not at all casual thing it is. It may have begun as a "conversation poem," but in its definitive form it is rather a series of associations. The images it contains could indeed be inspired by Delaunay's colorful, prismatic, many-faceted picture. Unlike Apollinaire's early verses on "The Virgin with the Bean Flower in Cologne," "Les Fenêtres" really is one of those poems that justify Baudelaire's saying that "The best *compte-rendu* of a picture can well be a sonnet or an elegy."

Apollinaire himself always thought highly of "Les Fenêtres." "I am very very fond of 'Les Fenêtres,'" he wrote to a friend during the war. ". . . It reflects a totally new esthetic. . . ."

During the months when Apollinaire was interested in Delaunay he was also engaged on something else—a project he had long meditated and which, now finally realized, combined his new esthetic ideas with those of all his years before.

As far back as 1904, in the *Festin d'Esope,* he had announced the imminent publication of a collected volume of his poems, to be called *Le Vent du Rhin;* and in 1905, in the unique issues of the *Revue immoraliste* and *Les Lettres modernes,* he had promised that it would be followed by another volume, *La Chanson du Mal-Aimé.* The announcements then ceased, and neither volume appeared. In 1910 *Paris-Journal* advised its readers that Apollinaire was putting the finishing touches to a volume of poems to be called *Eau de Vie,* and when Marcoussis etched his portraits of Apollinaire in 1912 he included in one of them *Eau de Vie*

Les Fenêtres

Du rouge au vert tout le jaune se meurt
Quand chantent les aras dans les forêts natales
Abatis de pihis
Il y a un poème à faire sur l'oiseau qui n'a qu'une aile
Nous l'enverrons en message téléphonique
Traumatisme géant
Il fait couler les yeux
Voilà une jolie jeune fille parmi les jeunes Turinaises
Le pauvre jeune homme se mouchait dans sa cravate blanche
Tu soulèveras le rideau
Et maintenant voilà que s'ouvre la fenêtre
Araignées quand les mains tissaient la lumière
Beauté pâleur insondables violets
Nous tenterons en vain de prendre du repos
On commencera à minuit
Quand on a le temps on a la liberté
Bigorneaux Lotte multiples Soleils et l'Oursin du couchant
Une vieille paire de chaussures jaunes devant la fenêtre
Tours
Les Tours ce sont les rues
Puits
Puits ce sont les places
Puits
Arbres creux qui abritent les Câpresses vagabondes
Les Chabins chantent des airs à mourir
Aux Chabines marronnes
Et l'oie oua-oua trompette au nord
Où les chasseurs de ratons
Raclent les pelleteries
Etincelant diamant
Vancouver
Où le train blanc de neige et de feux nocturnes fuit l'hiver
O Paris
Du rouge au vert tout le jaune se meurt
Paris Vancouver Hyères Maintenon New-York et les Antilles
La fenêtre s'ouvre comme une orange
Le beau fruit de la lumière

240

Apollinaire: Seven

The Windows

From red to green all the yellow languishes
When the macaws sing in their native forests
Giblets of pihis[4]
There is a poem to be made on the bird that has but one wing
We shall send it as a *message téléphonique*
Giant traumatism
It makes your eyes run
Lo, there is a pretty girl among the young women of Turin
The poor young man blew his nose into his white necktie
You will lift the curtain
And now the window is opening
Spiders when hands were weaving light
Beauty pallor unfathomable violets
We'll try in vain to take some rest
We'll begin at midnight
When you have time you have freedom
Winkles Lotte multiple Suns and the sea-urchin of the sunset
An old pair of yellow shoes in front of the window
Towers
The towers are streets
Wells
Wells are places
Wells
Hollow trees that shelter vagrant Capresses[5]
The Chabin rams sing endless tunes to the brown Chabin sheep
And the goose gabble-gabble trumpets northward
Where the racoon hunters
Scrape the pelts
Sparkling diamond
Vancouver
Where the train white with snow and nocturnal lights flees winter
Oh Paris
From red to green all the yellow languishes
Paris Vancouver Hyères Maintenon New York and the Antilles
The window is opening like an orange
The beautiful fruit of light

[4] One-winged birds found by Apollinaire in Chinese legend.
[5] Capre, Capresse. In the French Antilles, "cross-breed between negro and mulatto." *(Larousse)*

241

Guillaume Apollinaire

GUILLAUME APOLLINAIRE

among the titles of Apollinaire's books with which he decorated his plate. By this time, emerging from the trauma of the Santé, Apollinaire was finally working seriously at compiling a volume. No sooner was Marcoussis' *Eau de Vie* etching finished than the poet found a title that seemed to him more modern, less Symbolist: *Alcools*. In February, 1913, a Paris newspaper printed a literary gossip item saying that Apollinaire's book would soon be appearing, that it would be entirely without punctuation and

242

Apollinaire: Seven

would contain as frontispiece a portrait of the author by Picasso. The rumors were correct. *Alcools, Poèmes 1898–1913* duly appeared on April 20, 1913, over the imprint of the publishing house for whose monthly literary review, once the stronghold of the Symbolists, Apollinaire was continuing to supply his column "La Vie Anecdotique"—the *Mercure de France.*

Alcools, this selection by Apollinaire of fifty-five of the many poems written between his eighteenth year and his thirty-third, called by Albert Camus one of the most "astonishing" works, along with Rimbaud's *Les Illuminations,* that French poetry has produced, has become for the modern world one of the best known and most appealing volumes of French verse of any century. Why?

The essential answer and the obvious one lies in the quality of individual freshness—a freshness that characterized each poem when it was written and that for reasons varying with each continues to infuse most of them with life today. Some of the poems continue fresh because they continue to sing; in others the freshness seems to spring from surprising images, or from downright bizarreness, or from mystery, or from classic form, finish, and perfection. The poems or parts of poems dating from the summer in Stavelot, the poems from the Rhine and about Annie in Germany and England, those that came out of life among the painters, and later out of the Santé prison and the loss of Marie Laurencin—these poems are all very different, and the life of each springs from no common characteristic except their writer's genius.

244 However, the contents of *Alcools* also possess a unity;

"Portrait of Guillaume Apollinaire," etching by Picasso
(frontispiece to first edition of Alcools, *1913).*

245

Guillaume Apollinaire

and Apollinaire's careful arrangement and unification of his volume—a labor that engaged him that summer and autumn of 1912 and involved the writing of two long "major" poems at the last moment to give the collection a form he felt it needed—resulted in his providing it with a second kind of freshness, a freshness of the whole. It is this double freshness that makes *Alcools* unique among collections of verse: each poem in it lives a life of its own, and yet each of them seems to belong, inevitably, to *Alcools,* contributing its energy to the life and beauty of the volume. *Alcools* is a work of strange architecture, fascinating to analyze, yet defying complete analysis.

Of the fifty-five poems comprising it, for example, twenty owe their inspiration to Apollinaire's year in the Rhineland. (He wrote at least a dozen more out of that experience, which he excluded from *Alcools* even though he had already published some of them in magazines, these other Rhine poems being printed in volumes only after Apollinaire's death.) Of the twenty included in *Alcools,* nine are printed there as a group, collectively titled "Rhénanes" and separately titled as well. Why are the remaining eleven printed apart from them, scattered here and there through-out the volume? Why are only nine in the group? It is al-most as though the river Rhine itself were flowing through the book, never entirely absent, and in that one spot, as the volume approaches its end, broadening out into the "Rhénanes," an expanse of shimmering, romantic German water, complete with the bandit Schinderhannes, the Lore-lei, and the sound of church bells from villages along the shore. Or it is as though the Rhine wind—the *Vent du Rhin* that Apollinaire had contemplated publishing nine years before, and which would almost certainly have included *all* his Rhine poems, if only because of the small body of his work that then existed—were blowing through *Alcools:* it was, of course, the wind of Apollinaire's youth.

Three poems commemorate the loss of Marie Laurencin: "Le Pont Mirabeau," "Marie," and "Cors de Chasse"; they are not printed together.

Six poems commemorate the incarceration in the Santé prison: they are printed together as a group, collectively titled "A la Santé," with no separate titles.

Originally Apollinaire had planned to open *Alcools* with the "Chanson du Mal-Aimé": he changed his mind, and wrote "Zone," the present opening poem, specifically to occupy that all-important place. He had decided to close the volume with "Vendémiaire," a long poem on the theme of the modern world, and apparently he came to feel that to increase his book's impact the modern note should be struck also at the outset. Both "Vendémiaire" and "Zone" (which appeared in the *Soirées de Paris* for November and December respectively) are tinged with the "new esthetic" which in a few weeks was to flower more fully in "Les Fenêtres." Delaunay's "Orphism" or "Simultaneism" is evident in both of them, and they resemble also the highly colored urban pictures that the Italian Futurists were painting.

Alcools is thus framed by two poems of highly modern feeling. But "Zone" was skillfully composed to play its opening role in a volume that is, after all, made up of poems out of the poet's past. Michel Décaudin has called "Zone"   247 "the poet's reappraisal of his past, his artistic credo," and its reminiscent statement of the poet's ambivalence between the old world and the new leads the reader harmoniously onward (and yet backward) to "Le Pont Mirabeau" which immediately follows, and thence further back to "La Chanson du Mal-Aimé," which in the new order of the volume occupies third place.

Equally skillful was a double last-minute change that Apollinaire made in the proofs. He composed and inserted a new poem, "Chantre" ("Singer"), occupying a page to itself but consisting of a single line:

Et l'unique cordeau des trompettes marines[6]

It makes a break in the text, shocks, mystifies, and amuses; and to provide a page for it he arbitrarily chopped the entire last stanza from a long poem, "Le Larron." Nobody misses that last stanza. The blithe and successful excision of what one would think to be an integral part of an important poem, because that part happened to occupy a page alone, in favor of a one-line shocker, is as dramatic an example as one is likely to find of the freedom enjoyed by a poet as compared with practitioners of other literary genres.

Such, briefly considered, is what one is tempted to term the crazy architecture of the volume *Alcools*. There is nothing chronological, nothing logical, about it; the reader

[6] "And the single string of the marine trumpets" or "And the solitary row of megaphones." (Suggested translations by William Meredith.) Mr. Meredith says: "These strike only the two most obvious *double-entendres* in the line." What amused Apollinaire was doubtless the triple (at least) pun: *cordeau (corps d'eau)=cor d'eau=trompette marine*. A *trompette marine* is a one-stringed instrument. Critics have puzzled for years, playing with the puns and relating the single line of the poem of the single string of the instrument, to the horizon, to many things.

❯

Apollinaire: Seven

simply knows, by feeling, that it is successful; and about as far as one can go in summing it up is Michel Décaudin's statement that the only order in *Alcools* is "an order based on the esthetic and sentimental affinities felt by the author, or their discreet dissonances."

Alcools was published in an edition of approximately six hundred copies, the author receiving from the publisher —according to a rumor still current in the offices of the *Mercure de France*—not an advance on royalties, nor indeed any royalties or payment at all, but rather merely the publication of his book, for which service, as a special favor, he was allowed to pay, not in cash, but by his continued contribution to the magazine, without remuneration, of his more or less regular gossip column, "La Vie Anecdotique." Three hundred and fifty copies were sold the first year—a number "not at all to be scorned," in the opinion of Michel Décaudin, and testifying to "a certain curiosity" concerning the book. The curiosity did not persist—the second year, only four copies were sold, and the following two years seven and five copies respectively: it was some years before *Alcools* began to enjoy the steady popularity that has by now driven its editions well up over the hundred mark.

Michel Décaudin thinks that it was in part Apollinaire's personality, and in part the activity of the critics that was responsible for that first dizzy sale of three hundred and fifty copies. Perhaps something about the "certain curiosity" concerning *Alcools,* and perhaps something about Apollinaire himself, and even about his poetics, can be learned from a glance at two of the many reviews and from

Apollinaire's reply to one of them.

Nothing is more reminiscent of a junk shop [wrote Georges Duhamel in the June 15 issue of the *Mercure de France*] than this collection of verse published by Guillaume Apollinaire under a title both simple and mysterious: *Alcools*.

I say junk shop because these tawdry premises are filled with a number of disparate objects of which some are not without value but none is the product of the shopkeeper's own efforts. This is one of the hallmarks of a junk dealer: he resells, he does not manufacture. True, he sometimes resells unusual objects: occasionally you may find, among his grimy stock, a precious stone mounted on a nail. Heaven knows where the stuff comes from, but the stone, at least, is nice to look at. Otherwise, there is a jumble of faked paintings, exotic patched pieces of clothing, bicycle parts, and more or less unmentionable toilet articles. Instead of art we have an aggressive and bewildering assemblage of nondescript items. Through the rents in a moth-eaten chasuble we get an occasional glimpse of the ironic, candid expression on the face of the dealer himself: he looks like a mixture of Levantine Jew, South American, Polish squire, and *facchino*.

M. Guillaume Apollinaire's poems do indeed reflect a mixture of candor and shrewdness: nowadays one is perhaps expected to be impressed by this. However, it seems to me that in the presence of this mixture of dockside jargon and literary eloquence we are immediately aware that it is very different from the inspired delirium that we have found among the greatest of the Symbolists.

M. Apollinaire does not lack erudition. But we constantly have the impression that he is telling us everything he knows: he impudently defies even the loosest interpretation of the rules of moderation and good taste. For the poet, two ideas, distant though they may be from each other in the world of reality, are always linked by a tenuous, secret thread. The great artist knows just when to stop stretching this thread; the ambitious and clumsy workman overstretches it and breaks it. In other words, an image is the more surprising and suggestive the more distant from each other in real space and time are the objects it denotes, but an excessive

250

effort in this direction defeats its own purpose, and the link is snapped. There is nothing more obtrusive than such an abortive image.

M. Apollinaire is guilty of many such mistakes. The reason no doubt is that, instead of allowing himself to be guided by analogies, he is seduced by words. On the basis of these he established arbitrary analogies, and apparently derives pleasure from doing so. Are we to be blamed if we see through this, if we do not always tolerate his calculated incoherence?

The care and patience with which I am analyzing M. Guillaume Apollinaire's volume show that I find his effort neither negligible nor devoid of interest. M. Apollinaire seems to have set himself the task of combining all the defects of all the dead literary schools. As a crowning oddity, he eliminated all punctuation from the galley proofs: as a result, not a comma is to be found in his two hundred pages. Here M. Apollinaire missed a chance of puzzle his fellow men: he should have retained one or two commas and a single semicolon, concealed somewhere in his text, and promised, in his preface, a prize to the perspicacious reader who would discover them. In any case, whether or not M. Apollinaire is the first to omit punctuation, he seems to do so with unprecedented stubbornness: for this he will be remembered.

M. Apollinaire's book is not without its charms. Once or twice per page a line strikes the eye and the mind; the reader pauses, like a stroller who catches sight of a strange and precious crystal in the junk dealer's window:

Une famille transporte un édredon rouge comme vous transportez votre cœur[7]

But why must M. Apollinaire's best intentions be contaminated by literature? I am told that he is a scholar, a great frequenter of libraries: I can easily believe it. But I should prefer him to be illiterate, to write more often from the dictates of his heart: as it is, he writes only from books. Reading his collected poems we recognize a number of poets to whom M. Apollinaire pays praiseworthy but excessive homage. Sometimes it is Verlaine, often it is

[7] Literally, "A family transports a red quilt as you transport your heart."   251

Guillaume Apollinaire

Moréas; and as for Rimbaud, M. Apollinaire seems to feel that he must never forget his deep, terrible voice. More than that, I discern in the accents of the author of *Alcools* certain inflections that are more contemporary, for example those of Max Jacob, whose invention and psychological knowledge are certainly admired by Apollinaire, as well as those of André Salmon and Henri Hertz, whose roaming imagination is not without its influence on these poetic compositions by the author of *Hérésiarque et Cie.*

In connection with that latter curious work we may add that M. Apollinaire possesses one characteristic that is entirely his own—a many-colored cosmopolitanism, whose flavor must be acknowledged even though some will find it detestable. Thanks to this, M. Apollinaire's poetry smells not only of the library, but also of rare tobacco, palace hotels, deluxe trains, and exotic beverages.

It must be said, however, that M. Apollinaire has hidden in his volume one brief and poignant chapter. It comes near the end of the book, is six pages long, and consists of six short poems[8]: it doubtless evokes hours of real suffering. In writing these few lines M. Apollinaire set aside all literature, all false glitter, all desire to shock. He expressed simply human distress in the presence of misfortune. In my opinion, these fifty or so lines are worth more than all the rest of the book.

In the July-August issue of his magazine, *Le Divan,* Henri Martineau also reviewed *Alcools:*

This last month I have had to read many volumes of poetry. I shall not speak of all of them, but only of those which gave me some pleasure and captured my interest.

Among the young writers, M. Guillaume Apollinaire stands out as a likeable eccentric. I am fond of picturing him as a man of fine literary culture, who in his own writing amuses himself and is not afraid of flaunting his taste for the bizarre. We all know his

[8] The series on the Santé.

talent for practical jokes and mystifications: forewarned is fore-armed. Even before reading his verse, the moment we open his book we are struck by a deliberate novelty—all punctuation is omitted, and we are given two hundred pages without a single period or comma. But we are rewarded for our effort: Guillaume Apollinaire is a charming poet. Certainly not all his poems are on the same high level, but very few pages are without merit, and some lines are truly poignant. . . .

"Unfortunately I cannot quote more for lack of space," says Martineau, after printing passages from several of the poems, ". . . I cannot enumerate all the treasures collected by this enchanting junk dealer. . . ."

To Martineau Apollinaire replied in a letter which was printed in *Le Divan* only twenty-five years later, in March 1958:

July 19, 1913

Thank you, thank you for your article, thank you for having enjoyed my verse. However, it is not the bizarre that I like; it is life itself: when you know how to look about you, you see the most curious and the most attractive things! No matter what people say, I am not a great reader: I have kept reading and reread-ing much the same books since my childhood, and I have never read systematically. If I am cultured—and I think I am—it is rather thanks to a natural taste, which enables me to grasp the vital in-tensity, the degree of excellence, of a work, whether a work of art, or of literature, or anything else—it is, I repeat, thanks to a kind of intuition rather than to study. I have never indulged in practical jokes or mystifications concerning my work or the work of others. As for punctuation, I have eliminated it only because it seemed to me useless, and it actually is useless; the rhythm itself and the division into lines provide the real punctuation, and no other is needed. Almost all of my poems have been published as I

253

Guillaume Apollinaire

wrote them in first draft; I usually compose while walking, and while singing two or three tunes that came to me spontaneously and that one of my friends has transcribed. The usual system of punctuation would not be suitable. I think that my poems are not imitations, because every one of them commemorates an event in my life, most often something sad, but I also have joyful moments, and these too I sing. I am like the sailors who spend their shore leave at the beach—the sea provides so many surprises, so many sights that are always new—nothing boring. But the epithet "junk dealer" seems to me very unfair when applied to a poet who has written such a small number of pieces over a span as long as fifteen years.

Otherwise, I am extremely happy to have given you pleasure.

Yours with gratitude and devotion. . . .

Alfred Vallette, the director of the publishing house the Mercure de France, which published *Alcools,* was also managing editor and publisher of the magazine the *Mercure de France:* the review by Duhamel testifies to the freedom enjoyed by writers for the magazine. His article wounded and angered Apollinaire, who for a time did a certain amount of blustering about challenging him to a duel: he felt that Duhamel had written less dispassionately than vengefully, for (to skirt for a moment the quicksands of Parisian poetic politics) Duhamel was at that time "one of the leaders of the poetic school of the *Abbaye,* the *Unanimistes,* rival of the group known as the *Fantaisistes,* to which Apollinaire was often linked, though he himself denied the connection." The review also brought the *Mercure* a letter from Max Jacob, pointing out that Apollinaire had been writing verse since 1898, claiming that in 1905, when he and Apollinaire met, he himself had written nothing, and

254

concluding most illogically that therefore he could not have influenced Apollinaire. Duhamel replied that he continued to feel sure that Jacob had influenced Apollinaire *after* 1905, and he flatteringly added: ". . . one of the valuable characteristics of Max Jacob is that others can savor his rare and varied talent without needing to see his works. This has given him a reputation that will soon go beyond the limits of an intimate circle. This being the case, I have reason to believe that he may have impressed M. Apollinaire well before 1905."

Years later, in a radio broadcast devoted to Apollinaire, Georges Duhamel retracted many of his strictures concerning *Alcools,* and he consented to act as president of the committee of the Prix Guillaume Apollinaire, a prize awarded to young French poets of "Apollinairian inspiration."

It is not difficult to understand both Duhamel's strictures and his later recantation. Apollinaire's images are often bold, and comparing them with previous poetic practice Duhamel could well find his analogies overextended. And unquestionably his images do often give the impression of having been suggested to the poet not by perception of similarity between real objects or conceptions but rather by perception of similarity between words. Today, accustomed as we are to Surrealist[9] experiments, to free association, stream of consciousness, automatic writing, and the rest, Apollinaire often appears restrained in the use of his technique: Duhamel's later recantation perhaps shows that the critic "grew with the times."

[9] This is perhaps the place to mention, in anticipation of the event, that Apollinaire invented the word "surrealist." See page 317.

As to the title *Alcools* being "at once simple and mysterious," it is to us, rather, complex and revealing. Duhamel, who so loved "the greatest of the Symbolists," would certainly not have objected to Apollinaire's earlier choice of title, *Eau de Vie:* its dual suggestion of "inspired delirium" and life would have seemed to him entirely apt. Duhamel, a doctor turned literary man, later wrote a book scathing in its condemnation of the United States as the spearhead of the age of technology, and his bewilderment at the significance of the technical-sounding word *Alcools* may well reflect the same fear and distrust. It is clear today that the change from *Eau de Vie* to *Alcools* was an attempt by Apollinaire to help the reader understand the spirit of his book. It was another step that he took away from Symbolism, even though with his exoticisms and his erudition he always retained a certain Symbolist tinge. But in *Alcools* he went on to embrace the modern world. The atmosphere of *Alcools* is still one of "inspired delirium," of the poetic trance, but this trance is stimulated not only by the classic brandy but also by modern technological artifacts, which are as "exotic" and intoxicating to the poet as the Holy Grail, the pi-hi, or a bird that nests in the air. Apollinaire finds nothing incongruous in the mixture of the exotic and the commonplace, the medieval and the ultra-modern, the classic and the grotesque, that suggests to Duhamel the image of the junk shop and adjectives such as "disparate," "nondescript," and the like.

Martineau (he was an eminent Stendhal scholar) was obviously less resistant than Duhamel to the spell of Apollinaire's work. In speaking of "the treasures collected by this

Apollinaire: Seven

enchanting junk dealer," he is probably gently reprimanding Duhamel, and yet his willingness to adopt that image testifies to his feeling of the incongruousness of the charming mixture—not a full understanding of what Apollinaire was about. Martineau good-naturedly lays much of the strangeness of the poetry to prankishness, to Apollinaire's love of "practical jokes and mystifications." Despite Apollinaire's denial of this charge, some of his past conduct had certainly made him vulnerable to it: one need only think of the hospitality he had shown to the robber of the Louvre, his posing as the poetess "Louise Lalanne," and indeed his lifelong mystification concerning his own origins. But the critic was misled by such antics: they did not justify his assumption that as a poet, too, Apollinaire was in large part a jokester.

Duhamel and Martineau were far from being alone among the critics to be shocked by the absence of punctuation from *Alcools*. Apollinaire's defense, in his reply to Martineau, need scarcely be enlarged upon for the modern reader. In omitting punctuation, Apollinaire has thrown one more convention overboard: a throng of commas, colons, semicolons, periods, and exclamation points in *Alcools* would be like Victorian plush and clutter in a jet plane.

Apollinaire was perhaps carried away by his desire to persuade Martineau in the matter of punctuation when he maintained, in his letter, that "Almost all of my poems have been published as I wrote them in the first draft." There are still plenty of first, second, third, and later drafts of Apollinaire's poems in existence to show that he took his work   257 very seriously indeed and lavished endless care upon it. As to the "two or three tunes" that he was accustomed to sing while walking and composing, Mme Durry has transcribed one of them—preserved by the memory of Max Jacob and confirmed by Picasso. Here it is, with two of the lines that he might have composed to it:

Des-cen-dant des hau-teurs où pen-se la lu-mière

Jar-din rou-ant plus haut que tous les ciels mo-biles

In November 1911, shortly after his emergence from the Santé, Apollinaire had written in his gossip column in the *Mercure de France*:

I have met two Futurist painters, M. Boccioni and M. Severini. The former, who is, so to speak, the theoretician of the school, has a fearless, loyal appearance, which at once predisposes one in his favor. These gentlemen wear clothes of English cut, very comfortable. M. Severini, a native of Tuscany, favors low shoes, and socks of different colors. The day I saw him he was wearing a raspberry-colored sock on his right foot and a bottle-green sock on the other. This Florentine coquetry exposes him to the risk of being thought very absent-minded, and he told me that café waiters often feel obliged to call his attention to what they suppose to be an oversight, but which is actually an affecta-tion. I have not yet seen any Futurist paintings, but if I have cor-

258

rectly understood what the new Italian painters are aiming at in their experiments, they are concerned above all with expressing feelings, almost states of mind (the term was employed by M. Boccioni himself), and expressing them as strongly as possible. Furthermore, these young men want to move away from natural forms and to be the inventors of their art.

"So," M. Boccioni told me, "I have painted two pictures, one expressing departure and the other arrival. The scene is a railroad station. In order to emphasize the difference of moods I have not repeated in the arrival picture a single line occurring in the other."

In the light of this explanation, this kind of painting would seem to be above all sentimental and rather puerile. The Futurists defend it, if need be, by the use of "the big stick." Florence was recently the scene of one such brawl, in which the opposing parties were the Futurists, headed by Marinetti, and the group close to the magazine *La Voce*, M. Ardengo Soffici and his friends.

Of the four Italian Futurists whom Apollinaire thus mentions in so brief a space, Severini had been living in Paris since 1906, and Apollinaire had also previously met Marinetti. Marinetti's initial "Foundation and Manifesto of Futurism," signed by Boccioni, Carrà, Russolo, Balla, and Severini, had had its original publication in French on the front page of *Le Figaro* in Paris on February 20, 1909, shortly before appearing in both French and Italian in Marinetti's magazine *Poesia,* published in Milan; and now in 1911 Marinetti was arranging for a first Futurist exhibition in Paris, to take place the next year. The moment is well described by Joshua C. Taylor, in his volume *Futurism:*

In a hasty trip to Italy where he met Carrà and Russolo for the first time, Severini saw the works of his fellow Futurists and

259

was appalled that they so little resembled the paintings of his friends in Paris. Their resistance to principally formal pre-occupations struck him as old-fashioned. Impressed by his criticism, Carrà and Boccioni (and possibly Russolo), with the aid of Marinetti, made a brief trip to Paris in the autumn of 1911 to see at first hand the most recent trends in painting. Introduced to many artists by Severini and viewing hastily the Salon d'Automne they saw much that impressed them. With many new ideas in mind, they hurried home to complete old and make new works for the Paris exhibition, *more confident in their use of an international language.*[10]

Such was the occasion of Apollinaire's "I have met two Futurist painters. . . ." Perhaps the meeting took place in Montmartre, at the Café de l'Ermitage, which Fernande Olivier tells us had become the headquarters of the group around Picasso since he had moved from the Place Ravignan to the Boulevard Clichy, and which the visiting Futurists liked to frequent, their trousers "hitched up high" to show their vari-colored hose. "Along with Marinetti," Fernande says, "Soffici was the apostle of literary Futurism, and like him was inexhaustible the moment you displayed interest in his ideas. I remember spending an entire night with Apollinaire and Picasso in Marinetti's hotel room near the Place Pigalle. Dawn came after he had been talking uninterruptedly for ten hours. I must say we had not been bored." Boccioni, who also participated in the Parisian nocturnal conversation bouts, was apt to come away from them with somber thoughts. "Yesterday evening we dined, [Apollinaire,] Marinetti, and I in a celebrated restaurant on

[10] For that last discreet phrase (italicized by F.S.), one might rather read: "often adopting the technique of the Cubists."

260

the 'Rive Gauche,' " he wrote a friend during another visit to Paris. "We argued from seven to three in the morning. We came away drunk and exhausted. After these debates where victory is won by magnetism I find myself sad and discouraged. I wonder what I might have achieved by now if I had grown up in the atmosphere of Paris or Berlin. . . ."

Apollinaire's paragraphs in the *Mercure* about the Futurists were his first public mention of them. His next was in *L'Intransigeant* and *Le Petit Bleu,* on the occasion of their Paris exhibition, which was held, as arranged by Marinetti, at the Bernheim-Jeune Gallery February 5 to 24, 1912. For all his willingness to sit up all night talking with his new friends (he was also at this time in correspondence with Soffici in Florence, who was becoming more or less reconciled with the others), he maintained, in his reviews, the superior tone with which he had written earlier of their "puerility." He mentioned again, this time with contempt, their wish to express feelings, states of mind, and lamented their interest in subject. In his evaluations he displayed a goodly amount of French chauvinism—almost as strong, especially when he pointed out their evident debt to French painters, as the Italian chauvinism displayed by the Futurists, who loudly proclaimed their originality and their opposition to French schools. Apollinaire's only unqualified praise was for the Futurists' "audacity," as displayed in their presuming to exhibit such imperfect works, and in their choice of titles: "The new art being developed in France seems so far to have remained at the stage of melody. The Futurists have now taught us, by their titles, not by their works, that it could become truly symphonic." His   261

Guillaume Apollinaire

article in *Le Petit Bleu* ended: "As for Futurist art, it makes us smile a little here in Paris, but it is to be hoped that it will not make the Italians smile: if it should, so much the worse for them."

Naturally, we find Picasso and Apollinaire in agreement. From Apollinaire's "La Vie Anecdotique," *Mercure de France*, February 16, 1912:

> The painter Picasso was looking at a canvas by a Futurist painter. It presented a very confused appearance—a mixture of disparate objects, a bottle, a collar, the head of a jovial-looking man, etc. This chaos was entitled "Laughter."
> "It ought to be called 'Pell-Mell'," said Picasso, with a smile.

Condescension by Apollinaire-Picasso could scarcely go further.

It therefore comes as something of a surprise—or it would so come if by this time our poet were any longer capable of surprising us—to find Apollinaire composing for Marinetti, and distributing over his own name and address in Paris, before it appeared in Italian in the Futurist magazine *Lacerba* in Florence, a pro-Futurist proclamation entitled "L'Antitradition Futuriste."

We reproduce a portion of this four-page blast dated "Paris, 29 June 1913, day of the Grand Prix [at the Longchamps race track]," from "65 meters above the Boulevard Saint-Germain" (Apollinaire's flat being on the top floor of No. 202.) In it he makes lavish gifts of two commodities, *merde* and roses.[11] The *merde* is liberally sprinkled on various –isms and on a certain number of more or less great men, while a rose apiece is proffered to Apollinaire himself, to

262

members of groups with which he had been associated, and to each of the same Futurists whom he had so recently called puerile.

What was the occasion for this certainly puerile bit of iconoclasm? Was it perhaps an outburst of the pent-up irritation caused by the solemn disapprovals of *Alcools* that we have seen published by the worthy Duhamel in the *Mercure de France* for June 15, just two weeks before the date of the manifesto, and whose author Apollinaire had thought of challenging to a duel? In Duhamel's censurings, the hand of the past had come down rather heavily; perhaps Apollinaire —apparently solicited by Marinetti to write a "manifesto-synthesis"—had seized on the chance to strike back. Or there may well have been no immediate cause, with the blast simply taking its place along with, say, the elimination of punctuation from *Alcools* among the series of iconoclasms that can almost be said to have composed the life of the son of Olga de Kostrowitzky.[12]

[11] Apollinaire later explained his choice of those two substances on the basis of an incident he had once witnessed while walking with a friend near La Turbie, above Monaco. Children were tormenting a woman of noticeably soiled appearance; she turned on them, calling out *"Merde"* and they retorted in chorus *"Merda-rosa, merd'a ti ros'a mi."*

[12] Apollinaire later wrote to André Billy: "The word *merde* set to music in my manifesto did not apply to the older authors' works, but rather to their names used as a barrier against the new generations." In 1917 he wrote a preface to an edition of Baudelaire's *Les Fleurs du Mal*, which had just entered the public domain. There he offered Baudelaire more *merde*, this time in the form of a dubious accolade: "In him the modern spirit is incarnated for the first time . . . (but) he no longer participates in the modern spirit that proceeds from him."

263

Guillaume Apollinaire

L'ANTITRADITION FUTURISTE

Manifeste=synthèse

ABAS LEP ominir A liminé SS korsusu
otalo EIS cramlr ME nigme

ce moteur à toutes tendances impressionnisme fauvisme cubisme expressionnisme pathétisme dramatisme orphisme paroxysme **DYNAMISME PLASTIQUE MOTS EN LIBERTÉ INVENTION DE MOTS**

DESTRUCTION

	Suppression de la douleur poétique	
	des exotismes snobs	
	de la copie en art	
	des syntaxes *déjà condamnées par l'usage dans toutes les langues*	
	de l'adjectif	
Pas	de la ponctuation	
	de l'harmonie typographique	
de	des temps et personnes des verbes	
	de l'orchestre	
regrets	de la forme théâtrale	
	du sublime artiste	
	du vers et de la strophe	
	des maisons	
	de la critique et de la satire	
	de l'intrigue dans les récits	
	de l'ennui	

SUPPRESSION DE L'HISTOIRE

INFINITIF

MER . . . . DE . . . .

aux

Critiques
Pédagogues
Professeurs
Musées
Quattrocentistes
Dixseptièmesièclistes
Ruines
Patines
Historiens
Venise Versailles Pompei Bruges Oxford Nuremberg Tolède Bénarès etc.
Défenseurs de paysages
Philologues

Essaystes
Néo et *post*
Bayreuth Florence Montmartre et Munich
Lexiques
Bongoûtismes
Orientalismes
Dandysmes
Spiritualistes ou realistes (sans sentiment de la réalité et de l'esprit)
Académismes

Les frères siamois D'Annunzio et Rostand
Dante Shakespeare Tolstoï Goethe
Dilettantismes merdoyants
Eschyle et théâtre d'Orange
Inde Egypte Fiesole et la théosophie
Scientisme
Montaigne Wagner Beethoven Edgard Poe Walt Whitman et Baudelaire

ROSE

aux

Marinetti Picasso Boccioni Apollinaire Paul Fort Mercereau Max Jacob Carrà Delaunay Henri-Matisse Braque Depaquit Séverine Severini Derain Russolo Archipenko Pratella Balla F. Divoire N. Beauduin T. Varlet Buzzi Palazzeschi Maquaire Papini Soffici Folgore Govoni Montfort R. Fry Cavacchioli D'Alba Altomare Tridon Metzinger Gleizes Jastrebzoff Royère Canudo Salmon Castiaux Laurencin Aurel Agero Léger Valentine de Saint-Point Delmarle Kandinsky Strawinsky Herbin A. Billy G. Sauvebois Picabia Marcel Duchamp B. Cendrars Jouve H. M. Barzun G. Polti Mac Orlan F. Fleuret Jaudon Mandin R. Dalize M. Brésil F. Carco Rubiner Bétuda Manzella-Frontini A. Mazza T. Derême Giannattasio Tavolato De Gonzagues-Frick C. Larronde etc.

PARIS, le 29 Juin 1913, jour du Grand Prix, à 65 mètres au-dessus du Boul. S.-Germain

GUILLAUME APOLLINAIRE.
(202, BOULEVARD SAINT-GERMAIN - PARIS)

DIRECTION DU MOUVEMENT FUTURISTE
Corso Venezia, 61 - MILAN

"L'Antitradition Futuriste," 1913

Apollinaire among the Futurists: the interesting thing is the choice he made there. The Futurists had two sides to them—a raucous iconoclasm and rage for self-publicity, and a capacity for hard work and the creation of far from negligible paintings and sculpture. The worth of their work Apollinaire did not see—his usual dim vision was further clouded in this case by chauvinism; but he gleefully furnished them with *merde* and roses.

During these same months Apollinaire wrote, or completed, his poem "Lundi Rue Christine." It is a "simultaneous" poem: a number of things happen simultaneously in one place—apparently the same *"sinistre brasserie"* in the Rue Christine where he had taken his friends in 1903 to announce the birth of *Le Festin d'Esope*. In these stanzas the atmosphere of a low café-restaurant is evoked with extraordinary vividness by the simple device of recording verbatim overheard scraps of conversation interspersed here and there with the listener's own thoughts. Two men plan a burglary, someone mentions an urgent debt, others make malicious remarks on the habitués and exchange gossip, intimacies are suggested. Throughout, we are aware of the poet's own half-idle attention. Even literal translation is difficult because the underworld or semi-underworld conversations are recorded almost phonographically: a Parisian reading the poem in the original knows at once in what kind of a place he is. (For the poem and a translation, see the following pages).

Apollinaire the poet and Apollinaire the "art critic"; "Lundi Rue Christine" and the writings on the Futurists: one is impressed anew by the true ring of the one and the

266

hollow sound of the other. Like many other modern writers and artists, Apollinaire regarded criticism with only secondary seriousness. His own alternates between the pretentious and the offhand, between displays of erudition and slapstick manifestos.

And yet at this time Apollinaire was up to something else connected with painters and painting and was succeeding brilliantly at it.

Shortly before the end of his liaison with Marie Laurencin, he had met two of the few "really nice people" it seems to have been his privilege to know—a wealthy young Russian painter known in Paris first as Edouard Férat, then as Serge Férat (his real name, Serge Jastrebzoff, was difficult: Picasso called him "Serge Apostrophe"), and Férat's companion, the Baroness Hélène d'Œttingen, widow of a Baltic nobleman. The charming, warm-hearted young pair called each other brother and sister, but they seem actually to have been *"frère et sœur de lait,"* terms which identify them as having had the same wet-nurse as infants, without specifying their later relationship. Férat did a clever, charming, decorative, cubistic kind of painting, and his sister produced various kinds of literature under various pseudonyms, principally "Roch Grey." For a time during the summer of 1912, unable to bear the atmosphere of Auteuil after the break with Marie, Apollinaire lived in their house on the Boulevard Berthier, gratefully accepting their hospitality as we have seen him accepting that of the Delaunays.

With the issue of June 15, 1913, the *Soirées de Paris*   267

Lundi Rue Christine

La mère de la concierge et la concierge laisseront tout passer
Si tu es un homme tu m'accompagneras ce soir
Il suffirait qu'un type maintînt la porte cochère
Pendant que l'autre monterait

Trois becs de gaz allumés
La patronne est poitrinaire
Quand tu auras fini nous jouerons une partie de jacquet
Un chef d'orchestre qui a mal à la gorge
Quand tu viendras à Tunis je te ferai fumer du kief

Ça a l'air de rimer

Des piles de soucoupes des fleurs un calendrier
Pim pam pim
Je dois fiche près de 300 francs à ma probloque
Je préférerais me couper le parfaitement que de les lui donner.

Je partirai à 20 h. 27
Six glaces s'y dévisagent toujours
Je crois que nous allons nous embrouiller encore davantage
Cher monsieur
Vous êtes un mec à la mie de pain
Cette dame a le nez comme un ver solitaire
Louise a oublié sa fourrure
Moi je n'ai pas de fourrure et je n'ai pas froid
Le Danois fume sa cigarette en consultant l'horaire
Le chat noir traverse la brasserie

Ces crêpes étaient exquises
La fontaine coule
Robe noire comme ses ongles
C'est complètement impossible
Voici monsieur

268

Apollinaire: Seven

Monday Rue Christine
The concierge's mother and the concierge won't give any trouble
If you're a man you'll come with me tonight
All we need is one guy to watch the front door
While the other goes upstairs

Three gas lamps lighted
The patronne has T.B.
When you're through we'll play a game of backgammon
An orchestra conductor with a sore throat
When you come to Tunis I'll see that you smoke some kief

That seems to make sense

Stacks of saucers, flowers, a calendar
Pim pam pim
I owe my landlady nearly three hundred francs
I'd rather cut off my yes I would than give them to her

I'll leave at 8.27 P.M.
Six mirrors keep staring at each other there
I think we're going to get even more involved
Cher monsieur
You're a crummy one
That lady has a nose like a tapeworm
Louise forgot her furs
Me I have no furs and I'm not cold
The Danes smokes his cigarette as he consults the timetable
The black cat crosses the brasserie

Those pancakes were delicious
Got the clap
A dress black as her fingernails
It's completely impossible
Here you are sir

269

Guillaume Apollinaire

La bague en malachite
Le sol est semé de sciure
Alors c'est vrai
La serveuse rousse a été enlevée par un libraire

Un journaliste que je connais d'ailleurs très vaguement
Ecoute Jacques c'est très sérieux ce que je vais te dire

Compagnie de navigation mixte

Il me dit monsieur voulez-vous voir ce que je peux
   faire d'eaux fortes et de tableaux
Je n'ai qu'une petite bonne

Après déjeuner café du Luxembourg

Une fois là il me présente un gros bonhomme
Qui me dit
Ecoutez c'est charmant
A Smyrne à Naples en Tunisie
Mais nom de Dieu où est-ce
La dernière fois que j'ai été en Chine
C'est il y a huit ou neuf ans
L'Honneur tient souvent à l'heure que marque la pendule
La quinte major

270

Apollinaire: Seven

The malachite ring
There's sawdust on the floor
So it's true
The red-headed waitress eloped with the man from the bookshop

A newspaperman I know—not very well

Listen Jacques it's very important what I'm going to tell you

Shipping company freight and passengers

He said to me monsieur do you want to see what I can do in the way
    of etchings and pictures
I only have a little maid

After lunch café du Luxembourg

Once there he introduces a fat fellow
Who says to me
Listen it's charming
At Smyrna at Naples in Tunisia
But in God's name where is it
The last time I was in China
That was eight or nine years ago
Honor often depends on the time the clock shows
The major fifth

Guillaume Apollinaire

seemed to have reached its end. It had few subscribers or buyers—there was no reason why it should have had more; apart from Apollinaire's own contributions its numbers contain little of interest, and Apollinaire, held down by his colleagues from devoting as much space as he would have liked to his friends the painters, seems to have lost his enthusiasm for this magazine that had been founded for his own salvation. André Billy, who was apparently in a somewhat better financial position than the others, had for some time been paying expenses out of his own pocket, but could continue no longer. There were no issues for July, August, September, or October.

The *Soirées* proved to be a phoenix, however. In September, on Apollinaire's instigation, Serge Férat and the Baroness d'Œttingen paid André Billy two hundred francs, the amount of bills still outstanding, and the magazine's title and subscribers were theirs. Under the joint name of Jean Cérusse[13] they announced that they and Apollinaire were *co-directeurs,* and under the date of November 15 appeared Issue No. 18, the first of the new series. No longer so meagerly budgeted, it could afford illustrations; and its outstanding feature was a series of five black and white photographs of Picasso Cubist still-lifes, probably the first reproduction of such a group in any magazine. There were reviews by Apollinaire of the Salons d'Automne in Paris and in Berlin. (Each of these contains, as usual, more than one touch of the jejune, as when Apollinaire tags Jacques Villon as being *"à la récherche de sa personnalité,"* as though every artist worthy of the name were not perpetu-

[13] Cérusse = *C'est russe* ("It's Russian.")

272

ally engaged in such a search.) Certain articles and poems were clearly leftovers from the old *Soirées,* and there was a new dead spot, a series of notes on Chamonix by "Roch Grey." The Baroness d'Œttingen was to appear in almost every issue of the new *Soirées* under one or more of her pseudonyms. Apollinaire probably considered the presence of her interminable articles and dim little poems a small price to pay for the co-directorship of so splendidly revived and revamped a magazine. All his life the gentle Serge Férat, who lived until 1958, was to promote the writings of his beloved sister, which only he seemed not to find unreadable. The second (December 15) issue contained excellent black and white reproductions of paintings by Matisse, Marie Laurencin, Gleizes, and Metzinger, an article by Gabrielle Buffet (Mme Francis Picabia) on the Armory Show in New York, a postscript by Apollinaire to his remarks on the Salon d'Automne, his "Lundi Rue Christine," and poems by Max Jacob. In two bounds the new *Soirées* had become a brilliant magazine of the modern arts.

The editorial office rented by Férat and the Baroness at 278 Boulevard Raspail, near the *carrefour* of the Boulevard Montparnasse, became an *avant-garde* rendezvous. As Marcel Adéma puts it:

The premises were visited by the majority of those who had made or were to make for themselves a name in painting, poetry, or modern music: some day the history of the place will have to be written. Among the most assiduous visitors were Picasso, who had left Montmartre and now had a studio near the Montparnasse Cemetery, Kisling, Fernand Léger, the sculptor Zadkine, the always courteous Louis de Gonzague Frick, Archipenko, Maurice Reynal, Férat's friend Irène Lagut, Dalize, Cendrars, Modigliani,

273

the mysterious and monocled Max Jacob with his portfolio of gouaches under his arm, all the Italian Futurists, Severini, Soffici, Chirico, and his piano-breaking brother Savinio.

This was the beginning of the vogue of Montparnasse as a center of the arts, which had previously been represented there chiefly by Paul Fort's poetry readings at the Closerie des Lilas. Its post-war fame among the writers and painters of the international "lost generation" dates back to Picasso's move there from Montmartre and the flourishing of the *Soirées de Paris* in 1913–14. The first description of the new quarter was written by Apollinaire for his gossip column in the March 16, 1914 issue of the *Mercure*. It has a curiously post-war ring, with its picture of artists and models at the Rotonde, "estheticians from Massachusetts or the banks of the Spree" at the Dôme, the painters Dunoyer de Ségonzac, Luc-Albert Moreau, and André Derain sitting at tables:

> Though differing in mood from the old Montmartre, the Montparnasse of today is no less gay, simple and informal. The American-style garb worn by today's artists is no more loosely-fitting, and made of no different corduroy, than that favored by their predecessors; its looseness is simply of a different kind. And sandals, after all, are no less Germanic than those horrible elastic-sided shoes of yesteryear. I wager, without wishing for it, that Montparnasse will soon have its nightclubs and singers, as it already has its painters and poets. . . . Thomas Cook will be bringing busloads of sightseers. . . .

The entire January 15, 1914 issue of the *Soirées* was devoted to the Douanier Rousseau, with reproductions of his letters, poems, and paintings, a leading article on him by Apollinaire, and an account by Maurice Raynal of the

274

famous Rousseau banquet.[14] In February there were reproductions of Derain and letters of Jarry; in March, more Jarry letters, and reproductions, two of them in color, of Picabia. In April, reproductions of Braque; in May, of Matisse; in June, of Archipenko; in the July-August issue, reproductions of Vlaminck and Léger and notes on the Imagist poets. The *Soirées* also printed from time to time an article of an amusing character on an American subject. There was one in March, 1915 on "Popular American Epics" (Nick Carter, Buffalo Bill, Deadwood Dick, etc.) by Harrison Reeves, and another in July-August by Alan Seeger on "Le Baseball au [*sic*] Etats-Unis," which quoted in English all eight lines of "Take Me Out to the Ball-Game!" and rendered a certain well-known bit of baseball invective about umpires as *"Tuons l'arbitre!"*

That July-August issue was the end of the *Soirées.* Nowhere does one relive the fine fresh flourishing of twentieth-century art more intensely than in the pages of the new *Soirées de Paris;* nowhere does one have a keener sense of what "might have been," or feel more sickeningly the brutal stifling of it all when it had barely begun, the fatal descent of the curtain on August 1, 1914.

During the summer of 1913 friends had invited both Apollinaire and Marie Laurencin for a week-end on the Normandy coast. Marie refused to resume the old relationship, but something must have given Apollinaire hope, and he wrote her tenderly and passionately and they saw some-

[14] An event well covered in *The Banquet Years* by Roger Shattuck.

Guillaume Apollinaire

thing of each other. The following May he was invited to record three of his poems for the *Archives de la Parole*—the Archives of the Spoken Word—at the Sorbonne, and he read "Le Pont Mirabeau," "Le Voyageur," and "Marie," two out of the three being spoken, as it were, to her. The original recording can still be heard in Paris, and one of Apollinaire's readings, that of "Le Pont Mirabeau," has lately been reissued on a disk that also contains readings by other poets. His voice is resonant, grave, and slow; he gives full value to every final *e* and pauses after every line; the two poems to Marie he reads in a tone of anguish. No one knows whether she ever heard the record played back, but in any case it did him no good as far as she was concerned. The remainder of their story has been told by Louise Faure-Favier:

One day in May, 1914, Marie Laurencin said to me: "You know, Louise, things aren't going at all between Guillaume and me. Yesterday morning I took the boat at Auteuil and got off at Solferino and walked up the stairs to the Quai du Louvre. At the top, whom do I see right in front of me, leaning over the parapet, but Guillaume. I don't know where he had been all night, drinking and doing heaven knows what; he was all disheveled, his necktie was undone, his collar was dirty and his hair uncombed. And there was I in front of him all spic and span in my new dress and a fresh collar and my flowered hat. Guillaume asked me point-blank, 'Where are you going?' Without batting an eyelash I smiled and said 'To the Louvre.' But Guillaume wasn't as drunk as he seemed. 'The Louvre is closed on Mondays,' he snapped at me.

"You can't always think of everything," Marie added, philosophically.

However, two days later I ran into Guillaume and Marie walking down the Boulevard Raspail. They had been lunching at Montparnasse. Marie had one hand on Guillaume's arm and held a parasol in the other. Apollinaire was beaming and strutting along like a village bridegroom. The two of them looked as though they were posing for the Douanier Rousseau's wedding picture.

Imagine how surprised I was shortly thereafter when Marie confided to me that she was planning to marry Otto von Waetjen, a young German painter well known around Montparnasse.

How did Apollinaire react to this? Marie told me how she broke the news to him.

The scene took place in a bar in the Rue Vavin. They were both sitting on bar-stools drinking aperitifs. "I have a big piece of news for you," she said.

"I have news for you, too," said Apollinaire.

"Tell me what it is."

"No, you tell me yours."

"No, you first."

"No, *you* first."

"No."

"You began it."

Neither would give in, and they were almost on the point of leaving the place each in his own direction.

Finally Marie gave in. "Here is my news. I'm going to get married."

Guillaume at first didn't believe her, and burst out laughing. To convince him, Marie told him the name of her fiancé, whom he knew quite well, and the date of her wedding, which was to take place very shortly.

Guillaume made no answer. He frowned, clenched his teeth, paid the barman, and walked out without saying a word.

The marriage took place on June 21, so privately that I was not present. That same night the newly-weds left Paris for a beach on the Atlantic coast. They were there when the war broke out. They went to Bordeaux and thence to Spain, where they stayed for nearly five years.

Guillaume Apollinaire and Marie Laurencin were never to meet again.

277

Guillaume Apollinaire

Toward the end of July—after there had begun to appear in the *Soirées de Paris* a series of typographically complicated poems that Apollinaire first baptized *"idéogrammes"* and later *"calligrammes,"* and which were later to have a history of their own—he was commissioned by the newspaper *Comoedia* to go to Deauville with his friend the illustrator André Rouveyre to write a series of articles about the local "season," which would officially open August 1. What opened instead was an international "season" that was to last four years. Rouveyre had with him a car and chauffeur:

> We don't believe there will be a war [Apollinaire wrote a few days later in a mixed-tense diary-reportage for *Comoedia*], but still we think it wiser to leave. Our chauffeur Nolant gets the car ready. At the hotel, all the girls are perturbed by our departure. One German woman is terrified; she was probably unable to get away.
>
> We speed through the night. At Lisieux, a flat tire; we stop under a street lamp to be able to see; the lamp goes out. "A war omen?" asks Rouveyre.
>
> It is a marvelous night. We meet numerous cars headed for Deauville (the races are scheduled for the next day), and this reassures us. Probably Paris has learned that the danger is over. Another flat tire. While Nolant repairs it, dawn breaks. The sunrise is marvelous over the Seine, marvelous and unforgettable. Streaks of black floating and gradually melting in a sea of white; then a thousand dark celestial beasts turn purple; the stars fade; a deep golden blaze brightens the horizon. The east grows still paler, then blossoms into a prodigious garden of the Hesperides. It is adorably cool. Then everything takes fire—with grace, as though love itself were the arsonist. At that moment I had a feeling of infinite emptiness; and I was just falling asleep when the sun appeared. It tortured us with its burning rays, and we both finally dozed off in the car that was racing at full speed toward Paris.

278

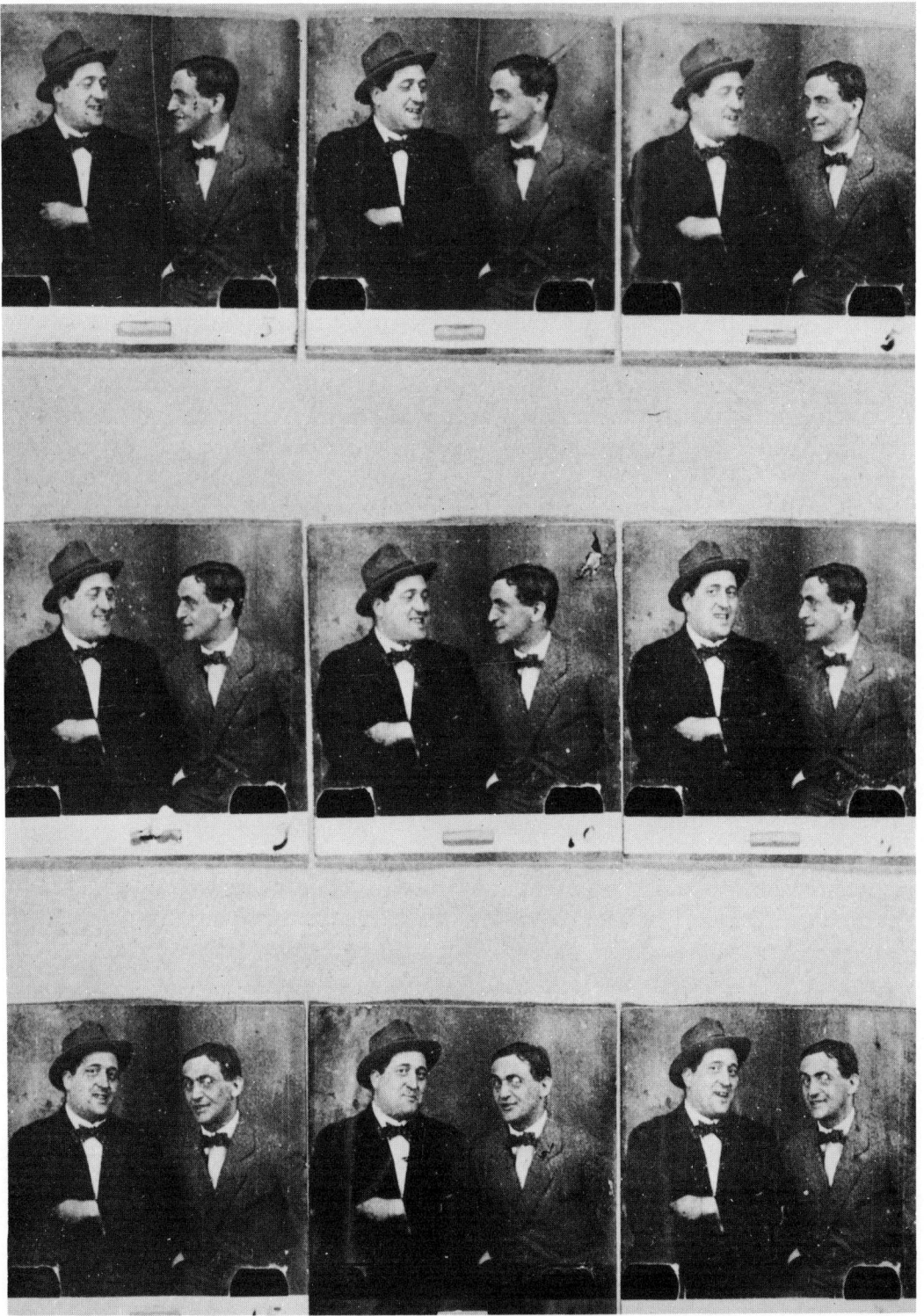

Guillaume Apollinaire and André Rouveyre, Paris, August 1, 1914

In commemoration of that ride Apollinaire wrote his poem "La Petite Auto," portions of which might be translated as follows:

The 31st of the month of August[15] 1914
I left Deauville a little before midnight
In Rouveyre's little auto

Including his chauffeur there were three of us

We said farewell to an entire epoch
Furious giants were casting their shadows over Europe

And when after passing that afternoon
Through Fontainebleau
We arrived in Paris
At the moment the mobilization notices were being posted
We understood my friend and I
That the little auto had taken us into an epoch that was New
And that even though we were both mature men
We had nevertheless just been born

[15] *Sic* (read July).

Apollinaire: Seven

Eight

Apollinaire's rebirth in the "new epoch" is inevitably a kind of epilogue. It was so brief, for one thing. Any look taken in August, 1914, at anything we have known before is a last look. If we keep looking, we see it change before our eyes into something different. Apollinaire changed into something different, and then he died.

This final chapter of his story forms no proper, smoothly flowing ending. It is like a cluster of bulletins—military, erotic, surgical, domestic, literary, obituary, much of it in the words of Apollinaire or his friends—added to the biography of Apollinaire the poet of *Alcools*. His life in the "new epoch" was to last exactly two days less than the war itself.

Within four months after his return from Deauville to Paris in the little auto he was enrolled in the Thirty-eighth Artillery Regiment of the French army.

Being a foreigner, he was not obliged to enlist. He could have sat out the war in a neutral country, or, like Picasso, in France itself; or he could have gone to New York and seen something of his friends Marcel Duchamp, Francis Picabia, and Albert Gleizes. But something drove Apollinaire to apply for enlistment early, on August 10. It must have been something deeper than the compulsion he certainly felt to throw in his lot with that of the French, a   281 becoming desire not to profit from the accident of foreign nationality when many of his closest friends were obliged to break off their normal lives. Something underlay that: some search for redemption on the part of a bastard who had been called a *canaille* by a magistrate and sent to the Santé. Nor would one be surprised to learn that he had been urged on toward military honors by Olga de Kostrowitzky, daughter of the Polish-Russian colonel and mistress of Francesco Flugi d'Aspermont, ex-officer in the army of the Bourbons. Throughout Apollinaire's service, Olga constantly sent him motherly letters of advice, food packages, warm socks, and other comforts: of his entire career this was the only part of which she seemed thoroughly to approve.

His first application to the army, made in Paris, was ignored. In early September he went to Nice—no one seems to know why—and it was there that he successfully enlisted, in December, and was sent to artillery barracks in Nîmes for training.

"I so love art that I have joined the artillery...."

So he wrote from Nîmes in a letter to a friend; and his career in the army was filled with quips, with poetry so celebrating the colors and sounds of war and of France at war that he is the dismay of pacifists, and with love for two women to whom he addressed countless letters and poems (often the same poems) from his barracks, from behind the lines, and from the trenches themselves. Apollinaire proved to be a steady, trustworthy soldier, cheerful amid rats, lice, mud, cold, and danger, and he made friends among officers and men.[1] What some have hailed as his "transformation" into a "new Apollinaire" was not to his advantage as an

282

artist—*Alcools,* the distillation of his previous life, remains his great poetic monument—but it provides a spectacle which as the French say is "not banal." It is not every poet who enters the artillery straight from opium-smoking and rises to a lieutenancy. The poet Apollinaire was determined to distinguish himself as Guillaume de Kostrowitzky in the war, and he was admitted to officer's training shortly after his enlistment.

He wanted to be French. His civil status was complex. He was considered by the French to be of Russian nationality because of his mother; Italy considered him Italian because of his birth in Rome. By language, by upbringing, and by occupation he was French already, but to become so officially required formal application and a long wait. The application he had made in the spring of 1914. Marcel Adéma has found the report made on his application by the appropriate governmental bureau, the "Renseignements généraux": it mentions his imprisonment in the Santé during the affair of the statuettes, but concludes that "As far as his patriotism is concerned, nothing has been reported that might cast suspicion on him. His name does not figure in

[1] Such friends did not forget him, and were sometimes picturesque in themselves. In the journal of the Père Marie-Alain Couturier, O.P., *Se Garder Libre,* there is the following entry: "9 November [1951], anniversary of the death of G. Apollinaire. Suddenly I hear the following story on the radio. A lecturer, perhaps the very man who is speaking, gave a talk on Apollinaire, I don't know when or where. Each time the poet's name was mentioned, a man in the audience rose from his seat, stood at attention, gave the military salute, and sat down again. This went on until the end of the lecture, when the lecturer was told that the man had served in Apollinaire's unit and that he always gave the military salute whenever he heard the name of 'his lieutenant.' I think that Apollinaire would never have wished for anything more fervently than for just such a tribute, such a human compensation."

283

Guillaume Apollinaire

the judicial records." The applicant thus unenthusiastically described was routinely awarded French nationality on March 9, 1916, just eight days before he was wounded in the head by shell splinters while in the service of the country that had so recently (he was not yet even aware of it) become officially his own. His activity at the moment of receiving his wound happened not to be particularly warlike: he was reading a copy of the *Mercure de France*. But the wound was a serious one. It necessitated trepanning and weakened his general health, making him an easy prey to the influenza that eventually carried him off.

In a letter written January 4, 1915, from his barracks at Nîmes to Serge Férat, with whom he seems to have been out of touch since before leaving Paris, he sketched briefly what had happened to him since they last met:

Happy New Year to you and Hélène.
Dear Serge, I am very glad to have news of you and your sister. On September 3, left for Nice. Joined a friend there. In my rooming house I had friends on every floor. Quickly got to know the officer in charge of the port, fliers, etc. Smoking parties, cocaine— the war was an artificial paradise. This went on for a month. It was then that I met the adored one. A month and a half of torment, passed my medical examination, then wildly happy, unable now to decide to sign up. Finally I did sign up, broke everything off, and left for Nîmes without leaving my address or my Polish name. The day after I reported to my unit she was at the door of the barracks and stayed here nine days. Then, on the thirty-first, at three A.M., I obtained leave and went to Nice until the midnight of the second. You can imagine how pleased I was to be back in Nice in uniform. Saw many old acquaintances who were much impressed, and here I am worn out from my leave. Revolver practice all morning and saber all afternoon. Tomorrow, riding

284

all day. I am well, and I feel that soldiering is my real trade. I like it very much. My friend tells me that the whole thing is like an opera to me, and she is right. I've had many tumbles from my horse, but it doesn't bother me. I really enjoy it. My behind gets rather sore, especially on long rides and on the rough downgrades. The big guns are interesting, too. I am fifteen or sixteen years older than most of the others, but I get good marks.

The "adored one," who so legendarily found her way from Nice to Apollinaire's barracks at Nîmes without knowing either his address or his Polish name, is famous in the Apollinaire canon as "Lou."

She is Louise de Coligny-Châtillon, descendant of an old French family whose most famous member, Admiral de Coligny, perished in the massacre of St. Bartholomew. Apollinaire's friend André Rouveyre had known her; it is probably through Rouveyre that they met in Nice. Rouveyre has described her as convent-educated from the age of four, as unhappily married at seventeen, and—to retain his careful adjectives—as *"spirituelle, dégagée, frivole, impétueuse, puérile, sensible, insaissisable, énervée, un peu éperdue en quelque sorte."* In the early 1960's she was living in the South of France, solitary, unapproachable, *farouche;* when Marcel Adéma called on her she pretended to be her own maid, and informed Monsieur that Madame was out.

She did follow Apollinaire to Nîmes; he did spend an ecstatic New Year's leave with her in Nice; then she threw him into despair by never coming to occupy a room he found for her in Nîmes near his barracks; indeed, when Apollinaire wrote his New Year's letter to Serge Férat, the carnal period of his affair with Lou was over, though he was unaware of it. But Lou was the recipient of seventy-six

285

Guillaume Apollinaire

passionate poems by Apollinaire, sent to her by him in a series of erotic letters written over the space of a year, from October, 1914, after the opium and cocaine in Nice, to September, 1915, shortly before he went into the front lines. Out of their short physical union the two strange lovers built a strange fantasy. Longing for her, he wrote her the passionate, explicit letters and the poems in the letters; she, having no intention of ever seeing him again, sent, until she tired of the game, equally explicit replies that inflamed him to further poems and further letters.

In 1955 Apollinaire's seventy-six poems to this partner in flesh and fantasy were published in facsimile, as he had written them in his letters. In some of them the writing forms pictures—a woman's head, a cigarette, the Maison Carrée at Nîmes: it is an old device that for a time Apollinaire made his own, calling the form *"calligrammes."* One poem is entitled "A Madame la Comtesse L—— ——y-——n": the poet was not insensitive to Lou's aristocratic name. The volume contains a double preface by André Rouveyre, and the preface tells the story of the projected publication not only of the poems but of all the letters with the poems included. Lou had consented to their integral publication. They were reproduced in facsimile by a Swiss publisher, each letter in its own envelope, the entire collection enclosed in a case and entitled *Lettres à Lou;* but when the edition was ready for distribution, Apollinaire's literary executors refused their permission because the letters were too free. They demanded cuts and revisions; Rouveyre and the publisher refused; the edition was "destroyed." How completely destroyed? Rouveyre implies total destruction,

Apollinaire: Eight

but there are copies of *Lettres à Lou* to be found here and there, quite apart from those few that were spared for certain individuals and institutions with the executors' consent. Persons who claim to be knowing hint that a stock of the edition exists, awaiting only the entrance of Apollinaire into the public domain to be marketed; certainly some day the world will have access to this product of a soldier-poet's erotic fantasy. Meanwhile we must be content with those few of the letters that were printed earlier, in a magazine,[2] and with the lyrics, which are now available to all in the Pléiade edition of Apollinaire's verse.[3]

But there exists another collection of Apollinaire's war letters, this one available to all who read French, and comparable in interest to the correspondence of such articulate artists as Delacroix and Van Gogh, and the literary equal of any volume of love letters ever published anywhere.

On January 1, 1915—the first New Year's day of the war—a young school teacher from Oran stepped into a train in the railway station at Nice. Her name was Madeleine Pagès, and she tells her own story:

It was in the train taking me back from Nice to Marseilles on January 1, 1915, that I met Guillaume Apollinaire. I had been spending my Christmas vacation at Nice, with the family of my older brother, a second lieutenant in the artillery. And I was returning to Oran by the boat leaving Marseilles that same evening, the *Sidi-Brahim*, I think.

[2] *La Table Ronde,* September 1952.
[3] The reader is cautioned against an earlier, faulty printing of a few of these poems in a volume entitled *Ombre de mon amour* (1947).

I was happy, I had enjoyed my vacation; my suitcase was full of presents that I was taking back to my mother, my sisters, and my younger brothers, all of whom were awaiting my return; I was wearing a pretty hat that I was very proud of, and the morning was glorious.

Buying my ticket for the eight o'clock train, choosing a second-class compartment in the center of the car—it all seemed easy and pleasant; I climbed confidently in, lifted my suitcase onto the rack, put down my book, my newspaper, and my sandwiches.

The station was empty except for the few employees on duty. Nicely settled in my corner, I was looking forward to enjoying the compartment all to myself as far as Marseilles, when a soldier came in, murmured an apology as he walked past me, and leaned out the window to speak to a lady who had come to see him off. Was he a private or an officer? I was never able to tell one rank from another; he was tall—yes, rather tall, only a bit short-legged and barrel-chested; and he wore his *képi* pushed back on his head—it was too small for him.

So much for my solitude. I wanted to move to the next compartment, but how could I without calling attention to myself? The soldier was saying something to the lady in a low voice: "Poetry? You want to read some poetry, you say? Then read Baudelaire's *Les Fleurs du Mal*."

Had he really said "Baudelaire's *Les Fleurs du Mal*?" In that case I would stay where I was.

The lady came into the compartment for a moment, to say goodbye to the soldier. She was tall and slender and seemed a little tired: I slipped quickly out into the corridor lest I seem indiscreet.

The lady returned to the station platform and I to my seat, and now the soldier was at the window again saying something else: "Don't stand there—you'll catch cold; go back to the hotel, the room is paid for till noon."

The train pulled out. The morning had grown even more beautiful; the car was well heated, and I smiled to myself as I thought of the odds and ends in my suitcase and of how happy my sisters would be when they found them. I longed to have someone to chatter with about it.

Apollinaire: Eight

Out the window I caught sight of the little pink beach with its pines where I had come with my brother at the time of his marriage the year before: then there was a marvelous glimpse of the sea. I must have exclaimed aloud, for the soldier left his own corner and came over and stood next to me: together we stared out at it, both of us enchanted by the beauty and the blueness.

We spoke of Nice, which we had just left and which he knew better than I did: I was fascinated to hear him tell me about the old quarters, with their Italian houses festooned with clotheslines and multicolored wash; he described the outdoor market, other parts of the city; his voice was pleasant, a little husky; I liked his profile and his hands, which were ringless and relaxed. He gave me a quick look, at one point, and I felt the better for it.

The roadstead of Golfe-Juan, with warships at anchor, and the little sails of the fishing boats that had gone out the night before, even though it was New Year's Eve, the cactus along the shore that reminded me of Oran, Algiers, and Bône, all of them cities that I had lived in and that were to my mind lovelier and livelier than the ones we were leaving. . . . By now I was smiling easily with him as we talked, and whenever I raised my eyes I found that he was looking at me. His eyes were brown, like his hair; his features were wonderfully handsome; he was much better-looking without his *képi*. Suddenly it was ten o'clock. With a blush I offered him one of my sandwiches, and he accepted politely. We proceeded to eat; now the train was going faster, and somehow its rhythm seemed to make us happy and unconstrained. I can't remember how we began to talk about poetry—I think that while he was swallowing a slice of ham, he asked and I answered that I loved it as much as I loved life itself, and that indeed I made no distinction between the two. He was so pleased that I almost thought he was going to kiss me; I sensed that he was about to tell me something, but he decided not to and spoke about poets instead. He asked me which ones I was familiar with, which ones I liked; now we began to vie with one another, laughing, mentioning various poets and reciting their verses.

Voici des fruits, des fleurs, des feuilles et des branches,

Guillaume Apollinaire

Sois sage ô ma douleur et tiens-toi plus tranquille
Some we recited together:
Sur le printemps de ma jeunesse folle
Je ressemblais l'arondelle qui vole

"Do you know Villon, Mademoiselle? I love him so."
And I burst out:
Femme je suis povrette et ancienne
Qui rien ne scay; oncques lettre ne leuz

The poetry made our mood more serious; the world seemed
to recede; and I leaned dreamily back in my corner and shut my
eyes.

The lines he had been reciting reverberated within me; never
before had I fully realized how wonderful they were. It was as
though he were holding them in his hand, enjoying the feel of
them as well as their sound. And yet he spoke them, or rather
murmured them, with a simplicity that it was beyond me to
match. I was entranced, overcome: I let him finish alone the verses
that I had begun.

At Fréjus the train stopped and a passenger entered our compartment: what a pity! But I had no further desire to talk, or even
read, and like a good little girl I closed my book and folded my
hands.

The new passenger sat down opposite us—the soldier hadn't
budged from his seat, as though to indicate that he and I were
traveling together—and I felt a little embarrassed at being surprised on such good terms with a stranger.

The soldier was disconsolate—I knew this from his restless
movements on the seat beside me; I felt sorry for him, and after
hesitating a moment or two I turned to him and smiled. His answering smile was so shy, so charming, that I was strangely upset.
It seemed to me that never before had anyone treated me with
this kind of respectful sympathy.

But the passenger began to talk to the soldier, asked him
questions about his company and his depot and other military
matters that I didn't listen to. Then he began to talk about business,
commercial difficulties, transportation tie-ups, all kinds of things.

Apollinaire: Eight

The soldier always answered him to the point. Then they discovered that they had acquaintances in common. They spoke of Monaco, and the soldier said that he had attended a Catholic school there: "So did I!" the passenger exclaimed. They introduced themselves, and I heard a foreign family name that I didn't catch, then the name Guillaume. They exchanged dates and discovered that the soldier's brother Albert had been a classmate of the passenger's. Whereupon the soldier turned to me, and to include me in the conversation told comic stories about a certain professor who had had a great deal of trouble with them—and indeed he must have, what with pupils letting beetles loose in class and throwing spitballs. I laughed, but I suspected that the soldier was showing off a little, that actually, when he was twelve, he must have been a quiet, dreaming, fattish, good-hearted boy, incapable—whatever he might be saying now—of harming a fly.

The passenger left the train at the next stop, and once again we were alone, a little more serious now. The soldier took up my closed book, played with it a moment. Gradually he began to say more about poetry, about how much it can express and about the way it gives life to things. Then he began a game of inventing images for the towns we had been riding through.

Nice, he said, was for him a rearing horse, a thoroughbred horse rearing in the midst of a great celebration, surrounded by Carnival cheering and a battle of flowers.

I said that I could see Villefranche as a great sea shell, wide open to sea and sky.

And, very softly, as though picking up a much earlier thread of our conversation, he murmured: "I am a poet myself, Mademoiselle. The pseudonym I write under is Guillaume Apollinaire. Have you ever heard of me?"

A poet! He was a poet! What a marvelous adventure to recount to my family! I was choking with delight, but I had to admit reluctantly that no, I hadn't heard of him . . . yet.

He was surprised. "It's obvious from what you say that people in Algeria are well up on the poets, so I thought. . . ."

"I have to confess to you," I said, "that most of what I know of the moderns comes from a cheap little volume of selections 291 called *The Hundred Best French Poems,* and in the edition I have there's nothing by you."

He assured me that the book must be very well put together anyway, judging from what I had learned by heart. "Still, I'd like you to know my poems. I'll send you a volume, *Alcools,* that was published in 1913, and if you feel like it you can tell me what you think of it." I thanked him with a smile and a nod.

By then the name had begun to awaken echoes, and I found myself wondering whether what I had told him was true. Guillaume Apollinaire! How could I have said that I had never heard the name?

Hadn't I noticed it one morning in a newspaper? I seemed to remember thinking it a lovely name—Apollo, Apollinaire: what a daring, amusing association!

But still I was uncertain, so uncertain that I didn't dare speak, and we both of us sat there silent, absorbed in our thoughts.

Perhaps the lady in Nice was at this very moment reading *Les Fleurs du Mal,* if she had been able to buy it at the station bookstall.

I looked in my bag. Was my railroad ticket safe? And my steamship ticket too?

I was going to have to think about getting rid of this soldier. Nicely, but firmly: after all, I couldn't be seen walking with him in the streets of Marseilles!

Suddenly I wasn't quite so sure of the beauty of the little gifts I was taking with me. Tiny pieces of Copenhagen ware, the size of a finger—a little vase with a design of blue flowers on a white ground, a miniature coffee set on a tray: up to now I had thought them delightful. The soldier, I felt, would have preferred the native Algerian "Nabeul" that I had once bought in Bône—primitive, sincere pieces of glazed earthenware.

He had leaned his head back against the cushions, and now he closed his eyes and suddenly looked depressed and tired: never before had I seen a face with closed eyes express so many things— it gave me a shock.

He opened his eyes, took a little notebook from his pocket and handed it to me. "Will you write your address?"

Apollinaire: Eight

I wrote it with his pencil, tracing my letters carefully. I did not write "Mademoiselle," and the omission seemed casual and amusing; but a minute later I reproached myself for having been so free—my name, unadorned there on the sheet of paper, seemed to me in wretched taste.

But the soldier smiled at me so sweetly that life was good again and I lost all sense of constraint.

We were coming into Marseilles. It was time to put on my hat—the poet got it down for me. Standing before the mirror I fluffed out my hair and gazed with astonishment at the new face I saw there: a little pale, the eyes overlarge. But behind my face, in the mirror, I saw the poet's face: his eyes were smiling, watching me closely in all my movements, and for the first time since leaving Nice I was able to take a long look at him. And as I was lowering my veil our eyes met in the mirror and I smiled at him: I was enchanted by the way he was looking at me so sweetly, so attentively, and I was overcome by a rush of feeling, all trace of which I had to banish from my eyes before leaving the mirror and turning around.

I drew my veil tight and pinned it at the back: it separated me from him a little. He was aware of this: I cast a timid glance at him and saw a sad look come into his eyes; his mouth drooped, too—his whole face was so expressive, and now that I had turned away from the mirror I didn't dare stare too long.

It was time to get down my suitcase; the train was pulling into the station: this was going to be a difficult goodbye to say, and I felt impatient to have it over with. Impatient to see the last of those caressing eyes and hear the last of that gentle voice; I couldn't bear the thought of touching his hand: I felt that I would begin to run the moment we left the train. I was eager to be on the station platform, on the boat, in my own home.

I wanted to think about him. And this, I knew, I could do only after he was gone.

The train had stopped. The soldier stepped off, carrying my suitcase; then he turned, helped me down chivalrously, kept my hand in his for a moment and kissed it. I don't know whether we said goodbye or not: I know that I began to run, my heart thudding. But before reaching the gate I turned and saw him still

293

Guillaume Apollinaire

standing next to the open door of our car: his arms were hanging at his sides and he was watching me run.

Had he seen me turn? He must have, for he began to run, too, to catch up with me, and as I was hastily, frantically giving up my ticket to the employee at the gate I felt his breath on my cheek and heard his voice again, this time murmuring *"Au revoir, Mademoiselle!"*

I did not turn around. Outside the station I jumped into a carriage and called to the driver: "The pier, *Compagnie des Transports Maritimes,* sailing of the *Sidi-Brahim!"*

And it was only when I was in my cabin, which the chief steward consented to open for me two hours before sailing time, that I began to regret my flight and to think of the words of farewell that I should have uttered.

I, who had fancied myself in the role of experienced traveler, a woman of the world, sophisticated in behavior and speech—I had acted like a badly brought-up little girl, or, even worse, like a mannerless little provincial, yes, that was it, a mannerless little provincial. What would he think of me?

Just that.

And then I had missed having lunch in Marseilles. The bouillabaisse at Basso's: I had been counting on it as a picturesque detail for the family chronicle—every trip I took was a new chapter.

Would they all be at the boat to meet me?

I would have to wait a little before mentioning the poet, to heighten my effects: besides, I would have to be careful about how I told the story, lest my mother begin to have ideas. But for that I could count, I felt, on the inspiration of the moment.

Stretched out in my berth I heard as though in a dream the preparations for departure that I knew too well to listen to. The chief steward had told me that I would be alone in my cabin because there were very few passengers at this time of the year, and I was glad that this was so.

Three shrill blasts from the siren. We were off. The sea that had looked so calm and beautiful that morning had turned rough: there was a real storm, lasting for the entire crossing.

294

My first storm, too.

The following April, Madeleine Pagès received a picture post card:

16 April 1915

Mademoiselle,

I have been unable to send you my book of poems because my publisher is in the army like me, and his business is suspended. I will send it to you as soon as I can.

Do you remember me, between Nice and Marseilles, on January 1?

My respectful greetings. I kiss your hand.

Guillaume Apollinaire

sender: *Corporal Gui. de Kostrowitzky*
38th Artillery
45th Battery
Postal Sector 59

Mademoiselle Pagès sent the corporal a box of cigars and a letter, and received the following reply:

5 May 1915

Mademoiselle,

What a wonderful surprise I found waiting for me last night about ten o'clock in the midst of an incredible bombardment of heavy guns sweetly accompanied by rifle fire and a steady rattling of machine guns. I was still on my horse, when in the black night of this forest where we are living in our huts the postman calls out to me: "A package from Algeria for you." And there was the lovely parcel from Oran, in the midst of the shower of Austrian 120's and 88's and the Boche 77's. A charming box of ammunition —the shells it contains are so fragrant and peaceful! I don't know how to thank you personally. But while waiting for a favorable opportunity, and since I haven't been the only one to benefit from your gracious gift, I send you the thanks of all the non-commissioned officers of the battery: like me they have sampled the cigars, and like me they find them delicious.

And now, sitting on a sack of oats, writing to you on a tree trunk, I see you as I saw you that day—the friendly little passenger

295

Guillaume Apollinaire

with the long eyelashes and the expressive face. A few hours in a train! A marvelous memory, against this background of war and rain and, from over toward Perthes, desperate deadly thunder. Here it is quieter than last night: from time to time a single shell goes whining over my hut.

. . . I resume my letter. Now, oh my discreet faraway messenger from sunny Africa, the wind and the rain have ceased entirely. All around me is the forest, with its caverns of blackness. Between the branches I catch a glimpse of sky, which gives me the impression of a dark blue eye, immense and faithful. Here we are at the furthermost edge of fighting France. Our artillery is very close to the infantry trenches, which at this point are sixty meters from the German trenches. There isn't a tree unscarred by shell-fire, and some of the trunks are smashed—chewed into pulp, like schoolboys' penholders.

> *Voici quelques pauvres fleurettes*
> *De merisier et de lilas . . .*
> *Si Mai chez vous a plus de fêtes*
> *Chez nous il a bien plus d'ECLATS*
> *Mais ce sont nos seules fleurettes*
> *Brins de merise et de lilas. . . . .*

I resume my letter for the third time by the light of a candle. In the meanwhile the postman has brought me a spray of lilac, too, in the form of your sweet letter. I must answer your post-script first. I know nothing of the village you ask about. I am not even in that sector. We are not allowed to send post cards showing views of the regions we are in: I am closer to the Cathedral, the earth here is *marneux.* I didn't dare write sooner, not having been able to keep my promise to send you *Alcools,* my book of poems. Nevertheless—I tell you this very frankly—I have thought of you often, very often. I am so far away that I can certainly tell you that without offending you.

Your letter took ten days to reach me, and now that I have your kind promise I won't have an answer for three weeks or a month. So write me a little oftener, and I will write you as often as I can too, if you would like me to, and in my next letter I will

Apollinaire: Eight

tell you about my life and about the trenches and about my horse
Loulou and about poetry, too, if there is room enough.

Unless, of course, a too-long silence gives you its own ample
information. . . .

Guillaume Apollinaire

They both wrote again:

11 May, 1915

Petite fée

We had the same idea, the same anxiety about each other:
neither of us must ever let the other go too long without news.
Your sweet card of today, sent the 3rd, gave me an even more
marvelous surprise if possible than your first letter, for I expected
nothing for three weeks. I wanted to write you these last few days
but I have had no time to myself.

I promised you details about the life here, and your new
card asks for them.

Today I will tell you about the infantry trenches. . . .

And with the long letter of description, in which he
tells her that he has baptized one of the trenches *L'allée
Madeleine,* he sends her, written on a piece of birch bark,
four of his calligrammes, stanzas whose lines are drawings
of the objects they describe.

Written normally, both lines level like the sky:

> *Le ciel est d'un bleu profond*
> *Et mon regard s'y noie et fond*

Written with the lines running together at one end,
like the tip of an artillery shell:

> *Un invisible obus miaule*
> *J'écris assis au pied d'un saule*

Written in the shape of a star:

> *L'étoile du berger déjà*
> *Comme l'aigrette d'un rajah*

297

Guillaume Apollinaire

Written in the form of a cannon:

Où comme une œillade chérie
Brille sur notre batterie

The piece of bark is signed:

Guillaume Apollinaire
at the front
15 May 1915

Such are the preface and the first few pages of the volume called *Tendre comme le souvenir*,[4] printed and issued in France quite normally by the publisher Gallimard in 1955, with a foreword by Marcel Adéma. It was the indefatigable Adéma who had discovered the whereabouts of Madeleine Pagès (she was now living in France), and persuaded her and Apollinaire's executors to permit the publication of the letters. Madeleine needed only a little guidance in the writing of her preface: in Adéma's words, "Madeleine is far and away, of all who were Apollinaire's women friends, the most cultivated and interesting. *Elle est très bien.*"

Nowhere is there a more "living picture" of a poet in a war than in *Tendre comme le souvenir,* or, outside of Stendhal, a more vivid picture of war itself. Journalism, that usual vehicle for the sights and sounds of war, shrivels be-

[4] The title is taken from a line in a poem in one of the letters, referring to a ring that Apollinaire sent Madeleine, made from an aluminum shell fragment. *"L'aluminium est un métal très tendre,"* he wrote in a letter; and in the poem:

Vous m'attendez ayant aux doigts
De pauvres bagues en aluminium pâle comme l'absence
Et tendre comme le souvenir
Métal de notre amour métal semblable à l'aube

298

side these letters and poems of Apollinaire's. Madeleine Pagès received dozens of them throughout 1915. About ten complete letters and about fifty passages here and there have been omitted from *Tendre comme le souvenir,* being considered, according to Marcel Adéma, "too free, erotic, personal"; without them the volume throbs sufficiently; if the little school teacher from Oran found Apollinaire so seductive in the train, one can imagine the effect of his burning letters, the "secret poems" in which he celebrates all the zones of her body. She did not know at the time that some of the same poems she was receiving were being sent in similar letters to the lady whom she had seen with Apollinaire in the train.

Throughout the months of 1915 the letters to Madeleine grow increasingly passionate and erotic; cries of physical longing are interspersed with autobiography; he wants his little girl to learn about his life, and he writes her about his mother, about Annie Playden, the painters, Marie Laurencin, the affair of the statuettes, his poetry, and even something about Lou. Much of what we know about Apollinaire's view of his own past and present comes from the letters to Madeleine. He writes to Madeleine's mother, asking for her daughter's hand; it is accorded; now they are engaged. He is promoted to sergeant; then he transfers to the infantry as second lieutenant; in the front-line trenches with his new regiment, under heavy bombardment, even he finds it hard to continue thinking of war as "beautiful" or "exciting": he experiences the full horror of the holocaust:

Nine days without washing, sleeping on the ground without straw, ground infested with vermin, not a drop of water except that used to vaporize the gas masks. . . . It is fantastic what one can stand. . . . One of the parapets of my trench is partly made of corpses. . . . There are no head lice, but swarms of body lice, pubic lice. . . . No writer will ever be able to tell the simple horror of the trenches, the mysterious life that is led there.

At the end of December he is given two weeks' leave, and spends them with Madeleine and her family in Oran;[5] Madeleine is loving but chaste; on his way back to the front he stops in Paris and tells his mother of their engagement; his mother, he tells her, "has nothing against it." He does not tell Madeleine that in Paris he is accompanied everywhere by an anonymous lady whom he met on the ship returning from Oran to Marseilles.

On March 14, 1916, he writes:

Mon cher amour, I have two letters from you. We are about to go to the front line. I am writing in haste, wearing my helmet. Don't know what we're going to be doing. At all events, I leave you all my possessions; let this be considered my will if things turn out that way. Well, let us hope that for the time being nothing like that happens. I adore you. The weather is glorious. I want you to be brave now and always.
Your Gui.

On the 15th he sent a military post card:

Mon amour, Haven't slept all night. No way to describe things here. Unimaginable. The weather is fine. I think of you. We sleep in the open. This morning, saw a sweet little squirrel, climbing up and up. I am tired, but cheerful at the same time. My mouth is full of dirt. I don't know whether there will be mail tonight. I hope there will be.
Your Gui.

[5] While waiting for the ship at Marseilles he made a pilgrimage to the Jas de Bouffan, Cézanne's house outside Aix-en-Provence.

Apollinaire: Eight

Guillaume Apollinaire with Madeleine Pagès, Oran, January, 1916

301

Guillaume Apollinaire

On the 18th another post card, written in pencil, almost illegible:

Mon amour, Yesterday I was wounded in the head by a splinter from a 150. It went right through my helmet. The helmet saved my life this time. I'm being admirably taken care of, and apparently it isn't serious. I'll write when I can.
Your Gui.

The following are the rest of Apollinaire's published letters to Madeleine:

19-3-16

Mon amour, I'm all right, but I still have that splinter in my head which they haven't been able to extract. I adore you, my love, but I am too tired to write, so I had better not. I adore you. *Gui.*

21-3-16
[Ambul. 1–55]
Sector 34

My love, I'll be operated on this morning. I send you my new address:
S/Lieutenant Gui de Kostrowitzky—Wounded
Hôtel Dieu—Château-Thierry
Aisne

22-3-16

My love, For the time being everything is going well, and after X-ray it seems there is no need to re-do the operation, which was performed in the ambulance at two in the morning on the 18th. I don't know yet whether I'll be evacuated to the rear, because head wounds heal quickly.

I was wounded just above the right temple—a narrow escape.

I am tired.

I adore you, my love, and I kiss you on the mouth.
Gui.

302

24-3-16

My love, I am better and I leave Château-Thierry to-morrow. If I am sent to the rear I will no doubt get sick leave; if not I'll get a regular leave and will come to see you. It tires me to write. I adore you, my Madelon.

> *Gui.*

25-3-16

My love, since my temperature didn't go down last night I'll not be evacuated today, but probably Tuesday.

I adore you, my darling, and I hope I get letters from you soon. I haven't had any since I was wounded.

Today I am better. We'll know more tonight, because temperature goes up at night.

I adore you.

> *Gui.*

[Telegram]
Château-Thierry 27 March 1916

EVERYTHING GOING WELL WILL BE EVACUATED TOMORROW PARIS WILL WIRE ADDRESS I LOVE YOU GUI

28-3-16

My love, I'm all right. We are waiting for the wound to close, but there's further cause for worry. I'll be evacuated to Paris today, and there they will complete the treatment. I adore you.

> *Gui.*

No letters from you since the 16th.

[*No date. Postmark 30-3-16*]

My love, I am a little tired from the trip and won't write very much. I am very comfortable at the Val de Grâce in Paris. I adore you and hope to see you soon. My wound is doing very well; it is almost all gone. Head wounds heal quickly.

I adore you.

> *Gui.*

303

Guillaume Apollinaire

Here is my address:

Sous-Lieutenant G. de K.
First Wounded
Hospital of the Val de Grâce, Paris

[Telegram]
Paris 12 April 1916

AM ITALIAN GOVERNMENT HOSPITAL 41 QUAI D'ORSAY RECEIVED
PARCEL I LOVE YOU GUI

2 April 1916

My love, I am supposed to do little writing or reading.

I am at the Val de Grâce (First Section Wounded). I am wiring you so you won't worry but I haven't sent the wire to you yet because it is probable that I shall go to the Italian Government Hospital, 41 Quai d'Orsay, in a few days. Then I will wire you at once. The weather is glorious and my condition is improving, but I tire quickly.

I adore you and kiss you. *Gui.*

6-4-16

My love, I am much better, but it still tires me to write.

So don't hold it against me, my darling. The weather was fine the first day after I came here. Now it is very bad, real Zeppelin weather. The wound is closing gradually. Everything is all right. I'm not even sure that I'll get a long sick leave. I was wounded at the Bois des Buttes, near Berry-au-Bac, a dangerous spot.

For several days now I haven't had a letter from you.

Write soon.

Embrace all the family for me.

I adore you.

Your Gui.

12 April [1916]

My love, your letters are reaching me regularly now, but it is clear that one whole lot of them has been lost. I go out a little these days. This means that I am better, but it will still take some

304

Apollinaire: Eight

Guillaume Apollinaire in the Italian Government Hospital, Paris, 1916

305

Guillaume Apollinaire

time before my wound is closed.

I left the Val de Grâce for the Italian Government Hospital, which is much more comfortable. There are only a few of us here for the time being. My medical attendant here is my friend Serge Jastrebzoff, who has a heart of gold, and we are looked after by the ambassador's wife, Madame Tittoni, who is a charming lady, rather like your mother. I never wrote you that I was at Rheims. I was wounded at the Bois des Buttes, west of the Choléra and Berry-au-Bac.

Your letters are exquisite, my darling.

I think you mentioned relatives of yours in Brittany, at Quimper, I think. My friend Max Jacob, who is from Quimper, also spoke of them to me.

Send me the poems for the volume, which will be published by the Mercure, I think.

I'll write more tomorrow because I am tired.

I love you.

Gui

[Telegram]
Paris, 19 April 1916

DONT COME NOW GUI

[Telegram]
Paris, 26 April 1916

SEND COPIES OF POEMS DONT WORRY BUT MUST NOT WRITE YET WILL HAVE LETTER SENT TOMORROW I LOVE YOU GUI

[*No date. Postmark, 1 May 1916*]

My darling love, I must not write at present or go out. I was doing well, and my wound is almost healed. I adore your exquisite letters but you must not be alarmed. I was forbidden to go out because I had a few accidents, such as fainting spells and trouble on my left side, particularly the left hand. But the opinion is that it will be nothing, so don't worry. I'll try to get post cards to write you every day but I have no one to do it for me.

The wife of the Italian ambassador, who looks after me, is

306

a kind and charming lady, but I don't dare ask her to write for me.

I am tired, so don't send me telegrams, they upset me too much.

Wait for news from me and don't worry, my darling.

I kiss you.

> Gui.

[Telegram]

Paris, 2 May 1916

RECEIVED POEMS LETTERS FOLLOW GUI

[No date. Postmark, 7 May 1916]

My dear little Madeleine, I am tired and I have so few friends in Paris at this moment that it makes me sad.

Everybody is selfish. I am much better, but I have great spells of dizziness and my left arm is out of action. I am not what I used to be, from any point of view, and I almost feel that I should become a priest or a monk. I am so far removed from my book, which has just been published, that I don't even know whether I had a copy sent to you. If I didn't, let me know, and I'll have one sent at once.

I kiss you a thousand times.

> Gui.

[Telegram]

Paris, 11 May 1916

OPERATION[6] PERFORMED SUCCESSFULLY AM AS WELL AS POSSIBLE GUI

26 August 1916

My dear Madeleine, You must not think of coming; it would upset me too much.

Most of all, don't write me sad letters; they frighten me.

I'll write you once a week. You do the same; I'm afraid of letters. I can't see anybody I know. I don't write to my brother or my mother, and I haven't seen Mother since April 15. She is distressed, but I simply cannot do it. I have become very easily upset,

---

[6] Trepanation.

307

Guillaume Apollinaire

and it will take me a long time to get over this.

Send me my notes, my record book from the artillery, because it is probable that I will be sent back to the artillery, my ring with the gold seal because now I can wear it again, and the ring with the German button.

I am going to start putting my notes in order, to pass the time, and will give my poems to the Mercure for publication the way they are unless I can improve them.

I am disgusted with Paris. So little is being done here toward winning the war that I feel a kind of despair.

As I see it, it is going to last at least another three years. Very unpleasant.

Don't send anybody to see me—visits from strangers frighten me. M.G. is no doubt very nice, but I get too upset when it's someone I don't know. But I think I can work a little. I'll try. But things have been going badly so long that there's no counting on anything. All the good jobs have been taken by the stay-at-homes; nothing much is left for someone who has been at the front. I kiss you a thousand times.

Gui.

16 September 1916.

My little Madelon, I have been rather poorly of late because of the coming of autumn. I have many, many dizzy spells and have become very irritable. Thank you for the parcel. It does not contain the notes I asked for: what I want are not notes about artillery, but notes I made while I was in the artillery. I jotted down things I heard the gunners say, and I should like to use them. I should also like my map and Dupont's letters, which I want to show to his family; they are collecting them because he was killed at Douaumont—seventeen shell splinters. I should also like to have the two water colors by M.L. which I want to send back: people returning here from Spain repeat things she said that I won't tolerate, so I'd rather send them back. I should also like the second copy of *Case d'armons*[7] that you have: I want to give it to Madame Tittoni; also some of my books that you have, especially one about

[7] A touching little sheaf of poems that Apollinaire had polygraphed in violet ink by a gelatine process at the front.

Apollinaire: Eight

the folklore of the Marne and a directory of the departments of the Marne and the Aisne. I need them for articles. My regiment has had its share of fighting and of honors; I think there is almost nothing left of it, but its flag was decorated.[8] My war comrades are almost all dead. I don't even dare write the colonel to ask him for details. I was told that he himself was wounded.

My friend Berthier's brother was killed a few days after being promoted second lieutenant.

All this is quite macabre, and with all these horrible visions in my mind I don't know what more to say.

I kiss you.

Gui.

There were a few more notes, which have never been published; but it is sufficiently clear from those that we have quoted that Apollinaire had made up his mind to break with Madeleine. Like Annie Playden, she had been an episode in his life; Annie had left him, now he left Madeleine. Both affairs were the occasions of some of his best writing, and certainly both women were for him muses rather than real persons. The real Annie Playden went to California, to a life of marriage and employment, ignorant of the career and the new name of the young tutor she had known in the Rhineland: indeed she had never even known that he wrote verse. The real Madeleine, bruised

[8] Apollinaire's regiment was cited collectively for bravery in action, and he himself was awarded the Croix de Guerre. The passage concerning him in the order reads: "Russian subject. Enlisted for the duration of the war in the artillery, where he was promoted sergeant; requested transfer to the infantry, where he was promoted second lieutenant; then became French citizen; at all times displayed exemplary composure and courage; was severely wounded in the head on 17 March 1916 during a violent bombardment."

Guillaume Apollinaire

and bewildered by the change of Apollinaire's tone and then by his silence, went on into a life of spinsterhood and teaching, learning by chance of his marriage and soon after of his death. Apollinaire never explained his change of heart concerning Madeleine. Perhaps she had merely filled an important wartime need for a lonely soldier. This lonely soldier was a special one: Madeleine was a precious correspondent for a poet facing death daily; he could send her his poems and other effusions with a reasonable certainty that they would be cherished and preserved. Did he ever really intend to marry her? His letters sound nothing if not sincere; and yet . . . there are those duplicates of the poems, sent simultaneously to Lou.

It seems incontestable that Marie Laurencin was the woman with whom Apollinaire had the most complete physical and spiritual relationship, and that her desertion of him was a traumatic experience that certainly influenced the course of his subsequent affairs. Even during the war he sent poems to Marie in Spain, via their common friend, Louise Faure-Favier. His wound and his trepanation were further traumas, and the condition in which they at least temporarily left him—"I am not what I used to be, from any point of view, and I almost feel that I should become a priest or a monk"—must also be part of the story of his desertion of Madeleine. His motives may not have been entirely selfish: his physical condition certainly brought with it feelings of inadequacy.

What had happened to Apollinaire is this:
After he was wounded above the right temple by shell

310

splinters (not a single splinter, as he seems to have thought), at four o'clock in the afternoon of March 17, 1916, while reading the *Mercure de France* in the midst of bombardment, his head was bandaged; and at two in the morning of the 18th, in an ambulance behind the lines, a military surgeon made a T-shaped incision in his scalp and removed the fragments. This seemed sufficient at the time; besides, the surgeon was overworked: the wounded, that night, were being brought from the front in an endless stream. During his convalescence at the Italian Hospital in Paris, where he had had succeeded in having himself transferred from the military hospital of the Val de Grâce because Serge Férat was working there as a medical aide, it became apparent that more damage had been done than had been supposed; there were the symptoms of dizziness and paralysis of the left arm of which he complained to Madeleine in his letter of May 7; and the surgeons ordered a trepanation, to relieve pressure on the brain. For the operation he was moved to a nursing home called the Villa Molière, which served at this time as a surgical annex to the overcrowded Val de Grâce. The writer Henri Duvernois, who was serving in the medical corps at the Villa Molière, has described the dangerous moment:

A new operation was decided upon. This time it would be a trepanation, the opening of a "window" to relieve the pressure on the brain. These brain operations are always cause for great concern; even the most skillful practitioner fears some unforeseen complication. Apollinaire knew. He talked about it easily, with his characteristic charming smile. "It's for tomorrow," he told me one day.

Next morning I was with him very early in his small white   311 room. He was lying on his bed, leafing through a manuscript with his good hand, and we wished each other good morning as though it were to be any ordinary day, to be passed in friendly talk, work, reading. It was hard for me to control my feelings. Soon the chisel and the mallet would be doing their work on one of the best organized brains of our time. I cast furtive glances at the head that was to undergo the ordeal, and at the door that would open at any moment. Apollinaire, so keenly perceptive, sensed all the apprehension and affection that must have shown in my eyes. His handshake was stronger and a little longer than usual. That was all. We immediately began to talk. He spoke to me about his plans with his customary enthusiasm and confidence. He talked about the play he was planning and showed me a few sketches he had just made for settings.

The door opened. "Ah, good, they're coming for me," said Apollinaire.

I can testify that his voice was steady, that he continued to smile as though someone had merely announced the arrival of his barber. There was no sign of a quiver on his face, nor did he change color. As he pulled on his heavy knitted stockings he picked up the thread of the conversation; there was not the slightest affectation or nervousness, just a courage that was completely natural.

He maintained this demeanor until the moment he was given chloroform. Then, at last, we had the right to show our worry. But what joy awaited us! The moment Doctor Baudet made the opening, the hoped-for reaction took place. On the operating table the fingers of the paralyzed hand feebly stirred. Apollinaire was saved.

What a joyous place an operating room can instantly become at such a time! The surgeon, his work done, breathes with relief; the light, so harsh a moment before, now seems warm and gay and triumphant; the nurses roll up the stretcher and place on it the body of a man who is inert and unconscious, but saved, saved.

Alas!

312   André Billy gives us a picture of the Apollinaire who

emerged from the trepanation:

An Apollinaire irascible and self-absorbed, dull-eyed, heavy-browed—that is what the trepanation had produced. His mouth was distorted with suffering—the same mouth that only a short time before had smiled so broadly as it uttered learned observations, jokes, delightful comments of all kinds. His pear-shaped skull (Guillaume did not like to hear that he resembled Louis-Philippe: he preferred Louis XIV or Racine) seemed flattened by the bandage, and his neck had become enormously thick during his enforced idleness in the hospital. A restless energy that felt itself to be fatally stricken and yet was endeavoring to collect itself. . . . His glance seemed sometimes to be veiled by a mist; his marvelous memory had moments of failure; his sudden outbursts of anger were so violent that we feared his head wound might reopen; we quickly calmed him, yielded on every point, and then he would regain control and laugh. After he left we would share our fears, and in the end someone would always say: "Oh, with such a marvelous physique he'll pull through all right."

As soon as he could, he resumed work. . . .

There was the threat, as soon as his period of convalescence ended, that he would be sent back to his regiment, and for this reason he sought employment in one of the military offices in Paris. He thought at first of the Maison de la Presse, but in those timorous circles the very mention of his name caused a flutter. Apollinaire, the champion of Cubism, at the Maison de la Presse? It would be the end of the place! I volunteered to sound out the Censor's Office, and there he was warmly welcomed. Behold Apollinaire a censor! One of war's oddities. . . . Apollinaire the censor deserves prominent mention among "the whims of Bellona," to employ one of his own expressions.

He was assigned to the periodicals department, and his special task was to read the little magazines.

With my own eyes I have seen the censor Guillaume Apollinaire, blue pencil in hand, scanning, with severe look, the galley proofs of the magazine *Sic*. What fitter person could have been found for the job? Was not Apollinaire the only man capable of

313

Guillaume Apollinaire

deciding whether a poem by Pierre Albert-Birot did not inadvertently shelter some indiscretion useful to the enemy? Nothing escaped his scrutiny, and when he signed his initials to a proof sheet one had no fears for the safety of *la Patrie*.

That little magazine *Sic,* which André Billy shows Apollinaire censoring with such burlesque solemnity, played a role in his brief return to the literary scene following his trepanation.

In one of his columns for the *Mercure de France* (he had continued to contribute them sporadically even from the trenches, and he now resumed them after his operation), he observed that "An *avant-garde* magazine founded since the outbreak of the war and devoted to letters, the plastic arts, and music has taken the name *Sic,* borrowed from the initials of three words: *sons, idées, couleurs.*" He became acquainted with the founder of *Sic,* the young poet Pierre Albert-Birot, who edited the magazine from his flat in Montparnasse; he contributed a few items, and in the Italian Hospital he allowed Albert-Birot to interview him about the new tendencies in the arts. The interview was published in *Sic* for October, 1916. Apollinaire had recently tried his hand at writing a movie scenario with André Billy, and in *Sic* he declared:

There is an art today that may give birth to a kind of epic feeling expressing the poet's love of lyricism and the truth of dramatic situations. This art is cinematography. Originally, epic poetry was recited to the assembled people, and nothing is closer to the people than the cinema. A man who projects a film today plays the role of the *jongleur* of old. The epic poet will express himself by means of the cinema; and in great epics combining all the arts, musicians too will be assigned a place, to accompany the lyrical passages recited by the protagonists.

Apollinaire: Eight

Concerning the theatre, his opinion was that:

The cameral or stage theatre will become less important. Possibly a circus theatre will come into being—more violent or more burlesque, as well as more simple, than the former. But without a doubt the cinema is the great theatre that will give rise to a total dramatic art.

Albert-Birot asked him to write, for production and publication by *Sic,* a play that would illustrate some of his theatrical ideas, including the wish he had one day expressed that the theatre of the future would be free of "odious realism." Apollinaire complied, coming up with a piece of the broadest buffoonery, which he claimed more or less seriously to have written in large part when he was twenty-three. In any case, he had long had an idea for a scene on a stage—a woman opening her corsage, out of which balloons would float up and bob about on strings: he was sure that it would make an audience laugh. And recently he had written a serious—or was it merely serious-sounding?—article for his column in the *Mercure de France:*

THE MILITARY SALUTE TO PREGNANT WOMEN

We see too few pregnant women nowadays. Needless to say, it is not on the boulevards or on café terraces that we would fain see them, more beautiful and more precious than Jupiter's head still heavy with Minerva, helmeted like our soldiers. Rather, we would have them appear in the parks and public gardens, in the Bois de Boulogne and the Bois de Vincennes, grave with the grace that makes for the charm of young matrons.

There is only one doctrine when it comes to children: the old French saying, "God blesses large families." Had there been more children in France, the war would not be dragging on so long. Great fortunes belonging to wealthy couples with only one child are almost always doomed to sterility; the heirs content

315

Guillaume Apollinaire

themselves with what they have, and most often squander it. And even when they are not squanderers, in most cases they do nothing to increase their inheritance. As a result, it diminishes, ruining thousands of other people.

Many children are needed, for the happiness of the home and of the nation.

I wish that soldiers, and especially officers, would adopt the habit of giving the military salute to pregnant women. Special honors should be instituted for the women who are the most exquisite orchards in the beautiful land of France.

Using that theme of the need for more French children, and treating it burlesquely, in the spirit of the woman with balloon-breasts (who in the play is a mere woman no longer, but a woman-man, Thérèse-Tirésias), he wrote a skit of two acts and a prologue that is well known today in a musical version later arranged and composed by Francis Poulenc. Apollinaire's original "drama," with incidental music by Germaine Albert-Birot played on a piano, and with Cubist sets and costumes by Serge Férat, was performed on June 24, 1917, in a small theatre in Montmartre. The *avant-garde* audience apparently seized on the occasion to make a kind of mid-Lenten free-for-all amidst the grim somberness of wartime Paris, and Apollinaire was delighted by the turbulence. "*Les Mamelles de Tirésias,*" he wrote to a friend, "was played in an atmosphere most suitable to a work which I think resembles nothing known, but which, if we must have comparisons, could be said to have affinities with Plautus and Beaumarchais, as well as Goethe."

Apollinaire's *Les Mamelles de Tirésias,* as distinct from Poulenc's opéra bouffe, has achieved its greatest fame through a word which Apollinaire invented to describe it.

316

He had first subtitled it *"Drame surnaturaliste,"* but he subsequently changed the adjective to *"surréaliste."* "All things considered," he wrote a friend, "I agree that it is better to adopt the term *'Surréalisme,'* rather than *'Surnaturalisme,'* which I first used. *'Surréalisme'* is not yet in the dictionary, and it will be more convenient than *'Surnaturalisme,'* which is already used by the philosophers."[9]

A number of young writers who were beginning to look on Apollinaire, especially after his interview in *Sic,* as the embodiment of the "new tendencies" he had discussed there, seized on the adjective "surrealist" and applied it to their own work. Apollinaire unquestionably invented the *word* "surrealist," but whether he can be said to have invented the surrealism later made famous by such younger men as Philippe Soupault, Louis Aragon, and André Breton could be—perhaps has been, undoubtedly will be—the subject of innumerable academic dissertations. Already this grave question is treated in considerable detail in Madame Durry's course on Apollinaire in the Sorbonne. Apollinaire has, in any case, always been much esteemed by the Surrealists. One of them, Philippe Soupault, has expressed some of the sentiments that Apollinaire apparently inspired in a good many *avant-garde* young literary men around Paris, Surrealists and others, as he began to circulate after

---

[9] Although the term "surrealism" has become accepted in English, the proper translation of the French *surréalisme* would be "superrealism," just as *surnaturalisme* is translated as "supernaturalism."

Apollinaire had apparently first used the word *Sur-réalism* in his program note to the Satie-Picasso-Massine ballet "Parade," which opened in Paris on May 18, 1917, about three weeks before *Les Mamelles.* (See LeRoy C. Breunig, *Guillaume Apollinaire, Chroniques d'Art,* 426.)

Guillaume Apollinaire

his trepanation. "Apollinaire was an egoist, like all artists, but less so than most," Soupault has said, "less exclusively concerned with his own little affairs, and he had a great sensitivity to other people and to his surroundings that made him irresistibly charming. He was hospitable and generous with his time to young writers and artists. Toward the end he perhaps tended to become a little conventional in his life, but never in his poetry: in that he grew ever bolder. But he always had a nostalgia for classical literature. He appreciated honors, but he probably could never have made himself into an academician: he loved his mystifications and practical jokes too much."

Apollinaire also contributed verse and prose at this time to several issues of the *avant-garde* magazine *Nord-Sud,* recently founded by the young poet Pierre Reverdy, the first number of which hailed him as a "tracer of new paths, opener of new horizons." Like Soupault, Reverdy always prized his acquaintance with Apollinaire. "Without my marvelous friendships," Reverdy has said, "without Picasso, Braque, Gris, Apollinaire, I would have amounted to nothing."

Apollinaire was also solicited by the Dadaists. He allowed them to print a pre-war poem, "Arbre," in their review, *Cabaret Voltaire,* but he contributed nothing current. According to Tristan Tzara, the Roumanian cofounder of Dadaism in Zurich, Apollinaire was, in those war years, too chauvinistic, too much of a Francophile, to be willing to associate himself with an international movement participated in also by Germans.[10]

[10] Tristan Tzara has also expressed the opinion that French wartime

Apollinaire: Eight

It is easy to see why the Surrealists and Dadaists should have sought out Apollinaire. Beyond the modern note of *Alcools,* beyond his provocative answers to the questionnaire in *Sic* about "new tendencies," his desperate experiences had given his fantasy at this moment a raw, strident wildness. Along with the gloom and melancholy that so disturbed his friends, he became more than ever the practical joker that Martineau had labeled him in his review of *Alcools.* "Apollinaire and I met not only in the Censor's Office," André Billy has written about this time. "We also worked together at *Paris-Midi,* where he translated English newspapers in a small room adjoining mine. Concerning foreign politics his ideas were just as personal as they were on every other subject. One day when I expressed my surprise at seeing him giving New York or London date-lines to despatches whose texts had sprung full-blown from his imagination, he said: 'There is no better way to influence events.' And you may be sure that he meant what he said."

The gross "symbolism" in *Les Mamelles de Tirésias* is in that vein, a far cry from the subtle music of the best of

chauvinism played a role in bringing the work of Braque to public attention. The beginnings and development of Cubism had been international, with the Spanish Picasso its founder, the Spanish Juan Gris a prime figure, and the German Kahnweiler its impresario. According to Tzara, during and after the war, Braque, a pure-blooded Frenchman, was pushed by French dealers and critics interested in Cubism, to show that it was not chiefly a foreign activity. Indeed Apollinaire wrote a letter to the *Mercure de France* in September, 1917, emphasizing the "latinity" of the school of Cubism, in which he speaks of "Second Lieutenant Georges Braque, wounded in the head and trepanned, who has been awarded the cross of the Legion of Honor and the Croix de Guerre with palm." As for Juan Gris, about whom Apollinaire had written little, once calling him *"le démon de la logique,"* he broke with him in 1917, following some hostile utterance by Gris concerning *Les Mamelles de Tirésias.* 319

Alcools. The previous autumn he had published a prose volume that might be called his fantastic, even his surrealist, autobiography, *Le Poète assassiné,* portions of which have been quoted in earlier pages of this book. Michel Décaudin, in his edition of *Le Poète assassiné,* has shown how its various parts were written separately, some as early as Apollinaire's twentieth year, and how they were altered into a pretense of relationship and patched together—a device that seems to stand a greater chance of achieving successful effects when applied to lines of verse than to chapters of prose. The short tales that form the second half of the volume were also written at various times during Apollinaire's life, and slapped onto the first part of the text; Apollinaire wrote and added a final sketch as the book was going to press, the *Cas du Brigadier masqué,* decorating it with a curious eagle mask [11] and a few of his calligrammes and giving it a modern, wartime air.

On the last day of 1916 a group of his old and new friends in the *avant-garde* organized a noonday banquet in his honor in a dining hall near Montparnasse; the names of the dishes were invented by Max Jacob, there were attempts at speeches foiled by raucous cries from those at the tables; Apollinaire wrote a friend that the lunch was "a kind of magnesium flash, just as it should have been, brilliant and dangerous, short, but carried to the point of paroxysm." The boisterousness of the feast was a kind of externalization of his own disturbed state of mind. It was as though somewhere within himself the wounded poet was conscious of

[11]Cf. p. 18 of present volume.

deep seismic tremors.

Les Mamelles de Tirésias marked the point at which these underground rumblings came closest to the surface. By the time the year 1917 approached its end Apollinaire seemed to have achieved, or regained, a certain equanimity, and in November he delivered, at the Théâtre du Vieux Colombier, a lecture on *L'Esprit nouveau et les poètes,* which though it reflects some wartime chauvinism is a remarkable and prophetic statement of a modern poet's esthetic. Unlike his recent interview in *Sic,* or his recent "surrealist drama," its tone is serious throughout. In it Apollinaire seems to have attempted to formulate his real convictions, and his sincerity is only underlined by a certain clumsiness that he displays in this type of expository, analytical writing.[12]

Also in 1917 he wrote a brief foreword to a volume of photographs of African sculptures published in a deluxe edition of sixty-three copies by the dealer Paul Guillaume, his first and only foreword to an art book. Since 1917 the writing of usually more or less bland or pretentious forewords to art books has become a major sideline for all kinds of persons more or less connected with the arts: probably Apollinaire, had he lived, would have been sought after as a writer of agreeable introductions, and probably he would seldom have declined such an opportunity to earn a modest honorarium. Indeed the number of art books Apollinaire almost certainly would have prefaced had he lived

[12] A translation of *L'Esprit nouveau et les poètes,* in which Apollinaire comes as close as he ever came to a logical statement of his poetic views, is included in the appendix of the present volume. The translation was made from the revised text of the lecture, published in the *Mercure de France* for December 1, 1918 (the month following Apollinaire's death).

Guillaume Apollinaire

until today—in 1963 he would be only eighty-three, no great age, especially among persons connected with the arts in France—would constitute a formidable *"musée imaginaire."*

And either late in 1917 or early the next year there was a sad little chance encounter with Lou. André Rouveyre tells us how she and Apollinaire met ". . . for a last time, accidentally, in Paris, in the Place de l'Opéra. By then Apollinaire had been trepanned. For a few moments they took shelter, to talk, within the great yellow doorway between the coffee store and Cler's jewelry shop. It was a distressing encounter for both of them. He was already a sick man, very emotional. Suddenly he found himself with a woman whom he had loved deeply and who had disappointed him. He uttered reproaches; the conversation was painful, a kind of flight on both their parts. It did not last long. They looked at each other with sadness, feeling that they would never meet again, as indeed proved to be the case."

The next year, Apollinaire's last, 1918, began with an attack of pneumonia that sent him back for more than a month to the Villa Molière. While there he was given the news that the French government had refused to decorate him with the cross of the Legion of Honor, an award that had been requested for him by friends, and that this Frenchman by everything except birth would have prized. Of course the Ministry of the Interior, subdivision Fine Arts, could not be supposed to know Apollinaire's war record—that was the business of the Ministry of War—and his implication in the affair of the statuettes was still working against him.

But it was at this time that he came to know a pretty, red-haired young woman named Jacqueline Kolb (her friends called her Ruby), a French bourgeoise, not at all a habituée of Montmartre or Montparnasse; and on May 2 they were married in his parish church of Saint-Thomas-d'Aquin, a few steps from the apartment at 202, Boulevard Saint-Germain, where they went to live domestically among Apollinaire's paintings by the Cubists and Marie Laurencin, the African sculpture he had bought along with Vlaminck and Derain, and his many shelves of books. Before their marriage Jacqueline had given him the title and some of the lines of one of his best known poems written after *Alcools*, "La Jolie Rousse" ("The Pretty Redhead"), which along with "Les Collines" might be called his esthetic in verse, as *L'Esprit nouveau et les poètes* is that in prose. Some people have wondered whether Apollinaire may have realized how frail he was, and suspected how numbered were his days, so intent does he seem to have been on stating his esthetic credo in those works that follow so closely the one on the other.

"La Jolie Rousse" is the last poem in the volume called *Calligrammes, Poèmes de la Paix et de la Guerre (1913–1916)*, Apollinaire's second collected volume of verse, published April 15, 1917, two weeks before his marriage. It differs from *Alcools* in the shorter span of years during which its poems were composed (four as compared with sixteen), in the greater number of poems it contains (over a hundred as compared with fifty-five), and of course in the more uniform modernity of its tone: all the poems were written

323

POIGNARDEE

ET LE J   AU

Douces figures poi**gnardée**s C**hères lèvres fleuries**

MIA   MAREYE
YETTE   LORIE
ANNIE   et toi   MARIE
o ù   êtes-
vous   ô
jeunes   filles
MAIS
pres d'un
jet d'eau qui
pleure et qui prie
cette colombe s'extasie

Tant d'explosifs sur le point **VIF !**

l'o^{ses} guerre
tu   en
si   toujours
mot   âme
un   mon
Ecris   dans   feu
d'impacts   le
points   crache
Les   féroce
troupeau
Ton

?

OMÉ**GAPHON**ᴇ

Tous les souvenirs de naguère Où sont Raynal Billy Dalize

O mes amis partis en guerre **?** Dont les noms se mélancolisent

Jaillissent vers le firmament Comme des pas dans une église

Et vos regards en l'eau dormant Où est Cremnitz qui s'engagea

Meurent mélancoliquement Peut-être sont-ils morts déjà

Où sont-ils Braque et Max Jacob De souvenirs mon âme est pleine

Derain aux yeux gris comme l'aube Le jet d'eau pleure sur ma peine

CEUX QUI SONT PARTIS A LA GUERRE AU NORD SE BATTENT MAINTENANT

Le soir tombe **O** sanglante mer

Jardins où saigne abondamment le laurier rose fleur guerrière

Calligrammes

324

Apollinaire: Eight

Guillaume and Jacqueline Apollinaire on the terrace of 202 Boulevard Saint-Germain, 1918

325

Guillaume Apollinaire

later than "Zone," which we saw Apollinaire hastily compose to increase the modern feeling of *Alcools*. Containing as it does "Les Fenêtres," "Les Collines," "Lundi Rue Christine," "La Petite Auto," "Le Musicien de Saint-Merry" and "La Jolie Rousse," as well as a number of the war poems sent to Madeleine and/or Lou, and the true "calligrammes" themselves with their witty typographical arrangements, the volume is so fresh and attractive that many think of Apollinaire as "the poet of *Alcools* and *Calligrammes*," evaluating the two well-known volumes more or less equally. But while in general *Calligrammes* may well equal or even surpass *Alcools* in charm, it is scarcely its rival in subtlety and the magic music of words. An interesting indication of this, perhaps, is that when Francis Poulenc came to set a number of Apollinaire's poems to music, he chose chiefly early verses from the *Bestiaire* and later ones from *Calligrammes:* one wonders whether he may not have felt that the music of the poems in *Alcools* is inherent, and that they need no second musician. *Alcools* will also always possess the added allure of presenting the autobiography of a young poet, his youthful adventures, and his poetic evolution from Symbolism to "Zone," as well as its inclusion of the matchless "Chanson du Mal-Aimé" and "Le Pont Mirabeau." But *Calligrammes,* too, alone, might well have made the reputation of any poet who had written the varied verses it contains.[13]

[13] Montaigne's slight opinion of earlier calligrammes, expressed in his essay "Of Vaine Subtilties, or Subtill Devices" (I, 54), is not without application to Apollinaire's:

"There are certaine frivolous and vaine inventions, or as some call them, subtilties of wit, by meanes of which, some men doe often endevour

326

Shortly before his marriage Apollinaire had been transferred from the Censor's Office to a more agreeable post in the Ministry of Colonies, where he worked with friends and had time to write magazine articles. Despite his wound and operations, the army did not release him, but in July promoted him to first lieutenant, *"à titre temporaire."* Friends say that he was proud of his new képi. In August he and his wife spent some time in Brittany, where he finished an operetta libretto, *Casanova,* and another play, *Couleur du Temps,* which can be considered yet another esthetic testament. He collected some of his articles from the *Mercure* into a small volume to be called *Le Flâneur des Deux Rives.*

And then, quite suddenly, everything was over.

"I'm not very well," Apollinaire said to André Billy, one morning in October. "I can't stop coughing." It seemed to Billy that he was suffering from a kind of asthma.

And on November 9, two days before the Armistice. . . .

Louise Faure-Favier tells us the story:

At seven in the morning on November 10 the ringing of my doorbell woke me with a start. It was still dark. Jacqueline Apollinaire's charwoman had come to tell me that the poet had died at six o'clock the evening before. Madame Apollinaire asked that I come to be with her: she was alone. I went at once. My feel-

to get credit and reputation: as divers Poets, that frame whole volumes with verses beginning with one letter: we see Egges, Wings, Hatchets, Crosses, Globes, Columnes, and divers other such like figures anciently fashioned by the Graecians, with the measure and proportion of their verses, lengthning, and shortning them, in such sort as they justly represent such and such a figure." (Florio translation.)

Montaigne was probably thinking of the earliest calligrammes of all, those composed by the "Graecian" Simmias of Rhodes.

Guillaume Apollinaire

ings as I climbed the stairs can be imagined. I passed a gentleman who was coming down—the doctor, I learned later from the weeping Jacqueline, who had come to sign the death certificate.

Poor Jacqueline clung to me. She was pale, touching in her grief. She opened a door and I saw Guillaume lying on their wide bed. I almost said "But he isn't dead!" so smiling was his face. I kissed him on the cheek—it did not feel cold, but when I touched his hands they were icy. I knelt and wept and prayed; "Gui, my Gui!" Jacqueline sobbed beside me; her grief was from the heart: I realized at that moment how deeply she loved her husband, her poet. She went into a fit of weeping that frightened me, and I led her to the outer room, where Apollinaire's identity papers were lying as the doctor had left them. As I helped her put them away she told me of Apollinaire's brief illness, which I had thought to be an ordinary grippe, and his brave struggle. He begged the doctor to cure him. She quoted words of his that I cannot forget: "Save me, doctor! I want to live! I still have so many things to say!"

It touched me to the quick, to hear those words while I could see him smiling there in death.

We returned to the bedroom and I helped Jacqueline dress him. I wanted to put a crucifix in his hands, but was there a crucifix in the house? "Yes," Jacqueline said; and she brought a plain black wooden one and asked me to place it as I wished. In a moment the image of the God of his baptism, of his first communion, of his marriage, was lying close to his heart. Together Jacqueline and I knelt to pray. How calm he looks, I thought; he seems happy. And his smile . . . !

I helped Jacqueline to her feet and offered to do anything else I could. Were there errands, telephone calls?

"Oh, no," she said, "stay with me. I sent a telegram to Gui's mother, Madame de Kostrowitzky, and I imagine she will be here before noon. Be here with me when she comes. Look, I'm not even dressed properly yet."

She changed to a black dress that made her look even slimmer and younger than she was, and she tidied her lovely red hair. Now she was ready for visitors.

328   The first to arrive was André Salmon. He had come to in-

quire after the patient, as he had done every day, and the concierge had told him the news. He went in at once to gaze at his old friend. I can still see him standing there, his face twisted in grief.

Others came with flowers. The news was beginning to spread. There were more friends, more flowers.

It was eleven when Madame de Kostrowitzky arrived. I was astonished at the sight of the lady. She was wearing a gala costume —jewels, furs, plumed hat; her tears were streaming down over her rouge. She uttered a heart-rending sob, one of those sobs that seem to come from the very entrails of a mother when she throws herself on the dead body of her son. "My little boy!" she whispered.

When some newly arrived friends came in and stood by the bed she rose and joined me in the outer room. I felt so sorry for her that I embraced her. Then she realized that her costume must seem strange. "I'm dressed for a wedding," she said, "a Jewish wedding. It would have been the first I ever attended. I was looking forward to it, and I was just leaving my house when the telegram came. The telegram about my son. About my son," she repeated. "I knew nothing about his illness."

Her voice thickened. I looked at her. How like her son she looked!

Guillaume's face had hardened in death. Now his smile was gone. His features had taken on an air of nobility that emphasized his resemblance to his mother, this woman of sixty who was still handsome and who must have been pretty.

She went in again and stood beside her son, and there she began to heap reproaches on Jacqueline for not having sent word earlier to her, Guillaume's mother. Jacqueline, in tears, pathetically answered that Guillaume had forbidden her to do so: "He didn't want to worry you and upset you." Madame de Kostrowitzky refused to accept the explanation. "You should have disregarded his instructions, Madame: you saw that he was dying."

And the loud recriminations continued, reproaches of all kinds, illogical and vehement.

Jacqueline was silent, slumped beside her husband's body, and then she began to speak to *him,* murmuring softly. She seemed

329

Guillaume Apollinaire

so weak! I pitied her, and I took it on myself to end the hateful scene. I said something, I don't remember what, to Madame de Kostrowitzky, and persuaded her to go into the other room. There, without a word, she stripped off her jewels—her earrings, her bracelets, and her necklaces—and threw them into her handbag.

In the afternoon, Madame de Kostrowitzky was no longer there. The room was too small to hold all the friends, and all the flowers that women in tears were placing on the deathbed.

Paul Léautaud, who had been responsible for the publication of "La Chanson du Mal-Aimé" in the *Mercure de France*—the beginning of the fame of that poem—tells us more in his *Journal Littéraire:*

Monday, November 11. This morning when I arrived at the Mercure, Vallette told me that Apollinaire had died on Saturday, the day before yesterday, at 6 P.M., after about a week of illness. Intestinal grippe complicated by pneumonia. I was appalled. In him I lose a friend whom I worshiped as a man and as a writer. He was destined to become someone. I immediately sensed in him a true poet, extremely individual and evocative, when I first saw "La Chanson du Mal-Aimé," which I had the *Mercure* accept a few years ago without passing through the usual readers. The evening before, I had met him on the Boulevard Montparnasse as I was walking my dogs. We strolled up and down together, and I asked him why he didn't send something to the *Mercure*. He said that he had sent some poems a long time before but had had no news about them. The next morning I had the pleasure of giving him news—I must have noted this at the time it happened. Five or six days ago we were recalling the incident, and he agreed that I had not waited for him to acquire a little reputation before recognizing his great talent.

I went to his house at once. Saw his wife and another lady. He was on his bed, covered with a blanket and a mass of flowers. Yesterday, Sunday, it was still possible to see him. This morning decomposition of the face set in. He has become unrecognizable. No one wants to remember him as he is now, and I could not look at him. . . .

Interesting detail concerning Apollinaire's death: The Armistice was signed this morning. The news reached Paris immediately, and everyone went wild. Crowds filled the Rue de Rennes, the Place Saint-Germain-des-Prés, and the Boulevard Saint-Germain. On the Boulevard, under the very windows of the small room where Apollinaire was lying dead on his flower-covered bed, crowds were shouting: "Down with Guillaume! Down with Guillaume!"[14]

Wednesday, November 13. Today, at noon, Apollinaire's funeral. Mass at Saint-Thomas-d'Aquin, burial in Père Lachaise. Many people. Military honors all the way to the grave. He had just been given his lieutenant's stripes. Madame de Kostrowitzky left the cemetery unaccompanied, his officer's cap held between her two hands in front of her, as though it were on a cushion. Everyone stared at her from a distance. . . .

How sad to see the earth cover so charming a human being, so dear a friend, so eager an intelligence!

It was the beginning of the end for Olga de Kostrowitzky and for all those around her. Something over two months later, on January 20, 1919, she paid her visit to Paul Léautaud at the office of the *Mercure de France,* in her furs and silk stockings, to seek her son's books.[15] On March 7 she died in her villa at Chatou, a victim of the same epidemic of grippe that had killed her son. Jules Weil, the gambler she had lived with to his end, had died in the villa a few days before. And a few months later Albert de Kostrowitzky, the younger brother who had picked so many mushrooms in the Ardennes, died in Mexico, where

[14] Meaning Kaiser Wilhelm II.
[15] See above, page 28.

331

in 1913 he had gone to further his banking career.

After the war Marie Laurencin divorced her German husband and never remarried. In later years she tended to express the opposite of gratitude to Apollinaire whenever his name was mentioned: with her own increasing fame as an artist came increasing reluctance to admit that he had played a role in her emergence.

Jacqueline Apollinaire, "la jolie rousse," still pretty, is living in the apartment at 202 Boulevard Saint-Germain, among the paintings by the Cubists and Marie Laurencin, the African sculpture, and the books, a few steps from the church of Saint-Thomas-d'Aquin where she and Apollinaire were married and whence he was buried, from the Café Flore where he sat with André Billy and the others and planned *Les Soirées de Paris,* from the little park at Saint-Germain-des-Prés where there now stands a sculpture contributed as a memorial to him by Picasso, from the little street that on November 9, 1951, the thirty-third anniversary of his death, was rechristened the Rue Guillaume Apollinaire.

332

The new spirit that will eventually dominate the entire world has in poetry nowhere asserted itself more clearly than in France. Thanks to the strong intellectual discipline followed by the French and the members of the French spiritual family, they are in a position to develop a conception of life, of art, and of literature that is neither a mere restatement of the classical traditions nor an appendage to the bright show-window of romanticism.

The new spirit whose coming we are witnessing seeks above all to preserve the classical heritage of solid good sense, sure critical principles, a comprehensive view of the world and the human soul, and a moral responsibility that tends toward austere expression, or rather toward containment, of feelings.

From the romantic heritage, it seeks to preserve the curiosity that leads to exploration of all domains capable of providing literary material for the exaltation of life in all its forms.

What mainly characterizes this new spirit is the will to explore the truth, to seek it everywhere, in the realm of the imagination but also in other realms—the ethnic, for example.

This tendency has always had its bold practitioners who were themselves unaware of it; for a long time it has been taking form and gaining momentum.

Only today does it emerge fully conscious of its own nature. Up until now the literary domain has been held within narrow limits. There were prose writers and there were poets. The form of prose was set by the rules of grammar. Poetry was governed solely by the laws of rhymed versification, which, though periodically subjected to attack, remained impregnable.

Free verse gave free rein to lyricism; but it was no more than

333

Guillaume Apollinaire

a stage in the possible explorations of the domain of form.

Since then, investigation of form has assumed great and legitimate importance.

Poets cannot but be vitally interested in this investigation, which may lead to new discoveries in the realms of thought and lyrical expression.

Assonance, alliteration, rhyme are conventions, each possessing its own merits.

Typographical devices, employed with great daring, have given rise to a visual lyricism almost unknown before our time. These devices are capable of being carried much further, to the point of bringing about the synthesis of the arts—music, painting, and literature.

All this is merely a search for new, perfectly legitimate forms of expression.

Who would dare maintain that rhetorical exercises like the fifteenth-century competition on the theme of *Je meurs de soif auprès de la fontaine* did not have a crucial influence on the genius of Villon? Who would dare maintain that the formal researches engaged in by the *rhetoriqueurs* and the school of Marot did not contribute to the refinement of French taste and its full flowering in the seventeenth century?

In an epoch when the popular art *par excellence,* the cinema, is in essence a picture-book, it would be strange if poets did not try to create pictures for meditative, more sophisticated persons who find the productions of the film makers too crude. Eventually films will be more refined, and it is possible to foresee the day when the phonograph and the cinema will be the only current forms of reproduction, and when as a result poets will enjoy a freedom hitherto unknown.

Let us not be surprised, therefore, that though the means at the disposal of poets are still limited, they are preparing themselves for this new art which is more vast than the art of words alone. One day they will direct an orchestra of prodigious dimensions, an orchestra that will include the entire world, its sights and its sounds, human thought and language, song, dance, all the arts

334

and all the artifices—more mirages than Morgan Le Fay conjured up on Mongibel to compose the book seen and heard by the future.

However, you will rarely find in France the so-called "free words" [*parole in libertà*] of the Italian and Russian futurists, who have carried the new spirit to excess: for France is averse to disorder. In France we are always willing to reconsider principles, but we abhor chaos.

Thus we may hope for an inconceivably rich freedom as concerns the content and the means of art. Today poets are serving their apprenticeship in this encyclopedic freedom. In the realm of inspiration, their freedom need be no more restricted than that of a daily newspaper, which on a single sheet touches on the most diverse subjects and tours the most distant countries. Why should the poet not enjoy a freedom at least equal to this? In the era of the telephone, wireless, and aviation, why should he be confined to narrower space?

Hitherto, modern poetry has not matched the rapidity and simplicity with which we habitually evoke, each time with a single word, entities as complex as crowds, nations, or the universe. Poets are filling that gap, and their synthetic poems are creating new plastic entities, as complex as the ones designated by those collective nouns.

Man has become familiar with the formidable beings called machines; he has explored the domain of the infinitely small; and new domains are opening to the activity of his imagination—those of the infinitely great and of prophecy.

You must not, however, suppose that the new spirit is complicated, languid, factitious, cold. Following in nature's own footsteps, the poet has rid himself of all turgid expression. We have eliminated Wagnerism; our young writers have cast off the obsolescent Wagnerian magic, the Germanic romanticism of the colossal, just as they have cast off the trappings of Rousseau's idyllic romanticism.

I do not believe that social development will ever reach the point at which it will no longer be possible to speak of a national literature. On the contrary, no matter what liberties we achieve,

335

Guillaume Apollinaire

these will serve only to strengthen most of the old disciplines, and new ones will arise which will be no less exacting than the old. That is why I think that no matter what happens, art will to an ever-increasing extent be national. Moreover, poets always express an environment, a nation; and artists, like poets or philosophers, constitute a social store which of course belongs to all mankind but remains the expression of a given race and environment.

Art will cease being national only when the entire world lives in the same climate, in dwellings all of the same model, and speaks the same language with the same accent—that is, never. Ethnic and national differences give rise to a variety of literary expressions, and it is this very variety that must be preserved.

A cosmopolitan lyrical expression would produce only ill-defined works, lacking accent and inner structure, the equivalent of the clichés of international parliamentary rhetoric. Note that the cinema, which is the cosmopolitan art *par excellence,* is already displaying ethnic differences obvious to all, and cinema fans can immediately tell an American film from an Italian. Similarly, the new spirit, which aspires to universality and has no intention of confining itself to this or that, nonetheless is and means to be a particular and lyrical expression of the French nation, just as our classical age is *par excellence* a sublime expression of the same nation.

We must not forget that it is perhaps more dangerous for a nation to let itself be conquered intellectually than militarily. That is why the new spirit speaks above all in the name of order and moral responsibility, which are the great classical qualities, the loftiest manifestations of the French spirit; and it complements them with freedom. This freedom and this order, which in the new spirit are inseparable, are its hallmark and its strength.

However, the synthesis of the arts which has been accomplished in our time must not degenerate into confusion. In other words, it would be absurd, if not dangerous, for instance, to reduce poetry to a kind of imitative harmony that would not even have the excuse of being exact.

Conceivably, imitative harmony might play a certain role,

336

but it can serve as foundation only for an art that will make use of machines. For instance, a poem or a symphony in which the phonograph will play a part might well consist of noises artistically chosen and lyrically combined or juxtaposed; whereas I, at least, cannot conceive of a poem consisting merely of the imitation of a noise that cannot be associated with any lyrical, tragical, or emotional meaning. If some poets indulge in this game we must see in it no more than an exercise, a kind of rough sketch of elements to be included in some given work. The "brekekekex coax" of Aristophanes' *Frogs* is nothing if it is separated from the play from which it derives its comical and satirical connotations. The "i i i i i" that Francis Jammes's bird utters for an entire line is a paltry imitative harmony if it is divorced from the poem whose fantasy it helps enhance.

When a modern poet gives polyphonic expression to the whirring of an airplane, we must see it above all as the poet's desire to accustom his mind to reality. His passion for truth drives him to make almost scientific notations which, if he wishes to present them as poems, err in being *trompe oreilles,* so to speak, efforts to create an illusion of auditive reality, to which reality itself will always be superior.

On the other hand, were our modern poet to attempt, for instance, to amplify the art of the dance and outline a choreography whose performers would not confine themselves to entrechats but would also utter cries suggestive of new imitative harmonies, his research could not be termed absurd; in all nations we find primitive dances of this kind, and war dances, for instance, are almost always accompanied by wild shouts.

To return to the concern for truth, for plausibility, which dominates all the research, all the efforts, all the experiments of the new spirit, we must add that it is not surprising if a certain number of these, indeed many of them, have remained momentarily sterile, or have even fallen into the ridiculous. The new spirit is full of perils, full of traps.

But all this is part of the spirit of today, and wholesale condemnation of these efforts and experiments would be an error of

337

Guillaume Apollinaire

the kind rightly or wrongly attributed to Monsieur Thiers, who allegedly said that railroads were no more than a scientific toy, and that the world could not produce enough steel to build tracks from Paris to Marseilles.

The new spirit thus admits even hazardous literary experiments, and these are sometimes far from lyrical. That is why lyricism is only one of the domains of the new spirit in today's poetry, which often confines itself to research and investigation, without looking for lyrical significance. These raw materials collected by the poet, by the new spirit, will form a store of truths which, though simple and modest, must not be scorned, for they may lead to great, very great, things.

Future students of the literary history of our age will be surprised that dreamers, poets, without even the pretext of a philosopher's stone, were engaged like alchemists in passionate research that exposed them to the jeers of contemporary journalists and snobs.

But their investigations will be useful. They will constitute the foundation of a new realism which will perhaps be not inferior to the realism of ancient Greece, which is so poetic and so intricate.

Also, thanks to Alfred Jarry, laughter, which used to grimace below stairs, has been ennobled, providing the poet with an entirely new type of lyricism. Gone are the days when Desdemona's handkerchief seemed impossibly ridiculous. Today even the ridiculous is cultivated, and it has its place in poetry because it is fully as much a part of life as heroism and all other qualities that have always inspired poets.

The romantics sought to endow things of crude appearance with a horrible or tragic meaning. Actually they preferred the horrible, giving it great precedence over the melancholy. The new spirit does not seek to transform the ridiculous: it assigns it its own flavorsome role. Similarly, it has no wish to ennoble the horrible. It preserves its horrible character; and it does not degrade the noble. *It is not a decorative art, nor is it an impressionist art.* It is entirely devoted to study of external and internal nature; it is entirely consecrated to truth.

Apollinaire: Appendix One

Even should it be true that there is nothing new under the sun, *the new spirit declines to abandon investigation of everything that is not new under the sun*. Good sense is its guide, and this guide leads it into corners that are unexplored even if they are not new.

But is there nothing new under the sun? Let us see.

X-rays were made of my head. With my own living eyes I saw into my own skull: is there nothing new about that? Tell others that if you wish—not me.

Solomon's words were probably addressed to the Queen of Sheba; and he so loved the new that his concubines were innumerable.

The air is being peopled with strangely human birds. Machines, motherless daughters of men, live lives devoid of passion and feeling: is there nothing new about this?

Scientists are constantly scrutinizing new worlds that are opening up at every crossroads of matter: and there is nothing new under the sun? Perhaps for the sun there is nothing new; bur for man. . . !

There are myriads of natural compounds that were never made by nature. Man conceives them and proceeds to make them, thus creating with the help of nature that supreme masterpiece which is life. It is these new combinations, these new works of the art of life, that we call progress. In this sense progress exists. But if progress be conceived of as eternal becoming, as a kind of Messianism as frightening as the myths of Tantalus, Sisyphus, and the Danaides, then Solomon has confuted the prophets of Israel.

But the new does exist, even apart from any consideration of progress. It is implied in *surprise*. So is the new spirit. Surprise is the most living, the newest element of the new spirit—its mainspring. It is by the element of surprise, by the important place it assigns to surprise, that the new spirit is distinguished from all earlier artistic and literary movements. Thanks to surprise it is set apart from all of them and belongs exclusively to our own time.

The new spirit is firmly rooted in good sense and experience. In evaluating things or feelings we are guided solely by considerations of truth, and we never try to render sublime what is by nature

339

Guillaume Apollinaire

ridiculous, or *vice versa*. The result is usually surprise, for our discoveries most often go against currently accepted ideas. Many of these truths have never before been perceived. It is enough to unveil them, to cause surprise.

A supposed truth, too, can be the occasion for surprise, when it is expressed for the first time. A supposed truth is not incompatible with good sense; otherwise it would not be a truth, even a supposed truth. For instance, if I were to assume that women no longer produce children, and that, such being the case, men could produce them,[1] I would be expressing a literary truth that could be called a fable only outside literature, and this literary truth would cause surprise. But my supposed truth is no more extraordinary or implausible than the old Greek truths, such as the legend of Minerva being born fully armed from the head of Jupiter.

As long as airplanes did not people the sky, the fable of Icarus was merely a supposed truth. Today it is no longer a fable. And our inventors have accustomed us to miracles greater than the production of children by men instead of women. I will go further: since most of the fables have come true, and more than come true, it is up to the poets to imagine new ones, which in turn will be translated into reality by the inventors.

The new spirit imposes on us this kind of prophetic task. That is why traces of prophecy will be found in most works conceived in the new spirit. The divine interplay of life and imagination opens an entirely new field to poetic activity.

For poetry and the creative process are one and the same thing. The name of poet should be given only to him who invents, who creates to the extent that man can create. The poet discovers new joys, painful though they may be to experience. It is possible to be a poet in every domain: it is enough to be adventurous and to explore new possibilities.

Because the imagination is the richest and the least known domain, a domain of infinite extension, it is not surprising that the name of poet has been especially applied to those who are

[1] Cf. *Les Mamelles de Tirésias*.

Apollinaire: Appendix One

seeking the new joys that stand out as landmarks in the tremendous spaces of the imagination.

The most insignificant fact may serve the poet as his premise, the point of departure for the immense unknown where multiple meanings blaze like joyous fires.[2] To set out on a voyage of discovery there is no need to choose, with the help of rules—even the rules of taste—a fact labeled sublime. An everyday fact can serve: the dropping of a handkerchief can be for the poet the lever with which he will lift the universe. We all know about Newton's apple and what it did for that scientist, who can well be called a poet. That is why the poet of today scorns no event in nature. He seeks to make discoveries in the vastest, the most ungraspable syntheses—crowds, nebulae, oceans, nations—as well as in what are seemingly the simplest facts—a hand fumbling in a pocket, a match lighted by friction, animal cries, the smell of gardens after rain, the birth of a flame on a hearth. Poets are not interested in the beautiful alone. They are also, and above all, concerned with the true, in so far as it enables them to penetrate into the unknown; and this is precisely why surprise, the unexpected, is one of the mainsprings of today's poetry. Who would dare maintain that for those worthy of experiencing joy the new is not beautiful? Soon enough, what was sublimely new will become commonplace and "reasonable"; but it must not be forgotten that it was the poet, sole dispenser of the beautiful and the true, who first proposed it.

By the very nature of his explorations, the poet is isolated in the new world that he is the first to enter, and his only consolation is that since men, in the final analysis, live only on truths despite all the lies with which truths are padded, it is he alone, the poet, who sustains the life in which mankind finds truth. That is why modern poets are above all the poets of ever-new truth. Their task

[2] Cf. "La Jolie Rousse":

> We want to give you vast and strange realms
> Where flowering mystery is there for all to pluck
> There there are new fires colors never seen
> Myriad imponderable fantasms
> Which need to be made real

341

Guillaume Apollinaire

is endless. They have surprised you and they will surprise you even more. They are already conceiving deeper schemes than those Machiavellian designs that were responsible for the useful and dreadful convention of money.

It was poets who invented the myth of Icarus, which has so marvelously come true today, and it is poets who will invent other fables. They will lead you, alive and awake, into the nocturnal, closed world of the dream, into worlds that throb ineffably above our heads, into those worlds both closer to us and remoter from us which gravitate around the same point in the infinite as the world we carry within us. And marvels more numerous than those that have been born since the birth of the oldest among us will eclipse the contemporary inventions of which we are so proud, and make them seem puerile.

In a word, it will be the task of poets to purify, by means of lyrical teleologies and arch-lyrical alchemies, the meaning of the divine idea, which dwells within us so alive and so true: that idea which enables us to renew ourselves perpetually, which is the very essence of the eternal creative impulse, of poetry continually reborn by which we live.

As far as we know, there are scarcely any poets today not writing in French.

All other languages seem to be silent, the better to enable the world to listen to the voices of the new French poets.

The world has its eyes on this light, which alone illumines the night around us.

And yet here these rising voices are barely heard.

Modern poets are thus creators, inventors, and prophets. They ask that what they are saying be examined for the greater good of the collectivity of which they are members. They turn toward Plato and beg him, if he banishes them from the Republic, at least to give them a preliminary hearing.

France, the depository of the whole secret of civilization— a secret that is a secret only because of the imperfection of those who try to guess it—has, as a result, become a seminary of poets and artists for the greater part of the world, poets and artists who every day add to the heritage of her civilization.

342

Apollinaire: Appendix One

And through the truth and the joy that they spread, they render this civilization, if not assimilable by every nation, at least supremely pleasant to all.

The French are bringing poetry to all nations.

To Italy, where the example of French poetry has provided an impulse for a young national school of superb daring and patriotism.

To England, where lyricism had become insipid, had dried up, as it were.

To Spain, above all to Catalonia, where an entire ardent young generation that has already produced painters who are an honor to both nations, follows attentively the production of our poets.

To Russia, where imitation of French lyricism has occasionally led to exaggerations—a surprise to no one.

To Latin America, where young poets passionately discuss their French precursors.

To North America, where French missionaries, grateful to Edgar Poe and Walt Whitman, have during the war been importing the seeds of a new production. What this will be like we cannot yet foresee; but it will doubtless be not inferior to the work of those two great pioneers of poetry.

France abounds in schools which preserve and pass on the lyrical tradition, in groups which teach their members to be daring. But one thing must be kept in mind: poetry owes its prime allegiance to the nation whose language it uses.

Before poetic schools embark on the heroic adventure of sending apostles to distant lands, they must actively reinforce, re-define, increase, immortalize, celebrate the greatness of the country of their birth, the country that nourished and formed them, so to speak, with the healthiest, purest, and best elements of its blood and substance.

Has modern French poetry done for France all that it could do?

Has it at least always been as active, as zealous, in France as it has been elsewhere?

Contemporary literary history itself suggests these ques- 343

Guillaume Apollinaire

tions, and to answer them we would have to evaluate all that is national and fruitful in the new spirit.

The new spirit is above all the enemy of estheticism, of formulas, and of every kind of snobbism. It does not combat any school whatever, for it does not want to be a school, but one of the great currents of literature encompassing all schools, beginning with symbolism and naturism. It fights for the restoration of the spirit of initiative, for a clear understanding of its own time, and for the opening of new vistas on the world around us and the world within us—vistas in no way inferior to those which scientists of all categories are discovering every day and which are enabling them to create marvels.

These marvels impose on us poets the duty not to let our imagination and subtlety lag behind those of the craftsmen who perfect a machine. Already there is a deep gulf between the language of science and that of poetry. This is an intolerable state of affairs. Mathematicians have the right to say that their dreams and their concerns often go far beyond the halting imaginations of poets. It is up to the poets to decide whether or not they will enter resolutely into the new spirit, apart from which only three courses remain open: imitation, satire, and lamentation, however sublime this last may be.

Can poetry be compelled to isolate itself from the world around it, to ignore the magnificently exuberant life that human activity is adding to nature and which is making it possible to machine-ize the world in the most incredible way?

The new spirit is that of the very time in which we are living. A time fertile in surprises. The aim of poets is to tame prophecy, that spirited mare that has never been mastered.

In a word, poets want eventually to machine-ize poetry just as the world has been machine-ized. They want to be the first to provide an entirely new lyricism for the new means of expression that are adding movement to art, i.e. the phonograph and the cinema. They are still at the stage of Incunabula, but wait! The marvels will speak for themselves, and the new spirit, which is causing the universe to swell with life, will manifest itself powerfully in literature, in the arts, and in all things known.

344

Apollinaire: Appendix One

Appendix Two
Another Visit With
Annie Playden Postings

A bright autumn afternoon in 1962 we set out from New York on our quest, a rather unusual one. We had learned that Annie Playden, the blue-eyed English governess known to admirers of the poet Guillaume Apollinaire as having been his Beatrice, his Laura, his Dark Lady of the Sonnets, at the moment of his poetic beginnings in the Rhineland, was now living in the Westchester suburb of Katonah with her sister, a Mrs. Vockins, who kept a dog kennels. LeRoy Breunig had made an appointment, and we were on our way.

We were three. LeRoy Breunig, in addition to being professor of French at Barnard College, is, along with two or three people in France, one of the world's leading "Apollinairiens"— students of Apollinaire and his poetry. Norbert Guterman has been a reader of Apollinaire since a friend in France sent him to his native Warsaw a copy of *Alcools,* Apollinaire's first collected volume of poetry, and since he subsequently went himself to Paris and the Sorbonne and found the young people there reading another Apollinaire volume, *Calligrammes.* Roy had seen Annie Playden once before, about ten years ago, shortly after a Belgian Apollinairien had discovered her whereabouts and written her, and for the first time she had an inkling that the French-speaking tutor whom she had called "Kostro" had become a famous poet and that she had been, and was known to have been, his muse. Roy well remembered the bewilderment she was still registering at that time. He had found her simple and unassuming, and we wondered whether she had grown accustomed to the new way she had to think about herself.

At the end of the parkway we turned left over the bridge to Katonah. We soon found Bedford Road, and after a mile or so there was number 221, a house half hidden by trees, with the name Vockins on the lawn, and, at a distance in the background,

345

the kennels. As we walked up the flagged path between over-hanging evergreens, we saw that the house was an old, rather small, post-Civil War one, probably originally clapboarded but now sheathed in shingles, painted grey. There was no answer to our knock on the front door, which led to a glassed-in porch. But the back door was opened quickly for us by a tall, spare, smiling lady with glasses and bobbed grey hair, dressed in a multicolored blouse and green wool slacks. "I'm Mrs. Vockins," she announced; and when Roy identified himself and presented Norbert and me she said "I hope you don't mind walking through my kitchen. Come to the front porch and I'll call my sister."

On the stove stood a gigantic metal caldron, almost as big as the kind used on farms for scalding slaughtered pigs. It was filled to the brim with a simmering brown mixture, as though a mess of rather sinister-looking hash were being prepared for a ravenous giant or for a crew of farm hands. "My dogs' dinner," said Mrs. Vockins. "I'll be feeding them before long." In the narrow front hall, which was carpeted in red and opened into a small living-room and dining-room, both of them somewhat heavily furnished in an old-fashioned way, Mrs. Vockins called upstairs. (The banister was machine-turned golden oak.) "Auntie! Auntie! Gentlemen to see you!" She pronounced "Auntie" with a broad English vowel. At first we thought she called "Annie!" but she quickly said, "I call my sister Annie 'Auntie' because I'm so accustomed to hearing her called that by my three sons."

She led us out onto the front porch, where we had originally knocked, and there we were almost immediately joined by the most delightful-looking person imaginable, plump, white-haired, rosy-cheeked. She was smiling, not only with her lips but with her eyes, too, which were of a gay cornflower blue, far brighter than the blue blossoms printed on the dress she was wearing. Here was the "Bluebird" sung by Apollinaire in "La Tzigane," a lyric about a man, a girl, and a gypsy fortune-teller. "Mr. Breunig," she said to Roy, "how nice to see you again!" In a moment we were all introduced and seated and she was telling us how she had retired a few years ago and was now living permanently here in

346

Katonah with her widowed younger sister, all of whose sons were in homes of their own. "I'm eighty-three now, you know," she said. "There are only us two old ladies here, but we're never lonely because of the—"

Just then, from beyond the evergreens and the lawn partly visible through them came an outbreak of barking, a chorus of frantic barks of different tones and pitches. We all laughed, and Mrs. Vockins stood up. She had seen a car drive into the yard. The dogs had seen it too, and had seen another dog in it: that was what had set them off. Mrs. Vockins explained that she had continued her husband's kennel business following his death some years before—"I've never known anything about dogs, really, but I seem to get along with them, and everybody begged me to keep the kennels open." She excused herself to greet the customer who was bringing a dog to board. When the customer drove off Mrs. Vockins rejoined us, bringing with her a tray with glasses of sherry and a plate of biscuits. By this time we were deep in things that had happened in the years 1901, 1902, 1903, and 1904, and the afternoon was passing rapidly.

As we talked, Norbert Guterman occasionally interjected a remark designed to remind Mrs. Postings of the fame that had gathered around Apollinaire and around her own name: she seemed, even after ten years, to need the reminding. "There's a street in Paris named after him," Norbert would say. Or: "A statue dedicated to him stands in one of the public squares." Or: "A course is given on him in the Sorbonne." Or: "France is already preparing to celebrate the 50th anniversary of his death, in 1968; if you go you'll be welcomed royally." Or: "Some of the poems he wrote about you have been set to music and are on records." When he said: "You must realize, Mrs. Postings, that Annie is immortal," she broke off her reminiscing and bowed her head, and we could see her pink cheeks flush brighter.

"You must sense how strange all this makes me feel," she said. "I knew Kostro did some writing in his room at the countess's, but I had no idea what he wrote. I didn't hear a word from him after we both left London in 1904. He'd been so *after* me that

Guillaume Apollinaire

I told my mother that if he wrote me she was not to forward the letters. I took a position in California. When I was twenty-seven I married Mr. Postings, and I was married to him for twenty-five years, until he died. And after that I had my position with Mr. and Mrs. Jackson in Santa Barbara for another twenty-five years. The little French that I knew as a girl is almost gone. I haven't been able to read the poems Mr. Breunig sent me. I really can't understand what all the things you tell me about have to do with *me*. Especially"—Mrs. Postings blushed again—"especially, since I was such an ignorant little English goose at the time, so much younger, really, than twenty. I was so *mean* to Kostro!"

We couldn't help smiling. "The whole French-reading world knows that," one of us told her. "In his poems he complains about it all the time."

"You mean, perhaps if I'd been good to him there wouldn't be the beautiful poems? Perhaps everything turned out for the best?"

The sudden shrewdness of it struck us: Mrs. Postings was clearly not one who had *read* much about poets profiting from their sufferings.

"I'm sorry, of course, if I was *too* mean," Mrs. Postings went on, "but what could I do? Kostro couldn't properly make love to me in words, since I knew so little French and his English was almost nonexistent, and neither of us spoke German—the countess hired us because we couldn't; she wanted Gabrielle to learn English and French. And I wasn't one to allow him to do anything else. I'd been warned so before leaving home. My sister and I were the most rigidly brought-up girls in Clapham. My father was so straitlaced that he knew it, and called himself 'the Archbishop of Canterbury.' 'Never speak to anybody, never be alone with anybody,' and all that: my parents kept dinning it into my ears. It was only because the countess's doctor in London was a friend of my father's that I was allowed to take the position and go to the continent: the doctor said he could vouch that I'd be with a respectable family. I don't suppose that at that time any of us had been told there was going to be a young man in the house. Kostro

348

was so intense! I refused to be alone with him, but sometimes the countess *ordered* the two of us to go out for a walk together. When she did that, she didn't know what she was doing; but then she thought Kostro was in love with *her,* she thought everybody was. I was amazed by his behavior to me. He terrified me. He'd take me on a dangerous mountain path and tell me that if I refused to marry him he was quite capable of hurling me down a precipice. He'd say to me, 'Each man kills the thing he loves!' When we traveled, if he saw me having the most casual, innocent conversation with anybody he'd stride up in a fury and order whoever it was to leave me alone, because, he said, I belonged to him. Then I'd be furious with him, and refuse to have anything to do with him, refuse to speak to him.

"He was extraordinary in London, too, both times he came," Mrs. Postings went on. "One day he bought me a hat, and a feather boa—he insisted on it. My mother was furious. She let me go out to dinner with him, once, but only when I promised to be home by nine o'clock. He took me to see an Albanian friend of his, a writer of some kind. His wife, I mean the girl he was living with, was expecting a baby. They weren't married, and she cried about it. She told me another woman kept coming to the street-corner opposite their flat and standing there and staring up; she was afraid that her 'husband' would go off with her. That was extraordinary company for me to find myself in—an archbishop's daughter! After dinner she started to make up a bed in the living-room, and I realized that she was making it up for *us,* for Kostro and me, and they all expected me to spend the night there with him. I said, 'Oh, no, I can't do anything like that. I must go home. My mother's expecting me.' Kostro got me home rather later than nine. My mother was furious."

"My mother was furious . . . my mother was furious": it was beginning to sound like a refrain.

"It was because Kostro became so insistent in wanting to marry you, in London, that you told him you'd taken a position in America, wasn't it?" one of us asked Mrs. Postings. "And having said that, you went out and got one?"

349

Guillaume Apollinaire

"I suppose it was partly that," Mrs. Postings said, "but somehow I'd picked up the idea that I wanted to go to a country beginning with 'A.' America, Australia—the offer from America came along first."

She seemed a little vague as she said that—the afternoon was wearing on now, perhaps we were keeping her too long; but it certainly sounded like a vague idea, perhaps more indicative than anything that had gone before of the greenness of the English girl when the young poet knew her.

"The great inducement that Kostro held out to me was that if I married him he'd make me a countess," said Mrs. Postings. "You know he always said he came from a noble Russian family, full of generals and heaven knows what. He mentioned his mother every once in a while, but there was never a word about his father. Somehow I had the idea that. . . . In fact I think you told me, Mr. Breunig, that. . . ."

Roy nodded. "You're right," he said. "Kostro's parents weren't married. His father was probably from a good Italian-Swiss family, and his mother's family was partly Polish; her father does seem to have been a colonel in the Czar's army before they left Poland and came to Italy, where Kostro's parents somehow met. But I don't think he could have made you a countess."

I thought of Kostro's mother, about whom we all knew a good deal more than Mrs. Postings did; the formidable Olga de Kostrowitzky, daughter of a Polish ex-colonel who in Rome became a papal chamberlain, and mother of two sons born out of wedlock, *entraîneuse* at the Monte Carlo casino, and—at the moment when her elder son was promising to make a young English girl a countess—living in poverty in Paris with her younger son Albert and her lover, an Alsatian gambler named Weil. I thought of Kostro as he later became—one of the joyous "bande Picasso" in Montmartre, losing his mistress Marie Laurencin because *her* mother (who was often "furious" too) considered him a ne'er-do-well and thought her opinion all too strongly confirmed when he was thrown into jail on suspicion of having been involved in the theft of the Mona Lisa from the Louvre. I thought of his two

350

wartime love affairs, one with "Lou" that began with an opium party, and the other, the "platonic" one, with a young school-mistress from Oran, that he broke off soon after there threatened to be some "reality" in it. He finally married, and was married for the last few months of his life; but in that short space of time, his friends have said, his bride found him decidedly *"orageux,"* and had they lived together much longer there would have been *"coups de revolver."* He certainly would not have made Annie a countess; he would scarcely have been a husband at all.

"I remember Kostro waving goodbye to me at the station," Mrs. Postings said. "Was it Waterloo? Victoria? He was half inside, half outside the window. That was the last I saw of him. I have a pendant he gave me. Would you like to see it?"

She went up the stairs with the golden oak banister and after a few moments came down carrying a box. It was large, flat, and of complicated shape; the inside of the hinged cover was of tufted white satin, stamped in gold with the name of a Parisian jeweler in the Chaussée d'Antin; the body of the box was grooved, almost like a maze; the long chain of the pendant lay in the curves of the grooves, forming a design that was somewhat heart-shaped; and at the bottom, in a hollowed-out space, lay the pendant itself. It was of a metal that I couldn't identify, quite elaborately chased, and decorated with black enamel and with a fringe of thin, pointed, imitation white pearls. Nothing about it was bright in color, but the design was what might be called "bright" in the extreme: it was a pure example of the style known as "Art Nouveau," or "Liberty," both concave and convex in its complicated, cartouche-shaped outline, a kind of 1900 baroque. It was a handsome, elab-orate, imposing piece, more showy than valuable, probably, but it gave one to think. Probably the last word in Paris when Kostro offered it to Annie, the pendant passed through whole decades in which it would have been classified by a jeweler or a person of fashion as démodé and impossible; now there is a revival of Art Nouveau among the more or less sophisticated. During those same years Kostro became Guillaume Apollinaire the poet, the friend of the *avant-garde* painters, the author of a book on the

351

Guillaume Apollinaire

Cubists. And all that time the Art Nouveau pendant lay in its Art-Nouveau-shaped box among the—probably few—possessions of Annie Playden, all during her first job, her twenty-five years of marriage to Mr. Postings, and her twenty-five subsequent years of service for Mr. and Mrs. Jackson in Santa Barbara.

Mrs. Vockins, who had taken little part in the conversation, now spoke. "I thought Kostro was charming," she said. "I was Annie's little sister Jennie. When she was twenty I was twelve. After Kostro came to London the first time to see her, he sent me a ring from Paris. I was thrilled: it seemed to me the most wonderful thing in the world to own a ring, especially one that a man sent me from Paris. My mother would only let me wear it once in a while, on some special occasion, and then I had to put it back in its box again. I still have it. I'll bring it down if you like."

Mrs. Vockins' box was tiny. Kostro's ring was a narrow band of metal set with a small pearl surrounded by diamond chips —a modest ring, but charmingly designed. Holding it between her thumb and forefinger after we had returned it to her. Mrs. Vockins said, quite casually, something that brought what must have been the barrier between Annie and Kostro into still clearer focus. "At the time Kostro gave us the ring and the pendant," Mrs. Vockins reminisced with a little laugh, "my sister said she was sure he'd stolen them from his mother."

Mrs. Postings looked shocked. "I *did?* Oh, I *was* mean to him!" She seemed to lose countenance just a little, and busied herself putting her pendant back into its box, guiding the chain along the heart-shaped grooves.

It was out in the open now, or so it seemed to the three of us—we talked of it later, on the way back to New York—how great had been the mistrust that had underlain the "meanness." The young English girl, "so much younger than twenty," had probably not "meant" what she had said to her sister about the exotic young tutor. Stealing jewelry from his own mother might not have been what she literally thought him capable of, but it was the image that had flown to her lips, her image of the quite possible family life of the strange, foreign Kostrowitzkys. In what

352

unexpected guise can a poet meet his muse!

Before we left, Mrs. Postings went upstairs again, and this time returned with a photograph of herself as she had been at twenty. It had once been published in a book on Apollinaire, although she seemed not to be aware of it. Here was the young girl, pretty, with the pompadour of the day, and eyes that could scarcely have been bluer then than they are today, but looking out at the world with a definite *méfiance*.

We said goodbye to the two sisters, one in slacks and the other in a blue print, each of them holding, incongruously enough there in Katonah, with the dogs barking spasmodically in the distance, the present of jewelry offered her by Guillaume Apollinaire —who was, incidentally, among other things, the coiner of the word "Surrealism."

Mrs. Postings' last words to us, as we drove off, were: "Thank you for coming. I think I'll have happy dreams tonight. You've made me feel that I haven't lived in vain."

353

Guillaume Apollinaire

Chapter One

MARCEL ADÉMA, *Guillaume Apollinaire le mal-aimé*. Paris: Plon (1952) *passim*, in this and all subsequent chapters. This is the basic biographical work on Apollinaire in French. There is an English translation, less dependable than the French original.

Anatol Stern's hypothesis was put forward in: "Apollinaire petit fils de l'Aiglon?", *Les Lettres françaises*, October 15 and 21, 1959.

"La Chasse à l'aigle," in APOLLINAIRE, *Le Poète assassiné*, Paris, Librairie Gallimard (1947).

An historically minded Monegasque. Eugène Trotabas, quoted in ANDRÉ ROUVEYRE, *Amour et Poésie d'Apollinaire*. Paris: Editions du Seuil (1955).

The Société des Bains de Mer was then, as it is now, the company controlling the Casino and other establishments in the principality.

PAUL LÉAUTAUD, *Journal littéraire*. Paris: Mercure de France (1956) III, 291–92.

Chapter Two

"The son of a gambling mother." Louis de Gonzague Frick. This French literary man was christened simply Louis, but as a young man beginning his career it occurred to him that the St. Louis for whom he had been named might just as likely have been St. Louis Gonzaga as any of the other, less sonorous Saints Louis, so he called himself thereafter by the fuller name. See *Le Flâneur des deux rives* (the magazine, not Apollinaire's volume of the same name), IV, 19.

"A schoolmate remembers." A. TOUSSAINT LUCA, *Guillaume Apollinaire, Souvenirs d'un ami*. Monaco: Editions du Rocher, (1954).

MICHEL DÉCAUDIN, in *Le Flâneur des deux rives*, III, 16.

The quotation from *Le Poète assassiné* is a slightly amended excerpt from *The Poet Assassinated* . . . translated from the French with Biographical Notice and Notes by Matthew Josephson. New York: The Broom Publishing Co., (1923).

GUY DUPRÉ, "Le Bâtard de Rome," *La Table ronde*, September 1952.

BERNARD GUILLEMAIN, "Mémorial pour rire," *Le Flâneur des deux rives*, V.

Chapter Three

FERNAND GREGH, *L'Age d'or*, 332-33.

GUILLAUME APOLLINAIRE, "Les mauvaises routes d'Allemagne," *Tabarin*, October 26, 1901.

Apollinaire: Notes

WERNER HEINEN, *Die Insel, Geschichte einer Kindheit*, Bonn.

"In 1915 Apollinaire, writing to a friend about his poetry": APOLLINAIRE, *Tendre comme le souvenir*, Paris, Gallimard (1952), 70.

L. C. BREUNIG, "Apollinaire et Annie Playden," *Mercure de France*, April 1, 1952. Here translated and presented in abridged form with the kind permission of Mr. Breunig.

GUILLAUME APOLLINAIRE, "Des Faux," *Revue blanche*, April 1903.

ANDRÉ BILLY, *Apollinaire vivant*, Paris: Editions de la Sirène (1923), 25–26.

Chapter Four

MICHEL DÉCAUDIN, *La Crise des valeurs Symbolistes*, Privat (1960), *passim*.

ANDRÉ SALMON, *Souvenirs sans fin*, Paris, Gallimard (1955), I, *passim*.

"Faïk Bég Konitza," in APOLLINAIRE, *Anecdotiques*, Paris, Gallimard (1955), 65–69. (Originally printed in "La Vie anecdotique," *Mercure de France*, May 1, 1912.) I have slightly changed the order of the sections quoted.

Apollinaire on Jarry in *Contemporains pittoresques* and *Il y a*.

ROGER SHATTUCK, *The Banquet Years*. New York: Harcourt, Brace and Company, *passim*.

LAFONTAINE, *La Vie d'Esope le phrygien*.

Chapter Five

M. ANDRÉ-ROYER to M. ADÉMA, *La Table ronde*, September 1952.

VLAMINCK, *Tournant dangereux, passim*.

VLAMINCK, *Portraits avant décès, passim*.

DENYS SUTTON, *André Derain, passim*.

Max Jacob on Picasso: quoted in L.C. BREUNIG, "Max Jacob et Picasso," *Mercure de France*, December 1957.

FERNANDE OLIVIER, *Picasso et ses amis*, Paris, Stock (1933), *passim*.

LE BARON MOLLET, "Les Origines du cubisme: Apollinaire, Picasso et Cie.," *Les Lettres françaises*, January 3, 1947.

MAX JACOB, "Souvenirs sur Guillaume Apollinaire," *Le Flâneur des deux rives*, VI.

GUILLAUME APOLLINAIRE, "Art et curiosité, Les Commencements du cubisme," *Le Temps*, October 14, 1912. Reprinted in GUILLAUME APOLLINAIRE, *Chroniques d'art (1902–1918). Textes réunis, avec préface et notes, par L. C. Breunig* Paris, Gallimard (1960).

"Chef d'école of Cubism." SIDNEY GEIST, *Arts Magazine*, January 1962.

"Perhaps the greatest critic of our century." Lionello Venturi, *L'Espresso*,

355

August 27, 1961.

Georges Braque, conversation with the author.

"... very different from that of the Montmartre group ..." *Le Cubisme, 1907–1914.* (Catalogue of exhibition at the Musée d'Art moderne, Paris, 1953.)

"... a paragraph recently composed ..." By Mr. Douglas Cooper, Picasso's friend, historian of modern art. Included in a letter to the author and printed here with Mr. Cooper's kind permission and with the author's thanks to Mr. Cooper for his help in this and other particulars.

DANIEL-HENRY KAHNWEILER, "Reverdy et l'Art plastique," in *Mercure de France,* January, 1962.

MARIE LAURENCIN, *Le Carnet des Nuits* Genève, Pierre Cailler (1946), *passim.*

MICHEL DÉCAUDIN on "La Vierge à la fleur de haricot à Cologne," in APOLLINAIRE, *Oeuvres poétiques,* Bibliothèque de la Pléiade.

Mr. Horst Vey, of the Wallraf-Richartz-Museum, letter to the author.

Monet-Manet "Déjeuner sur l'herbe." Kindly confirmed by Mr. John Rewald, in a communication to the author.

Quotations from Apollinaire's art writings from WILLIAM C. SEITZ, *The Art of Assemblage,* The Museum of Modern Art, New York, 1961.

"... a man of good will ..." Anonymous, "Pablo Picasso, The Artist as Subject." *Times Literary Supplement,* December 22, 1961.

"... literary cubism ..." GEORGES BRAQUE, *Oeuvre Graphique,* Paris, 1960 (Catalogue of exhibition at the Bibliothèque Nationale), No. 128.

"La 'poésie cubiste?' Terme ridicule!" Pierre Reverdy, conversation with the author.

"She is bright, witty. ..." LOUISE FAURE-FAVIER, *Souvenirs sur Apollinaire,* Paris, Grasset (1945), *passim.*

"... he had acquired a graceful mistress ..." ANDRÉ ROUVEYRE, *Apollinaire,* Paris, Gallimard (1945).

"... née d'une mère normande ..." Courtesy of Mr. Joseph Morton.

"They had a song about her ..." ANDRÉ SALMON, *Souvenirs sans fin,* II, 117.

"I cannot find words ..." Quoted in L. C. BREUNIG, *Chroniques,* 53, from Apollinaire's review of the Salon des Indépendants, 1908, for the *Revue des Lettres et des Arts.*

"A Henry Kahnweiler." *50 Ans d'édition de D.–H. Kahnweiler.* Galerie Louise Leiris, 1959.

"Guillaume Apollinaire never gave me the impression of being completely natural. ..." ALICE HALICKA, *La Table ronde,* September 1952.

"L'Enfer de la Bibliothèque Nationale," *La Parisienne,* 1956.

Fernand Fleuret, quoted in J. de Saint-Jorre, *Fernand Fleuret et ses amis* (Imprimerie Bellée, Coutances).

ROGER SHATTUCK, *op. cit.,* 212.

The questionnaire: "Une Enquête et une réponse," *La Revue des lettres modernes,* Spring 1962.

356 Letter to Natanson, *Le Flâneur des deux rives,* III.

Apollinaire: Notes

Chapter Six

"And the guard that watches the gates of the Louvre." Reprinted in L. C.
BREUNIG, *Chroniques.* The quotation is from François Malherbe, "Consolation à M. du Périer."

JOHN GOLDING, *Cubism, A History and Analysis, 1907–1914* (George Witten-
born, Inc., 1959), *passim.*

GUILLAUME APOLLINAIRE, *Tendre comme le souvenir, passim.*

ANDRÉ BILLY, *op. cit., passim.*

"I don't trust her an inch!" Anecdote by courtesy of Mr. W. G. Constable.

"M. Gilbert Prouteau tells the story a little differently." Conversation with
the author.

ALBERT GLEIZES, "Apollinaire, la justice et moi," in *Cahier Spécial de Rimes et
Raisons consacré à Guillaume Apollinaire,* 1946.

Chapter Seven

LOUISE FAURE–FAVIER, *op. cit., passim.*

L'Aurore, September 13, 1911.

ANDRÉ SALMON, *Souvenirs sans fin,* II, 118.

". . . a much more purely abstract kind of painting . . ." JOHN GOLDING, *op.
cit.,* 35.

L. C. BREUNIG, "Apollinaire et le Cubisme," in *La Revue des lettres modernes,*
Numbers 69–70, Spring 1962.

MICHEL DÉCAUDIN, *Le Dossier d'Alcools* (Droz, Minard, 1960), 38.

". . . one of the leaders of the poetic school of the Abbaye," and "Many years
later . . ." MARCEL ADÉMA, *op. cit.,* 158 and 159.

"The premises were visited . . ." *Idem,* 173.

MARIE-JEANNE DURRY, "Un secret d'Apollinaire," in *Le Flâneur des deux rives,*
IV, 13–14 and V, 36.

"Yesterday evening we dined . . ." and "Apollinaire, completely pacified . . ."
JOSHUA C. TAYLOR, *Futurism* (The Museum of Modern Art, 1961), 134
(where an English translation only is printed; the Italian original has
not been seen), and *passim.*

L. C. BREUNIG, *Chroniques, passim.*

FERNANDE OLIVIER, *op. cit.,* 212–13.

MARIE LAURENCIN, *op. cit.,* 40.

Apollinaire's reportage for *Comoedia,* entitled "La Fête manquée," was
printed in the newspaper only after his death, on August 1, 1920. It is
partially reproduced in ADÉMA, *op. cit.,* 185–86.

357

The quotations from those of Apollinaire's letters not in *Tendre comme le souvenir* are from ADÉMA, *op. cit., passim.*

HENRI DUVERNOIS, "L'Opération," in *Vient de Paraître,* November 9, 1923.

ANDRÉ BILLY, *op. cit., passim.*

GUILLAUME APOLLINAIRE, *Anecdotiques,* 227.

Tristan Tzara, conversation with the author.

Philippe Soupault, conversation with the author.

Pierre Reverdy, conversation with the author.

ANDRÉ ROUVEYRE, *Apollinaire,* 202.

LOUISE FAURE-FAVIER, *op. cit.,* 203–7.

PAUL LÉAUTAUD, *Journal littéraire,* III, 283–84.

The author wishes especially to thank the Librairie Gallimard for permission to quote from works by and about Apollinaire published by them and listed individually in these notes. Of the poems printed in French, "Clair de Lune," "La Chanson du Mal-Aimé," "L'Emigrant de Landor Road," "Le Pont Mirabeau," and "Chantre" are from Alcools; "Les Fenêtres" and "Lundi Rue Christine" are from Calligrammes; "Vae Soli" and "La Vierge à la fleur de haricot à Cologne" are from Le Guetteur Mélancholique; all three volumes are published by Gallimard.

Apollinaire: Notes

Index

Guillaume Apollinaire

Apollinaire Index

361

Guillaume Apollinaire

Apollinaire Index

364

Guillaume Apollinaire